MARY STOTT was born in Leicester in 1907, the daughter and granddaughter of journalists. She began this career herself at the age of eighteen, working on various provincial newspapers including the *Manchester Evening News*, where she became its first woman sub-editor. She was Woman's Page Editor of the *Guardian* from 1957-1971. In 1937 she married Kenneth Stott, who became northern editor of the *News Chronicle*, and has one daughter and two granddaughters. Her widowhood, in 1967, proved a watershed in her life. She moved to London where she now lives and works. Always involved in the cause of women, she was a founder member of Women in Media. She has also been very active in all campaigns concerned with equal pay and anti-discrimination legislation.

She now divides her time between her family, her writing, her passionate interest in music, and her continued work for the women's movement.

In *Before I Go*, her sequel to the much-praised *Forgetting's No Excuse*, Mary Stott offers a wonderful blend of reminiscence and controversy in writing about her lifelong concerns and interests as journalist, campaigner, mother and grandmother.

Before I Go ...

Reflections on my life and times

Mary Stott

Published by VIRAGO PRESS Limited 1985
41 William IV Street, London WC2N 4DB

British Library Cataloguing in Publication Data

Stott, Mary
Before I Go.
1. England — Social life and customs —
20th century
I. Title
942.082'092'4   DA566.4

ISBN 0-86068-404-0
ISBN 0-86068-409-1 Pbk

Typeset by Clerkenwell Graphics and
printed in Great Britain by
Anchor-Brendon Ltd,
of Tiptree, Essex.

Dedication

I dedicate this book to my friends. Their names are:
Alison, Amelia, Amy, Angela, Ann, Anne and Anna,
Anthea, Audrey.
Barbara, Bea, Bel, Beryl, Betty, Beverley, Bridget.
Calliope, Carol, Caroline, Carolyn, Carmen, Catherine,
Celia, Charlotte,
Christine, Clare, Clink, Connie, Constance.
Dale, Daphne, Deborah, Deirdre, Diana, Diane, Doreen,
Doris, Dorothy.
Edna, Eileen, Elaine, Ella, Elizabeth, Elsie, Emily, Enid,
Esther,
Ethel, Evelyn, Eve, Eva.
Fay, Felicity, Fiona, Frances, Felicity.
Gertrude, Gill, Gillian, Grace, Georgina, Gladys, Gwen.
Harriet, Harriette, Hazel, Heather, Hilary, Hilda.
Io, Ira, Irene, Isabel.
Jackie, Jacqui, Jan, Jane, Janet, Jean, Jennifer, Jenny, Jenyth,
Jo, Joan, Joyce, Julia, Judith, Juliet, June.
Katharine, Kathleen, Kaye.
Lena, Lily, Linda, Lyn, Lynne, Lennie, Lesley, Liz, Louise,
Lucy.
Madelon, Margaret, Margo, Marguerite, Marion, Marjorie,
Mary,
Maude, Megan, Marie, Mikki, Molly, Monica, Muriel.

Nancy, Naseem, Nell, Nesta, Nora, Norma, Norrine.
Olive, Olwen, Olly.
Pamela, Pat, Patricia, Pauline, Penny, Peggy, Phyllis, Polly,
Prue.
Rachel, Rita, Robin, Rose, Rosie, Rosemarie, Rosemary,
Rosalie, Ruth, Ruthie.
Sally, Sandra, Sandy, Serena, Sheila, Shelley, Shirley, Sonia,
Sue, Susanne, Suzanne, Susannah, Suzie.
Tamar, Trixie, Taya, Thelma.
Una, Ursula.
Veronica, Vera, Valerie, Victoria, Vicki, Virginia.
Wendy.
Yvonne.
Zoe.
There are also a number of people named David, Michael,
Peter, Tony and John; and some named Bill, Brian, George,
Jim, James, Kenneth and Richard. Also there are
Andrew, Alan and Allan, Arthur, Aubrey, Cyril, Dennis and
Denys, Gordon, Joe, Jordie, Nigel, Norman and Don and
Ron.

Contents

Foreword

This book is for my friends . . . not just the great company whose names I list gratefully on the facing page but for those others I picture out there somewhere, reading what I write, listening to what I say; the friends who sometimes write to me out of the blue or come up to me at meetings; the friends who make the hard chore of writing worthwhile. It is to them that I want to offer this summing up, in my seventies, of my attitudes and beliefs. To me this book is half a dialogue – I have to imagine the other half.

Some of my known and unknown friends, mostly those set in positive political convictions, will think – quite affectionately, I hope that I am 'naïve' or 'wet'. Some, chiefly the 'Trads', members of the older women's organisations with which I have been involved since my youth and whose work for the betterment of women's lives I have so long admired, may think some of my views too permissive. Some of the younger women, the 'Libs' whom I have come to know and love in the last decade in the women's liberation movement, may think me moralistic, prejudiced and soaked in out-of-date sex prejudices. All these have their own views; I have mine.

I tend to think of myself as a 'Trad-Lib' – a lifelong campaigner for the equality of the sexes who wishes and endeavours to keep a foot in both camps . . . not only for ideological reasons but also out of affection for all, of whatever allegiance, who are committed to The Cause. I know full well that one of my sticking points which irritates both Trads and Libs is my stubborn preference for 'chairman'. Trads prefer 'Madam chairwoman'; Libs prefer 'chairperson' or even 'chair' (as if a person were no more than a structure made of wood or metal).

What I want to establish is not only that 'chairman' is simply a label for a function, like president, manager, mayor or magistrate, but that we must work towards establishing the use of 'man' as a genderless word indicating a member of the human race, or inventing a new genderless word. Dear readers, do not let us go on carving up functions . . . whether we are Trads or Libs.

1

Going public

It was in the spring of 1925 that I joined the *Leicester Mail*, straight from school, and for nearly sixty years I have continued to be a journalist, briefly as a news reporter, then editing women's pages and a women's magazine and writing women's columns. For five years I sub-edited news on the *Manchester Evening News* and for fifteen years edited the women's page of the *Guardian*. I have written books, I have broadcast and lectured, but it is as a journalist that I regard myself and have expected always to be regarded by others.

And yet . . . since I retired from the *Guardian* at the beginning of 1972 a rather different Mary Stott seems to have taken over, and must have written quite a lot of this book. Much to my own surprise I seem to have become a 'public woman'. When a *Guardian* colleague confronted me with this I said rather feebly, 'Do you think so?', adding defensively, 'Well, my mother was.' When my brother said, 'Just like your mother; can't stop organising something or other', I wondered 'Can he be right? Or is he just, in the way of older brothers, pulling my leg?'

But now I can see that not only has there been a change from back-bench girl in newspapers to public woman, but that it has also been a gradual development, not something that happened suddenly when my husband died or when, a few years later, I retired from the *Guardian*. It was not the outcome of a need for new preoccupations or for supportive women friends. I had, in

fact, dipped a toe into the world of committees, of taking the
chair, even of making speeches when I was in my early
twenties.

I think that the very first time I got shakily to my feet was at
a meeting of the Leicestershire branch of the National Union of
Journalists. My first Union card is dated 1926; my first
appearance at an annual delegate meeting was as a delegate from
the Bolton branch in 1932. (I was telephoned during the
conference to be told that my father had suffered a fatal heart
attack.) The NUJ remained my chief interest outside work
when I moved to Manchester (to edit the women's and
children's publications of the Co-operative Press) and I became
the first woman chairman of the Manchester branch in 1937. K
Stott and I – I was Mary Waddington then – had to arrange
the date of our wedding so that it did not conflict with the
branch meeting. Soon K became branch treasurer and at one
ADM an amiable delegate composed a ditty to the tune of
"Two Sleepy People" which included the line "You make the
speeches while I do the sums."

I fear speechifying must have been in my genes or in my
conditioning, for while working for the Co-operative Press I
used to give little talks to Co-operative Women's Guilds about
what we aimed to do in our little magazine *Woman's Outlook*
and how we hoped members would help to popularise it. For
these talks I was always paid half a crown (an admirable
principle), but as I took the view that this was part of the job
for which I was paid quite a good salary, I always dropped the
coin in the charity box on the chairman's table. A young friend
in the CWS publications department told me he saved up his
half-crowns to get married.

From the time my daughter was born until she went to
continue her education in Switzerland my public activities were
cut to a minimum, for my husband worked at night (on the old
News Chronicle) and I by day. We had nanny housekeepers, of
whom the first and far the best was my good Lancashire

mother-in-law, but alas her health broke down and we had a series of paid helps until I decided on semi-retirement – soon after I left the *Manchester Evening News*. Becoming women's page editor of the *Guardian* in 1957 greatly enhanced my prestige, of course, and I began to be asked to speak at functions like school Speech Days. The first time I presented the prizes was at a girls' school near our home. I was exceedingly nervous but came to enjoy having such a splendid pulpit from which to air my views. I can't resist quoting from this first effort:

When I was sitting down there instead of standing up here, what saved me from boredom was going off into a private daydream about the time when *I* was distinguished enough to present the prizes. Of course I don't feel particularly distinguished now, and I have discovered that my part of the proceedings is much harder than yours. You only have to try not to embarrass the staff by showing your boredom too plainly. I have to try to prevent any of you from being bored, and as some of you are only eleven, some are young women in their later teens, some are parents, some are grandparents and some are teachers, it is quite a tough task.

I never did get to present the prizes at the Wyggeston Grammar School for Girls, which I attended, and which is now a sixth form college, but I was the prize-presenter for a co-educational comprehensive in Manchester's Free Trade Hall, a truly daunting task. Barely a week later I had to respond to a cry for help from a headmistress whose prize-presenter had let her down at the last moment and so found myself on the platform of the Free Trade Hall once again, and this time – for it was a Catholic school run by nuns – there was a solid row of Catholic priests behind me. I never discovered how they reacted to the views of a feminist agnostic who came from a long line of Nonconformist radicals, but it would be wonderful if I made them think a bit. I probably said to the girls that they must not be so silly as to think only of the time when they would leave school, fall in love, marry and settle down for the rest of their lives to care for husband and children. I'm sure I cited three women prime ministers, Mrs Indira Gandhi of India, Mrs Bandaranaika of Sri Lanka and Mrs Golda Meir of Israel. All, like Margaret Thatcher, were mothers; so are many women life peers, Nobel Prize winners, scientists, judges, professors, doctors, accountants. 'So don't let anyone tell you,' I would say in my best platform style, 'neither your parents nor your teachers, that you can't do things because you are a girl.'

I used to say the same sort of thing when I had the rare opportunity to speak to boys, either at co-educational or at single-sex schools. 'You may dream of being a prime minister, a Lord Chancellor, the chairman of the Bank of England, a pop star or a rugby international, but I think it would be a pity if you got it into your heads that in due course you will find some beautiful blonde who will look after you when you go out into the world and become famous . . . someone who will sew on your buttons, make your favourite puddings and look after the kids while you are at work. Girls are people too and having an education much like yours they aren't suddenly going to turn into half-people whose job is to wait on you and say "Yes darling".' Once I said to a group of sixth form grammar school boys, 'You had better accept that that beautiful blonde you eye as she gets on the bus may one day be your boss.' I could have imagined it, but it seemed to me that a wave of hostility swept back at me.

I think that the best speech I ever made was my 'thank-offering' address to the governors and academic board of Manchester Polytechnic, on behalf of the newly appointed honorary fellows, in November 1972. This was a wonderfully happy day, arranged in the old Manchester College of Art with imaginative ceremonial, and the new honorary fellows included two knights, the Dean of Manchester, the Very Reverend Alfred Jowett, for whom I had an affectionate admiration, and one or two other very distinguished men, so I felt truly honoured to speak on their behalf. The one passage I wish to recall is this:

I will remind you that the heart of Manchester does not reside and never has resided only in its men, but also in its women. Women have also helped to bring it renown. [I quoted some of the city's most distinguished women and then added]: I have a profound conviction that if there were many more women in responsible jobs it would help to bring about the peaceful revolution we all want. There would be fewer battles for power, fewer soulless managements, fewer take-overs throwing people on to the scrap heap, less stress and strain. For in so far as women are different from men I believe that, perhaps by nature, perhaps by nurture, and certainly by life experience, they have the edge over men in caring more about people and less about personal power and status, and even about money.

To quote any more would be self-indulgent. I recognize that public speaking is still important and that it is probably what has made me come to be regarded as 'a public woman', but it does not *equate* with being a public woman in my sense of the term. Speaking on a platform you may influence people's opinions, but what is the use of that unless you convince them that something needs to be done, by acts of parliament, by decisions of local authorities, by trade union bargaining or by any other democratic process? Prating on public platforms seems to me a fairly superficial involvement in public life compared with setting in motion processes which may right wrongs, prevent abuses and improve the quality of life for our fellow citizens. I believe the true public woman is one who devotes herself to participating in such initiatives and, at least as important, maintaining their momentum.

I had precious little time for this kind of participation while I was still a fully employed journalist, but a year or two after my husband died, when it was still hard to see much point in such a chopped-in-half life, the new women's liberation movement established itself in the United States and began to stir the imagination of British women. In 1970 the well-known *Guardian* columnist Jill Tweedie recruited me to a small group of women journalists who had begun to meet monthly in a dreary room at the Kingsway Hall. This group, which included women from newspapers as diverse as the *Guardian*, *Telegraph*, *Morning Star* and *London Evening Standard*, soon decided to call itself Women in Media and to set about campaigning against discrimination against women not only in newspapers, and in recruitment and job opportunities at the BBC, but also in all walks of life.

It was my involvement in Women in Media that really led to my 'going public' in the sense that is really important to me – getting things moving. Since my young days I had been a convinced feminist. The cause that involved me wholeheartedly in my last year or two at the *Guardian*, and for the next decade, was the campaign to eliminate all forms of discrimination against women, in law, custom and practice.

Women in Media was an *action* group. We went on a picket or two and a march or two, but mostly we lobbied, went on deputations – such as to heads of government departments, including Margaret Thatcher when she was Minister for Education – drafted and sent out questionnaires to editors about staffing ratios in all editorial departments and to MPs about anti-discrimination legislation, compiled reports for Royal Commissions, gave evidence to Committees of Enquiry and wrote endless letters. I shall not forget a young activist who complained at a Women in Media meeting that we didn't seem to do anything except write letters. She little guessed how many hours those letters took – often a single letter would take me as long to write as one (well-paid) article. There is also the matter of records . . . Even in the most open and non-hierarchical women's group there usually comes a time when some kind of records have to be kept – of membership, of subscriptions paid and other financial matters, of decisions taken and plans made.

To people not involved in 'public work' this may sound extremely boring. But think of the compensations for this 'boring' labour. In the Women in Media campaign for anti-discrimination legislation there were moments of real joy and triumph. How can we forget that great meeting in Caxton Hall, Westminster, in February 1973, when MPs came over from the House to urge us on? Everyone who hurried off at the close of the meeting in the direction of Westminster was given a torch to carry. As I had been taking the chair, I was last out and felt a trifle forlorn when I looked down Victoria Street and saw all my friends had gone on ahead. Then in the distance I saw lighted torches moving out of Parliament Square, and I ran and ran – as I could not run now – and caught them up as they were processing up Whitehall. I walked between Deaconess Una Kroll and Mikki Doyle, women's editor of the communist *Morning Star*, until we got to Downing Street. One of our prime movers, Shirley Conran (now a best-selling novelist), joined me as I stood at the barrier. Sergeant Garnham of Cannon Row Police Station came up and told us that, if we wished, two of us could deliver a written message at Number Ten. Shirley and I had pens and pencils handy, of course – but no paper to write on. Sergeant Garnham tore a page out of his notebook for us and we wrote our message to the Prime Minister, Edward Heath, and marched up to the door of Number Ten with it. Sometimes the British way of life is very endearing.

So, the battle for a Sex Discrimination Act was won in 1975, and I had been deeply involved in campaigning, had taken the chair at great meetings, had come to be known to quite a wide range of organisations and had been recruited to the Fawcett Society, the oldest campaigning feminist organisation in the country – one which traced its history through various name changes back to 1866. In the summer of 1979 I was elected chairman of the Fawcett Society – truly a public woman now! – and in the following December at a Women in Media Christmas party-cum-daylong reappraisal of our aims and function, it was decided that we needed to try to inject a new enthusiasm into the women's movement. The Sex Discrimination Act was on the statute book. It purported to outlaw discrimination on the grounds of sex or marriage in employment, education, training, the provision of goods and services and various other aspects of life. It also set up an Equal Opportunities Commission with headquarters in Manchester which was empowered to undertake research, foster public education in 'equality' practices and institute investigations into discrimination by firms or businesses. But it seemed to us that four years after the EOC had been set up, women were still greatly disadvantaged in many aspects of their lives both public and private.

It also seemed to us, perhaps especially to me, that we must try to combat a sort of 'sag' in the women's movement and prevent the possibility, if we could, of a sag in interest in our own group. It is my strong conviction that all organisations must be seen to be *doing* something if they are to retain old members and recruit new ones. So at this Women in Media party the decision was taken to undertake the organisation of a 'Women's Action Day'. My chairmanship of the Fawcett Society gave me the opportunity to commend the idea also to this body of doughty fighters for equality. And so joint plans were laid for an event which was another of the shining memories of my 'public life'. First, of course, it was back to the old grind of writing endless letters and of making endless phone calls to beg for money, to beg for support on the day, to solicit ads for our programme. It was back to the old routine of tracking down every organized women's group which might possibly be represented at a conference at Central Hall, Westminster, and of keeping them in touch with our plans. There were not, I think, more than a couple of dozen of us, from both the Fawcett Society and Women in Media, involved in this eleven-month exercise, and often there would be only a handful at our planning sessions in the peaceful top-floor rooms of the then headquarters of the London Women's Liberation Movement in William IV Street, Charing Cross. We brought together representatives of sixty-seven societies and groups, whose total membership we calculated to be over two million. The thoroughly traditional large-scale organisations like the National Federation of Women's Institutes and the National Union of Townswomen's Guilds supported us. So did Kent Women's Aid, the Child Poverty Action Group, the Co-operative Women's Guilds, the UK Asian Women's Conference, Sappho (the Lesbian women's group), the Associations for the Improvement of the Maternity Services, the Iron and Steel Trades Federation, the National Labour Women's Advisory Committee and the Women's Liberal Federation . . . I dip into the list of sixty-seven supporting women's organisations almost at random.

Two members of our group drafted a 'Women's Agenda' which, when it had been approved, was debated during Action Day. It covered education, employment and training, public and political life, the law, the family, health and the media, and representatives of the various organisations led discussions on the subjects especially important to them. During the afternoon the representatives walked, two by two, across to the House of Commons to deliver to the Prime Minister, Mrs Thatcher, letters containing their agreed views on various aspects of the agenda. The degree of consensus on women's issues among these widely differing organisations and groups was remarkable.

My job was to sit on the platform at the side of the chairman for the day, Mrs Jane Finlay, then deputy chairman of the Equal Opportunities Commission and also, of all things, to deputise for one of the best-known women of the western world, Merlina Mercouri, who was prevented from being with us by developments in the Greek parliament, of which she is a member. But what I would really have liked to do was to mingle in the foyer with the women who crowded around the stalls displaying the literature of many of the participating organisations. That, I was told afterwards, was where the feeling of real commitment and sisterhood was most in evidence. We ended the day singing Ethel Smyth's 'March of the Women', a suffragette rallying song, and Sandra Kerr's 'We are Here', with its potent lines:

> For the world was meant for sharing,
> Equal giving, equal caring,
> Growing, learning, doing, daring.

I don't think anyone who was at this Women's Action Day will ever forget it. I know I shall not . . . and perhaps what I shall remember most will be the words of one of the finest 'public women' I ever knew, Dame Margery Corbett Ashby, who started her career as a feminist and internationalist in 1907 and who came up from Sussex at the age of nearly ninety-nine to be with us. 'The best thing that has happened in my long life,' she said, 'is that women have learned to trust and to work with one another.'

It was not only Mary Stott the committed feminist who was drawn into public life. It was Mary Stott journalist, writer, author. One of the organisations with which I have been most deeply involved is the National Association of Widows, which was launched not long after I had written in the *Guardian* and in my book, *Forgetting's No Excuse*, about 'learning to be a widow'. When the NAW was able to hold its first national conference I was invited to appear on a BBC programme compered by Frank Bough, and found myself talking to June Hemer, its founder and secretary. June was in the Birmingham studio, I was at Shepherds Bush, but as we looked at one another on the monitoring screen we felt, I am sure, that we were friends.

The next day I was on the stage of the Greenwich Theatre looking out over a darkened auditorium filled with widows. I found it almost impossible to talk when it came to my turn; I was thinking of all those women who, like me, were going home to a 'lonely bed' that night – and, most of them, every night for the rest of their lives. Only those who have suffered that kind of pain, I believe, can help those who are also experiencing it. The most expert, trained counselling cannot compare with the rush of loving sympathy that flows towards the newly bereaved from a widow who, through bleak and sometimes agonised months and even years, has learned to cope, after a fashion.

So I became a patron of the National Association of Widows and then a trustee of the Widows Advisory Trust, of which the Baroness MacLeod of Borve, widow of the distinguished politician Ian MacLeod, is the chairman. She will forgive me, I hope, for recalling our first meeting at an annual meeting of the NAW. After hearing a very warm tribute to her husband from Bruce George, a local MP, she turned to me and said, 'I think I could do with a cigarette.' From that moment I felt to her as a friend. As for June Hemer, words are inadequate to express my admiration. Her education was limited. After being widowed she worked in a small business and when she had the urge to set up an organisation for widows she knew no Important Persons and had no political clout, but within a very few years she was able to talk to members of both Houses of Parliament, to important civil servants and heads of trusts, and to travel abroad to make contacts with similar organisations. Somehow she finds the time, with only a colleague or two, to write on widows' problems to every candidate of all the major parties when general elections are called. Would one not feel ashamed to sidle out of giving support to a woman like that?

More people have heard of that admirable organisation for widows, Cruse, and may wonder why there is need for another one. There are two reasons. The NAW believes that the help one widow can give to another is greater than that which can be given by professionally trained counsellors who have not themselves been bereaved. Also, the NAW is a campaigning pressure group which Cruse, a charitable organisation, cannot be. Widows suffer many disadvantages which could be rectified. The overlapping benefits rule for example, prevents their drawing any kind of benefit – sickness, unemployment, even a grant for retraining – on top of the widow's pension. But the disadvantage that has always made me deeply angry –

and I am not a person easily moved to anger − is the operation of the cohabitation rule which makes it possible for a social security officer to requisition a widow's pension book on the *suspicion* of her entertaining a man on the premises. Surely this must be the only instance in British practice where a person can be assumed to be guilty without trial?

The National Association of Widows, through June Hemer and its adviser, Ann Stanyer of Lanchester Polytechnic, has fought many of these cases in social security tribunals. I went with Ann Stanyer to one such an appeal on behalf of a widow who had taken in a elderly man, rather slow in his limbs and in his wits. She was the kind of woman who enjoys taking someone under her wing − she had cared for parents and for her late husband. The idea that the lodger and the landlady were virtually man and wife and that therefore he ought to be maintaining her was ludicrous, and so the chairman of the tribunal clearly thought it, for he said some tart things about the haste in which the investigating officer had rushed to her conclusion and about the waste of time and public funds which had been caused by her. The widow won her case.

On another occasion I sat in the House of Lords when Lord Gardiner, a former Labour Lord Chancellor, introduced a debate on the cohabitation rule, and saw a very old widow in the public gallery, obviously distressed and bemused. She had been accused of cohabiting with a friend of her son's for whom she was keeping house. Her suffering made me sick to the core. Sometimes the journalist and the public woman aspects of Mary Stott can act as one. I feel I must quote from an article I wrote for the *Guardian* women's page in which I voiced my anger:

In the present framework of Social Security there is only one valid reason for withholding pension or benefit, and that is that the claimant is, by reason of some other source of income or maintenance, not in need. 'Cohabitation' is not a reason unless it means being fully, or even partially maintained.

It is impossible to escape the conclusion that women who are accused of cohabiting, in its current sense, are harassed, even persecuted, more because they are 'immoral', therefore undeserving, than because they are fraudulently concealing a source of income or maintenance. Nasty, isn't it? Sickening, if you consider that the woman who receives a lover occasionally may be assumed to be paid by him, as if she were 'a common prostitute'.

If a young nurse, represented as pregnant without her knowledge or consent [in an advertisement widely displayed at the time], can sue for damages, why not a widow or separated wife branded as immorally cohabiting because a man's trousers are found in her wardrobe? (In one case of this kind the accused widow was able to establish that the trousers found in her wardrobe were her son's.)

I wish I could get into the mind of any member of an appeals tribunal who equates man-about-the-house with illicit maintenance. I wish I were young enough to be at risk, for if anyone accused me of immorality as well as of defrauding the State, on the grounds of having a male lodger or an occasional overnight visitor, I would institute an action for defamation of character.

Wouldn't you?

I wrote this with the more passion because I was aware of one widow, in debt to the gas and electricity boards for bills run up when her husband was dying, who had been accused of cohabiting with her lodger and deprived of her pension book. She had been rescued by him in the nick of time from a suicide bid.

It was my writings that drew me into involvement with the National Association of Widows and my editorship of the women's page of the *Guardian* that gave rise to invitations to be involved in other public works. People who become moderately well known as broadcasters are apt to be asked to be patrons of this, vice-presidents of that, trustees of the other. It is very flattering to be asked, but sometimes I wonder if one ought to be selective. Perhaps I ought to ask myself, 'How much good can I do them now?' as well as 'Can I afford the time – and the money – that commitment to this organisation may involve?' However, my next trusteeship I undertook, and still fulfil with great goodwill, was for the National Housewives' Register. This rather unfortunately named but excellent organisation grew out of a letter to the *Guardian* women's page from a young mother, Maureen Nicol, in 1960. She suggested that 'perhaps housebound housewives with liberal interests and a desire to remain individuals could form a national register, so that wherever one moves, one can find like-minded friends'. Her idea was an instant success, and the register quickly established itself all over the country – mainly because Maureen Nicol and her successors as national organiser were prepared to do a great deal of donkeywork, at their own kitchen or dining tables. Now that NHR has a membership approaching 30,000 in something like 1,200 branches in Britain and overseas, it has to have an elected National Group and a paid (though elected) national organiser. It felt obliged to obtain charitable status which meant appointing trustees. They were Maureen Nicol, of course, Betty Jerman whose article in the *Guardian* women's page prompted Maureen Nicol's letter, and me, editor of the page at the time. Betty Jerman was a regular contributor during my editorship and I knew her well, but I did not meet Maureen until the twenty-first birthday celebrations of NHR in 1982. 'I think,' I said as I held out my hand to her in greeting, 'I ought to say "Mrs Livingstone, I presume?" ' Being a trustee does involve some responsibility, some decision-taking, but that the organisations formed in the 1960s as a result of letters and articles in the *Guardian's* women's page also recognise me as their 'midwife' gives me great satisfaction. Not only the National Housewives' Register but also the National Association for the Welfare of Children in Hospital and the Pre-school Playgroups Association invited me to their twenty-first birthday celebrations.

It was, almost certainly, not on account of my 'public' activities but because of my fifteen years' editorship of the *Guardian* women's page that I received from the hands of the Queen my OBE in the New Year's Honours list of 1975. Of course it was all rather exciting, right from the moment I was called to one side after a London Press Club committee meeting by Sir Trevor Evans, distinguished *Daily Express* industrial correspondent and, I believe, friend of the then Prime Minister, Harold Wilson. 'Have you had any interesting letters lately?' he asked me. 'No,' I said, puzzled at this odd question. 'You will,' he said. And a letter arrived a few days later from 10 Downing Street offering 'to our trusty and well-loved Charlotte Mary Stott' appointment as 'an ordinary officer of the Civil Division' of the 'most excellent order of the British Empire'.

For weeks I kept this unexpected honour a dead secret, and only at the last moment suggested to my only surviving brother that he might look in the Honours List on 1 January. From then on, of course, it became rather fun. My daughter Catherine drove up the Mall with her little daughter Charlotte and as we parked I waved to Dr Alex Smith, principal of Manchester Polytechnic (which had previously honoured me), who was to become Sir Alex that day. Catherine and Charlotte were ushered into the grand drawing room where, to the sounds of music, the ceremony was to be performed, and I settled myself down uneasily in the large ante-room where the CBEs, OBEs and MBEs were assembled. Time passed. I got into conversation with the late Mia Kellmer Pringle, director of the National Children's Bureau, and with a distinguished trade union officer, Audrey Prime. When would we be summoned? Audrey Prime said with a grin, 'I wonder if anyone ever gets fed up with waiting and goes home?' But of course nobody did. We got our medals from her gracious Majesty and went on our way. At least my daughter, her daughter and I did . . . we were in rather a hurry to get to other engagements. When my daughter dropped me off it began to rain. The expensive hat I had bought for this occasion got very wet. I have not liked to throw it away, but it never looked the same again.

Actually I have always been slightly embarrassed about this honour. Some years earlier I had written in a *Guardian* column that I would like to see most of the lesser honours falling into disuse,

not because they are so often 'undignified and unfair' as a *Guardian* leading article once said, but because they have become rather silly. What do you do with your OBE or MBE once you have been to the Palace to look at the Queen? You can hardly ever wear it; it isn't worth anything intrinsically; you can't sign the letters after your name except on a few official occasions without sounding pretentious. Thousands of people must have these medals tucked away in a drawer, and there isn't even a British Empire any more.

I feel exactly the same today – the OBE, a gilt cross with a pretty coral-pink ribbon, sits in its small black box on a table in the hall of my flat and is only shown off to some curious visitor, most often a child. The only time I sign myself OBE is when I am giving a reference for a job to some worthy young woman. Why doesn't Her Majesty the Queen institute an Order of her own, more appropriate to our times, honouring especially *voluntary* service, and let the Orders of the British Empire fall out of use? The accolade that pleased me much more than the medal was a comment at the time by Katharine Whitehorn in the *Observer* headed 'Three Cheers for Mary':

Mary made her pages a forum for all the serious vital interests that women have. On it she fought all the battles for women's rights: to maintenance, to a place by their child's bed in hospital, to a decent return for their labour: hardly a pressure group in the fifties and sixties didn't get its impetus, or even its origin, on her pages.

That accolade was more worth having than any I could earn as a 'public woman'. If I had been allowed, I think I should have stayed at the *Guardian* until I dropped, for I was accustomed all my working life to have a desk to sit at, a secure base from which to operate, a very definite job with known perameters to work within. But then I should never have had the experience in the Fawcett Society of working alongside able women from other walks of life – academics, civil servants, lawyers, economists, business women, a chemist, a prison governor, a librarian and a baroness or two, including the present leader of the Liberal Party in the House of Lords, Lady Seear, president of the society. When, as chairman, I was working out with such as these, policies and tactics for a Cause instead of for a women's page, I felt no more than a *prima inter pares*, as I hope I always was as women's page editor.

My writing experience was useful to the society in compiling its newsletter and writing a pamphlet or two, but I had to learn a range of new skills for chairing its executive committee – which is much, much harder than chairing even quite a large meeting, for it is essential to hold the reins both loosely and firmly. One has to try to give every member of a committee a chance to speak and yet not to let the discussion drool on endlessly. One has to bear as patiently as possible with the occasional awkward, opinionated or too-verbose member and try to find an outlet for her talents – and almost by definition every committee member has something useful to contribute. One has to try to convey a feeling of leadership without being bossy, of being concerned in all members' interests and problems without being wet. In the three years I did this job I learned a great deal – including a degree of humility in the face of women who carry this sort of responsibility for far longer than I felt able to do, and also in face of the sad fact that there are some desperately sincere supporters of causes who are unable to work as part of a team. One tries very hard to integrate them but with a few it is not possible. Very sadly one has to let them go.

In these years as Fawcett chairman I came to be accepted as the representative of a top-ranking women's organisation and to meet as colleagues many admirable women at a variety of conferences and receptions. I confess I greatly enjoyed all this, but by far the best reward for 'three years hard' as Fawcett chairman was the friendship, the affection and the scarcely deserved acclaim that was lavished on me. I am deeply grateful for having had the chance to work with so many fine women for such important ends.

In two other ways I have 'gone public' in my later years, both of them arising from my writings. I was recruited to the Voluntary Euthanasia Society many years ago by Professor Harry Ree, who latched on to something I had written in the *Guardian*. I became a life member and attended one or two annual meetings when I moved to London. Nicholas Reed was then the society's general secretary, and he suggested that I might let my name go forward for the presidency of the society – the *Guardian* connection was, I think, the reason for this proposal. Honesty compels me to say that it was as much cowardice as modesty that made me refuse the invitation. I did not want either to distress my family or to become involved in acrimonious public debate. I was right, of course, in my apprehensions. I was certainly not a big enough person, either in character or status, to carry the burden when Nicholas Reed was charged with aiding suicide and sentenced to a prison term. I could not agree with some of his policies or methods; I thought he was very wrong to allow, let alone help, any member of the society to take part in 'counselling' potential suicides, and I was very glad when the society, which in Nicholas Reed's time had been known as 'Exit', decided to return to is original name and its original aim to win support for a Bill to legalise euthanasia under strictly controlled safeguards. During the society's 'Exit' days I took part in debates at both the Cambridge and Oxford Unions . . . at Cambridge with the TV personality Hughie Green, where we won, and at Oxford with Lord Listowel, where we lost. I am still a vice-president of the society. I still have, locked away, a copy of its 'Guide to Self-Deliverance'; I still fully endorse its aims and have a great admiration for its present able and courageous chairman, Barbara Smoker.

My public appearances as 'an elderly person' give me some amusement; they seem also to give some amusement now and then to gatherings of nurses, social workers, home helps, members of Help the Aged, Age Concern, the British Association for Service to the Elderly, the London Boroughs Training Committee, Pensioners Link, Pensioners Action and many other organisations concerned with the problems of old age. Sometimes I think sardonically that the one growth industry in this country is 'concern for the aged'. But what I have been doing, since my book *Ageing for Beginners* was published, is to talk, when invited, about the ability of the newly retired to help in the care of the really old; to beg those concerned with the care of the elderly to regard us as people, not as geriatrics who are inevitably going deaf, blind and probably dotty; and to tell stories, of which I have plenty, of the good, clever, kind, funny and independent old people I know. In recent times I have often shared a platform with one of the very best 'elderly persons' of my acquaintance, Mrs Ollie Hollingsworth, founder of Tooting Action for Pensioners (TAP), which has not only done wonders for old people in its area but also taken part in national campaigns. In my view she is, like June Hemer of the National Association of Widows, one of the public women before whom we should all bow the knee.

I am very glad myself to have become a public person, even if not quite of their quality. It means that wherever I go I am almost certain to be greeted by people who know me, personally or by repute, on account of my writings or on account of participation in my 'causes'.

This friendliness, this appreciation of what I try to do, makes all the trudging up and down to London on public transport, all the preparation and delivery of speeches, all the letter writing, all the answering of phone calls seeking information, all the fatigue, more than worth while.

2

The Cause

This chapter *has* to be called 'The Cause' – which is what Ray Strachey called the seminal history of the women's movement she published in 1928, when I was just of an age to be fired by it. I mean *the* cause, the one overriding cause for most of my life (after all, I hurried up to be born just after the militant suffragettes got going!) Ray Strachey's book covered well over 100 years of campaigning. In a book as discursive as this one I must be very much less ambitious in my account of how the present-day women's movement seems to me.

It was comical to discover that having decided to start with a year, 1968, in which a great deal happened of importance to women, I had in fact hit on what you might call *the* year in the last quarter of a century. The United Nations designated 1968 Human Rights Year and, not unnaturally, feminists in many parts of the world celebrated it with gatherings, taking their stand on the United Nations Declaration on the Elimination of Discrimination Against Women which had been passed by the General Assembly in 1967.

And how far did that get us? In December 1979 the UN Assembly thought it necessary to reaffirm that 1967 resolution and to declare that 'discrimination against women is incompatible with human dignity and the welfare society'. The years 1975 to 1985 had been designated The United Nations Decade for Women. What progress towards ending discrimination against themselves have women made in twenty years of benevolent UN patronage? Very little, I should have thought, looking at the worldwide scene, but my knowledge, especially of the third world, is so limited that I must concentrate on a narrower perspective – on what has been going on in the United Kingdom, of which I can write with more knowledge, more involvement and perhaps even more insight.

Was there something in the stars favourable to the women's cause in 1968? It almost seems so. It was, of course, the year of the golden jubilee of the granting of the vote to British women, and this was celebrated with tremendous flair at a great meeting in Central Hall, Westminster, called by the Status of Women committee, whose chairman was Dame Joan (now Lady) Vickers, and organised and orchestrated by two remarkable public relations officers, both dedicated feminists, Pamela Anderson and Heather McConnell. Had there ever been such an assembly on one platform of notables of all parties? There was the Prime Minister, Edward Heath; the Leader of the Opposition, Harold Wilson; the Leader of the Liberal Party, Jeremy Thorpe. There were Margaret Thatcher, Shirley Williams and Edith Summerskill; hunger-striking suffragettes like Grace Roe and Leonora Cohen; the young women presidents of the Oxford and Cambridge Unions. I was there, sitting on the platform beside my friend and colleague Lena Jeger, and when I pointed to the woman in front of us and whispered to her, 'That's Dame Kathleen Courtney. She's ninety,' Leonora Cohen, ramrod straight, looked around and said sternly, 'I am ninety-two.' This meeting was a milestone I can never forget.

But then, on the other side of the Atlantic, there was a happening which got worldwide publicity and echoes through the media still. At a protest meeting against the whole concept of beauty contests, a group of young women in Atlanta City responded to a call to dump their bras and girdles into a 'freedom trash can'. A news agency reporter covering the event added the flames and so started the myth of the burning bra –

a far more potent event than the symbolic gesture of Christabel Pankhurst on the steps of the Free Trade Hall, Manchester, when she was arrested for spitting at a policeman. Like the bra burning, it was a fake, for Christabel only pretended to spit. She had no other means of getting herself arrested for assault. This was, in fact, the start of suffragette militancy, but it never became a delicious joke to young men, as did 'Have you burned your bra?'

In this *anno mirabile* there was another memorable call to action. Joyce Butler (Labour MP for Wood Green) introduced, for the first time in the British Parliament, a Little Anti-Discrimination Bill under the Ten Minute Rule. It was a simple Bill to make discrimination on grounds of sex illegal and to set up procedures for preventing it. She said later that it was greeted almost with ridicule (just as John Stuart Mill's amendment to the Reform Bill 100 years earlier, in which he proposed to substitute 'person' for 'man', caused hilarious mirth in the Commons). Many who supported Joyce Butler's Bill did so in rather a shamefaced way because it seemed such a trivial exercise, of interest to such a small number of people. Years later she told me, surprisingly, that it was actually the Queen's previous Christmas Day speech, urging more participation by women, that had inspired her to get the Bill drafted.

One more significant 1968 event: that valiant campaigning 'Six Point Group' led by Hazel Hunkins Hallinen, a notable American feminist resident in the UK, published an influential little book *In Her Own Right*. In it Lena Jeger wrote about 'Power in our Hands'; the Reverend Elsie Chamberlain told about the little boy who was rebuked by his sister for saying the preacher at their church next Sunday would be Mr X – 'You know,' said she, 'that MEN can't preach'; and Marghanita Laski flayed 'the cult of servility' after watching a TV interview with Cambridge undergraduates who said 'No,' they didn't think of going into politics because 'men want girls to be feminine'.

So that's where we were in 1968. You might say that long-time feminists like me were ready for off, for we knew that Betty Friedan's *The Feminine Mystique* had been the spark for a vigorous new women's movement in the United States. It was only later, when she published her second book *It Changed My Life*, that we learned how that powerful body, the National Organisation of Women, came into being in 1966. It happened in Washington, when Betty Friedan went to cover a meeting of the state commissions on the rights of women and invited some of the women involved into her bedroom one night. When she was asked, 'How did you recognise one another?' She replied, 'We recognised the honest fire.' The women at first seemed reluctant to accept her suggestion of starting up an organisation, 'but the next noon those women were waiting for me, fighting mad, because they couldn't even get a resolution on the floor at the Convention.' They had even been told officially that this conference of the Status of Women Commissions of all the sovereign states had no power whatever to take any action, even pass a resolution, not even on ' sex discrimination. So Betty Friedan and her friends took two tables for lunch at the Washington Hilton, passed scribbled notes around, 'and under the very noses of the organisers of the Convention' Betty Friedan wrote on a paper table napkin the words which launched the National Organisation of Women (NOW): 'to take actions needed to bring women into the mainstream of American society, now, full equality for women, and fully equal partnership with men'.

There was nothing so dramatic or eventful in the upsurge from about 1969 of the new women's movement in this country, but we too, I think, recognised 'the honest fire' among our like-minded friends. In her essay in Michelene Wandor's collection of pieces on *Gender and Writing*, Angela Phillips wrote: 'It would be hard to express, even to today's feminists, what sisterhood meant in the early 1970s. It was like falling in love.' Those words speak for me.

I had always, partly because of my work, taken an interest in

women's organisations, been a member of the National Council
of Women and helped in their Manchester campaign to abolish
the limit on widows' earnings without deduction from their
pension, but here was something new and stirring. Even before
Jill Tweedie recruited me to the group that became Women in
Media, in 1970, I was putting out feelers to the new liberation
groups. What is the use of being a women's page editor if you
aren't *listening*? I knew about that first conference at Ruskin
College, Oxford, in 1970, the idea of which came from a group
of women historians who rebelled against the domination of
the Ruskin history workshops by men who seemed to assume
that women had no part in history. They spread the word
around among the liberation workshops that had begun to
proliferate all around London and in some universities, and
hoped that 200 to 300 might turn up. In fact there were almost
600 who, according to *Sweet Freedom* (a history of the struggle
for women's liberation by Anna Coote and Bea Campbell)
'knew they were on to somethig. They discussed proposals to
lobby for the Sex Discrimination Act; to research into women's
history, to campaign for free contraception and abortion on
demand; and to study alternatives to the nuclear family and
conventional ways of bringing up children.' Several known
women journalists were there, and among those who came
expecting to jeer was the distinguished writer Mary Holland,
who stayed to applaud, and to involve herself in the
movement.

The group of women journalists who started meeting in a
bleak classroom in Kingsway Hall (now taken over for
women's organisations by the GLC) included Bea Campbell
and Mikki Doyle, women's page editor of the communist
Morning Star. As Women in Media, a name it decided on quite
soon, the group has been meeting ever since – which must be
something like a record for a liberation group of the period.
The names on our first membership list in 1971 include
Corinna Adam, then of the *New Statesman*, Pat Barr (now a

best-selling novelist), Lynne Edmunds of the *Daily Telegraph*, Margaret Howard (now presenter of 'Pick of the Week'), Mary Kenny (now well-known columnist), Emily MacFarquar (*Economist*), Bel Mooney, Joan Shenton (then working for 'Nationwide'), Anne Sharpley (*Evening Standard*) and Jill Tweedie (*Guardian* columnist). One of our first jobs was to draw up a statement of aims. It remains much the same today, and still contains one clause which I would fight to the death to keep: 'Above all we must assist women to know, like and trust one another, so that the changes we seek should genuinely be the result of self-knowledge and mutual understanding.'

In those euphoric days it seemed possible for gradualist, 'liberal-minded' traditional feminists like me to work in close accord with the new young radicals. So I set off, on behalf of Women in Media, with a freelance photographer, Serena Wadham, on an overnight bus to Manchester for the third national women's liberation conference. It was a remarkable experience, both disconcerting and exhilarating. Serena found herself not particularly welcome, because of her camera – 'libbers' as we were then called had had some pretty horrid experiences at the hands of the popular press. I, reared in the tradition of very experienced chairmen operating with a standing orders committee, found the procedural muddles irritating and the lack of respect for the chair disconcerting. But the sheer size of the gathering was exciting, and its passionate support for women of other countries was heartwarming. I am afraid I was scornful of the group of lesbians who clung to one another, tearfully protesting that men should not be allowed to attend the evening party. They may well have been right, though, at that stage of the development of the movement, when women had to separate themselves from their husbands and boyfriends in order to think out their own, independent line. My friend Helen Fletcher, with whom Serena and I stayed, came with us to the conference though she was not at all involved in the feminist

movement. She said a thing that astonished me at the time, in
that turbulent gathering: 'It's very restful to be at a gathering
of women where they are not competing for the attention of
men.' I understand that better now.

In this spring tide of hope there was much coming together
of 'Trads' and 'Libs'. Through Anna Coote and a few other
socialist feminists calling themselves 'The Women's Lobby',
and through Pamela Anderson and Virginia Novarra of the
Fawcett Society, it was agreed to launch a bi-monthly journal,
Women's Report. The Fawcett Society provided the finance and
Women's Lobby the 'staff'. After a year the *Women's Report*
collective decided to be completely free and independent,
though no one has ever said, so far as I know, that the Fawcett
Society tried to interfere, much less censor the journal's
contents. It was a valiant effort by a quite small group of
exceptionally able and dedicated women and lasted for seven
years. I think it was evidence of the strength of the British
devotion to the 'voluntary' method, and also of the fact that
the 'collective', totally unhierarchical way of doing things can
work successfully – on a small scale, at least.

The *Women's Report* collective's farewell, in June 1979, is
worth quoting:

We have monitored news sources; attended press conferences;
classified the information which may be needed for the magazine;
done additional research necessary; discussed, drafted, rewritten and
edited articles for publication; read books and publications, arranged
typesetting; laid out and pasted up the typeset copy, adding
cartoons where and when we felt able; answered letters, collected
anything from 2-3000 copies, posted to subscribers, arranged for
copies to go to bookshops, kept the accounts . . .

All the members of this gallant band had full-time jobs. They
deserve a retrospective cheer. The journal was often funny as
well as informative, especially in its feature 'Thanks, and a free
consciousness-raising session to . . .', a forerunner of the
Guardian women's page's 'Naked Ape' feature. All contri-

butions were unsigned, evidence of a remarkable degree of agreement and mutual support among the 'staff'.

'Trads' and 'Libs' (my shorthand, as I explain in my foreword, for the old-established, constitutional organisations and the post-1968 non-structured groups) came together to a considerable extent in the lobbying on the Sex Discrimination Act. To a notable extent this was organised and publicised by the dedicated enthusiasts of Women in Media. Women's liberation activists also participated, of course, which led to occasional stresses and strains with our basically Trad group. I remember with particular pleasure, though, passing the word around in the public gallery of the House of Commons when the Bill was being debated that if the young women there objected to any speaker they must not protest noticeably or they would be removed by the solid, implacable parliamentary attendants. But they could smile beatifically and *hiss* without being spotted, which they did. One of the 'hissed at' was Sally Oppenheim who, at a celebration in 1978 of the extension of the suffrage to women held near the statue of Emmeline Pankhurst in the gardens near St Stephen's Tower, actually said that the suffragettes 'never lost their dignity'! Unlike, she seemed to imply, those fierce young 'libbers' of the 1970s . . . to their vast amusement, and to mine. (She obviously did not know of the suffragette mother of an acquaintance of mine who took a pair of scissors with her on demonstrations and snipped the braces of any policeman who tried to restrain her!)

An example of how Trads and Libs divided came during the general election of 1974 when some members of Women in Media persuaded Una Kroll, family doctor and ordained deaconess of the Church of England, to stand as a Women's Rights candidate in Sutton and Cheam. We expected flak from the Liberals, who thought their candidate had a chance of winning the seat from the Tories, but we did not expect it from younger sisters in the women's movement. But the *Women's Report* collective announced that for reasons held by three different groups among them, they could not support Una's candidature: (1) 'She has no political stance on any but feminist issues'; (2) 'No party should be sure of the women's vote and we should seriously weaken our political power if we did not confront *all* candidates', and (3) 'We should just say that elections are a load of rubbish.' Una's reply spoke for me exactly: 'I have marched with you from the beginning, when we were few. You gather power as you work, march and suffer together; if we had waited for the power first we should never have started.' Not unlike what I said at a workshop at the fourth women's liberation conference in Acton when one of the women said that we should never be free from male domination without a socialist revolution: 'I'm too old. I can't wait that long. I want to achieve something *now*.'

Being a gradualist, a believer in constitutional processes, I soon found my natural home in the Fawcett Society – recruited, in fact, by Pamela Anderson (who herself was drawn into it as an activist through that memorable 1968 Central Hall rally). She set me to work with that fine campaigning feminist Virginia Novarra, to produce a statement of aims for the society called 'What Next'. The society's history had long fascinated me and though I have often told it, in articles and a pamphlet called *The Long March To Equality*, I think it is necessary to say again here that it claims to be the oldest feminist society in the country and proudly claims on its letterhead 'Campaigners for equality between the sexes since 1866'.

In 1865 a group of women calling themselves the Kensington Ladies Discussion Society debated women's suffrage; decided, rather to their surprise, that they were in favour of it, and put out feelers to the political philosopher, John Stuart Mill, who was then Member of Parliament for Westminster. He agreed to move an amendment to the Reform Bill then going through Parliament if the ladies would get up a petition with a creditable number of signatures. Within a fortnight their petition had been signed by 1,500 people, including women of the stature of Harriet Martineau, Josephine Butler, Emily Davies (who later founded Girton) and those famous headmistresses, Miss Beale and Miss Buss. Out of this exercise came the first women's suffrage committee, and from then on they and their descendants went on campaigning for the vote until it was fully achieved in 1928. Millicent Garrett Fawcett, newly wedded wife of Henry Fawcett, later to become the Postmaster General, sat in the Ladies Gallery when J. S. Mill moved his amendment to substitute 'person' for 'man' in the 1867 Reform Bill, and she sat in the Distinguished Strangers Gallery more than sixty years later when the Lords passed the Bill that put women on the same level as men as parliamentary and local government electors. What a record.

During all those years, as the society waxed and waned, it had a number of names. During the massive suffragette campaign before the First World War it became the National Union of Suffrage Societies, with Mrs Fawcett as its president. During the war it became the Women's Service Trust (which still exists, in fact, as a trust responsible for the funds which had accumulated), but by 1953 its function seemed to be moving again towards parliamentary campaigning. Kathleen Halpin, an active member then and, in her eighties, an active member now, offered a book prize for a new name for the society. The suggestions ranged from 'Society for Women's Service' to 'Society for Promoting Equity and Promoting the Interests of Women'. The minutes at the next annual meeting record that the suggestion 'Fawcett Society' was proposed by that remarkable woman Philippa Strachey, sister of Lytton Strachey, who was secretary from 1907 to 1956. They do not record whether Kathleen Halpin then handed 'Pippa' the book token – but as the secretary and minute taker, she would not be likely to blow her own trumpet, would she?

This is not the place to tell the story of the Fawcett Society's campaigns and commitments in the fifties and sixties, which tended to focus on the issue of equal pay. The early 1970s were difficult and often painful, because the validity of the Women's Service Trust from which the Fawcett Society draws its income had to be tested in the courts, and meantime money was exceedingly tight. The society had to move, too, from its comfortable lodge in Wilfred Street, Victoria, which meant that the Fawcett Library of over 20,000 volumes, many of them of priceless value to the women's movement, like first editions of Mary Wollstonecraft's *Vindication of the Rights of Women* (1792), then housed at Wilfred Street in somewhat cramped and higgledy-piggledy fashion, had to find a new home. After much discussion, sometimes very tense, the Society accepted the invitation of the City of London Polytechnic, where the head of library and information services is Rita Pankhurst, a granddaughter-in-law of Emmeline Pankhurst and wife of Sylvia Pankhurst's son Richard. Even those who worried about this move are now satisfied that the library is in safe keeping, and students from all over the country and from abroad research there for theses, for women's studies courses, and for yet more books on forgotten feminists or unrevealed aspects of women's history.

They were good years for me, the Fawcett years, when I was elected first to the executive committee and then to the chair. Even before this period, when my time was so utterly absorbed by seminars, campaigns, meetings and committees concerned especially with education, employment (including the new technology), pensions and income tax, I had been learning about other areas of women's organisations. The National Union of Townswomen's Guilds (NUTG) celebrated its golden jubilee in 1978 and I was asked to write its history — one of the most rewarding jobs I ever undertook, for it involved research into the history not only of the Townswomen (whose foremothers were the same women who were ancestors of the Fawcett Society), but also of the other major women's societies. I learned, of course, about that hierarchical, rule-bound structure which the new young women's groups of the 1970s were so determined to avoid, and came to understand why it was set up and how it worked. Sometimes, when reading the letters and documents lent to me in the Townswomen's headquarters, I was astonished at the rigidity with which the 'no politics' rule was applied . . . but that was all in aid of maintaining 'the common ground'. The motivation of the Townswomen as expressed by one of the founders, Dame Margery Corbett Ashby, was: 'We realise we cannot serve the common good unless we first educate ourselves. We must pull ourselves up to a new standard of intelligent knowledge and experience.'

From 1953 the NUTG came to see that 'no politics' did not mean no debate on public questions but rather no commitment to any one party political view. They did, in fact, mount and collaborate in many campaigns, from those which today's campaigners might think trivial, like litter (some Townswomen cleared out filthy local ponds themselves), to matters that certainly should not be derided, like moving towards a multiracial society and building international links. (They were the first major women's organisation to hold out a hand of friendship to the West Germans after the war, and went on many study tours, including one to Russia.) The Townswomen supported Mrs Butler's first Anti-Discrimination Bill in 1967, as well as Willie Hamilton's in 1972 and Women's Action Day in 1980. The National Federation of Women's Institutes (which was, in fact, the pattern for the NUTG) has similarly moved on into the world of broad-based political activity and has supported equal opportunity legislation. But as operating costs increase, neither of these great organisations has been able to be complacent. The NUTG, for example, has moved from its headquarters in Kensington to Birmingham, where costs are expected to be lower. During the late sixties and early seventies, the NFWI was losing members at the rate of about 7,000 a year, slipping from at least half a million in its heyday to around 355,000. What were the reasons? No younger woman should shrug and say, 'They are too stuffy. They are

not really part of the women's movement anyway.' Neither is
true. An essential component of the women's movement is the
coming together of women for the common good of their sex as
well as of society as a whole. 'Sisterhood is powerful' is one of
the most telling slogans of the women's liberation movement.
It applies in a more personal but still important way to the
traditional guilds and institutes whose members are mutually
supportive to a very high degree.

The most important factor in the decline in membership of
the guilds and institutes was probably that much of what they
were set up to provide – education in a variety of fields,
including music, drama, crafts and 'public questions' – came
to be provided on a large scale by local education authorities.
Not since 1965 has the NUTG employed specialist advisers in
these fields. Moreover, as increasing numbers of women began
to take paid jobs outside the home they were less able to spare
time for sharing the work of keeping societies going by taking
office. In the case of the women's institutes, the whole pattern
of life in rural Britain is changing – many villages have
become commuterland. Though the craft and produce markets
flourish, even they may decline in importance as more and more
village dwellers invest in deep-freezes and stock them up from
the nearest small-town supermarket. However, the membership
decline which gave such cause for alarm in the early seventies
did seem to have been halted by 1984. The Women's Institutes
have, by means of a promotional drive in 1983-84, built up not
only the number of members but also the number of institutes.
(Perhaps cuts in local authority spending on adult education had
something to do with this?) The year 1984 also saw the decline
of the Townswomen's Guilds reversed, with a similar influx of
new members and guilds.

The oldest women's organisation apart from the Mothers
Union, the Co-operative Women's Guild, founded in 1883, has
shrunk from a peak of 87,000 in its great peace campaigning
days just before the Second World War to 15,000 at the time

of writing. Its members are seriously questioning how and even whether the CWG can survive or indeed have a continuing usefulness in the community when the great consumer co-operative movement itself has so altered its character. Women's guilds were firmly based on the local retail shops. Now many a would-be co-operative shopper has no store within even a reasonable bus journey, let alone within walking distance.

Not much younger is the National Council of Women which, surprisingly, started life in 1891 as the Central Conference Council of Women Workers, usually called the CCC. This turned itself into the National Council of Women in 1918 when it affiliated to the International Council of Women, and it became one of the most influential women's organisations of its day. Its annual conference was often called 'the women's parliament' for it drew together many of the most experienced town and city councillors, magistrates and so on, and was often consulted by members of the government. A recent national president, apologising for concentrating so much of her time on fund-raising, wrote, 'It is not possible for staff or officers to cover the same volume of work as we did ten years ago with a staff and a membership twice the present size.' (Several years earlier, at the annual meeting of 1977, the then national president, Mrs Helen Waldsax, asked that the government should 'acknowledge in some constructive form the public service given by so many voluntary organisations to this country' and warned that unless this was done, many organisations would have to function at half strength, or even disappear, which would mean the loss of 'the source of supply of many specialist skills'. She added, 'a very important democratic principle is at stake here', but there has been no sign that Prime Minister Thatcher, who so heartily approves, she says, the voluntary principle, has taken any notice.

Economy – of effort, if not of money – was probably the reason why the National Council for Social Service, now the National Council for Voluntary Organisations, withdrew financial and office support from Women's Forum – rather abruptly and ruthlessly, it appeared to me. This was indeed a sad casualty of changing patterns in the voluntary field. Originally set up by Margaret Bondfield during the Second World War as the Women's Group on Public Welfare, and with fifty affiliated societies and close links with a nationwide network of 'standing conferences of women's organisations', Women's Forum was a very useful consultative body and repository of information. It was Women's Forum which compiled the invaluable 'list of women's organisations in Britain', now maintained by the Women's National Commission. Other smaller but still influential campaigning organisations have folded, like the Six Point Group, the Status of Women Committee and the National Association of Women Citizens. They are missed, but some at least of what they were doing has been taken over by other bodies.

There is no doubt that the setting up of the Women's National Commission in 1969, and the Equal Opportunities Commission in 1975, has lessened the need, or at least the *perception* of the need, for some of the older societies – especially, I think, for the National Council of Women. Probably the NCW itself suggested to some member of the government of the day the desirability of a 'women's consultative committee'. In 1969 this was turned into the Women's National Commission by the Labour Government under Harold Wilson, and it has always had two co-chairmen, one appointed by the government and one chosen by the affiliated voluntary societies. Its great advantage lies in its government funding, its respect-worthy status as a quango and its paid director (always a civil servant), small staff and office just off Whitehall.

Its disadvantage lies in its apparently inflexible constitution which limits the number of affiliated organisations to fifty, insists on their 'nationwide' membership, and seems to have no way of adapting to the great changes that have taken place in the nature of women's organisations. Member organisations include eight trade unions, among them SOGAT, the Transport and General Workers and the General and Municipal Workers, Boilermakers and Allied Trades – none of them notable for commitment to the women's cause. Few of those useful and 'caring' organisations like Gingerbread or the National Association for the Welfare of Children in Hospital are included. Nor is the Fawcett Society, because it is 'too small'. Surely it is time that a new look was taken at this potentially useful body? It *is* a possible channel for the women's view in a way that the Equal Opportunities Commission can scarcely be, since that is a civil service department under the aegis of the Home Office. (Lately the WNC has been recruiting women from non-member organisations for enquiries.)

At first look, The Cause seems to have suffered a serious loss of strength among its older supporters. What about the injection of new life from the women's liberation movement which inspired us with such joy and hope in 1970-71? In some ways I find that story even more depressing. In fact there are young women who have dedicated years to the women's liberation movement who doubt if it still exists as a recognisable movement. There has not been a WLM national conference since 1978; there has not been an issue of that vigorous journal of the groups, *Shrew*, since 1979, and that was a one-off 'special' after a long gap. The only channels of communication now remaining seem to be *Spare Rib*, a monthly feminist-oriented journal; WIRES (Women's Referral and Enquiry Service), at present operating from Oxford, and the Feminist Library and Information Centre (formerly Women's Research and Resources Centre). There are also local newsletters, the best-known and most widely circulated being the *London Women's Liberation Newsletter*, put together, typed and circulated by a collective at A Woman's Place, the long-running centre for the movement in the London area, now excellently housed at Hungerford House on the

Victoria Embankment.

It is wrong to evaluate the new women's movement in terms of membership and 'branches'. Its aim has never been to affect legislation, but to change thinking. At its very core and heart were, and perhaps still are, the 'consciousness-raising groups' which enabled women to look keenly and honestly at their lifestyles and to consider to what extent they were dominated by male thinking, male conventions and male power, physical and economic. I have never laughed at what some people unkindly call 'breast-beating' sessions, though I have not joined in them when invited, saying loftily (but really because of great personal shyness), 'My consciousness was raised years ago.' It is very important for women to learn to put a proper value on their own opinions, attitudes and work, inside or outside the home.

It took those of us who might be described as 'Trads with Lib Connections' some little time to realise how deep were the differences between us. Most of us had (and still have) reservations about the Sex Discrimination Act but would not have declared, as *Women's Report* did, that it was 'tokenism at its worst'. The women's liberation conference in Manchester protested against 'obvious, fundamental omissions of discrimination such as pensions, taxation, social security, etc.', and resolved, 'we demand of the government a comprehensive Sex Discrimination Bill, so that women no longer are defined as dependants, and a Bill that provides for no less than equality under the law for both sexes.' However much we Trad-Libs might have agreed with these sentiments, we knew that to cover all these areas was impossible under our parliamentary system which prevented *financial* provisions from being included.

When I marched with a great number of friends in the International Day March of 1971, the four demands proclaimed on banners were equal pay now; equal education and job opportunities; free contraception and abortion on demand; free twenty-four-hour nurseries. Only inexperienced campaigners would have presented their demands in that way, for a call for twenty-four-hour-a-day nurseries actually convinced a great many homemaking women that the Libs were weird women who were prepared to dump their babies in care right round the clock while they went off and campaigned or otherwise enjoyed themselves. Many Trad-Libs would have supported the demand as it was later revised: 'free, community controlled childcare', just as they would have supported the fifth demand in 1974: 'legal and financial independence for women'. It was the two demands added in 1978 that indicated a great divergence:

An end to discrimination against lesbians.
Freedom from intimidation by the threat or use of violence or sexual coercion. An end to all laws, assumptions and institutions that perpetuate male dominance and men's aggression against women.

Most Trad-Libs, I would say, regard discrimination against lesbians as absurd as well as unjust. Some people (including a few MPs during the debate on Jo Richardson's Private Member's Bill on sex discrimination in 1983) make a great song and dance about the 'harm' lesbians might cause in girls' schools — as if promiscuous heterosexual men could not do a very great deal more harm, both in school and out of it. But I personally do not believe that prejudice and discrimination against lesbians can be dealt with by Act of Parliament. There is, of course, now no legal basis for prosecution for male homosexual acts performed in private, and society is, I hope, gradually growing more tolerant of gays. There never has been any legal basis for discrimination against lesbians, and I should have thought that their best tactic by far would be to go their own way without fuss or fervour except in the comparatively rare cases of overt discrimination, as in the case of lesbian mothers being refused custody of their children. Society has to get used to the idea that same-sex relationships are valid and here to stay, and in my view this acceptance will be more quickly accomplished by calmly and quietly ignoring out-of-date prejudices than by demanding special places on public bodies for lesbians, along with ethnic and other minorities. (If for lesbians why not for grandmothers? There is ageism as well as sexism! . . . But of course grannies do sometimes campaign for recognition, so why, some would argue, should not lesbians also?)

As for that last 'demand' about freedom from intimidation by the threat or use of violence or sexual coercion: Trad-Lib groups are as much concerned with violence on the streets and in the home as the women's liberation groups. What bothers them is the fear that campaigning against 'male dominance and male aggression' appears to involve an overall hostility to men . . . to husbands, fathers, brothers, sons. Indeed, it cannot be denied that this *is* one strand in the tangled ideologies of feminism.

A statement published by the Women's Rights and Resources Centre in 1977 puts very well the basic stance of the women's liberation movement at the time:

It is a movement of women who believe that women in our society are oppressed and discriminated against because of their sex (i.e. sexism) and who are committed to changing that situation. It is not an organisation that you 'join', as you might join a church or a political party. It doesn't have a head office, a president or a book of rules. Since it challenges one of the most fundamental power structures – power based on sex – it has consciously sought to be non-authoritarian, believing that women can work and campaign together without the need for arbitrary rules and officials.

This concept of women working together in a non-authoritarian, non-hierarchical way was the most inspiring thing about the WLM in the seventies. It obviously worked at *Women's Report*; it worked and to a considerable extent still works at *Spare Rib* and A Woman's Place. But there has to be another step, not yet thought through, let alone accepted, whereby decisions can be taken and abided by in a democratic but non-hierarchical way by larger bodies and by groups scattered all over the country – that is to say, passed through an established and accepted chain of communication – not vertically, from top to bottom, as in the Trad organisations, but horizontally, from group to group.

Accounts of WLM conferences in *Women's Report* in its later years recognise this difficulty and suggest the need for 'an honest reappraisal of conference procedure, and indeed organisation'. Its account of a socialist feminist conference in 1979 was a notable example of practical analytical assessment:

Even when something must be organised – this conference for example – there is no mechanism for doing so. A self-selected group of women, the planning group, decided how the conference should be run . . . Little input from other women was sought, hence little could be learnt from experience . . . The movement is frightened of co-ordination. It tends to consist of many isolated autonomous groups pursuing their own policies and aims, ignorant of what others are doing and thinking. A loose network devoid of binding principles is fine so long as we have some network – else no progress can be made. We will be doomed to retrace the same steps over and over again.

The task of pulling together this large, incoherent mass of groups and individuals, often ideologically divided about strategy, always extremely wary, and sometimes quite paranoid about structure and hierarchies, has so far proved impossible. The WLM was to some extent split from the beginning into radical feminists and socialist feminists, and now, to my mind, is more destructively so, because attitudes seem to have hardened and become more positively divided. The very language of debate seems to have become more and more politicised. When I read sentences like the following I want to shrink into myself or run away: 'Both sides have developed highly complex political analyses which are still being developed . . . from an early stage each has had different analytical approaches and different strategic priorities.' The old woman who matriculated in 1923 and the young woman with a CSE from her comprehensive in 1983 are likely to be equally baffled by this talk of 'highly complex political analyses', but in simplified terms the two wings of the WLM are the 'politicos' who say 'the system's the problem' and the 'feminists' who say 'men are the problem' – according to definitions usefully offered by Amanda Sebestyen in a pamphlet, *Feminist Practice*.

The radical feminists' overriding belief is that in any situation the deciding factor must be 'what is best for women' – which obviously could result in attitudes as basically oppressive and unjust to men as men's have for so long been to women. Asserting that a change in the political system will not necessarily mean a change in the situation of women can and sometimes does lead on to the assertion that women should curtail their involvement with men. Socialist feminists, on the other hand, tend to take the line that only when society's fundamental basis is just to all can there be justice for women. Bewildered Trads often find themselves wondering whether anyone but a working-class socialist lesbian can qualify as a true feminist! I think the words of the philosopher Mary Midgley in a *Guardian* article are worth noting:

It is true that women must not build their freedom on the bondage of others. They are not just one more blindly competing interest group. They are half the human race, trying to think for the whole of it. There is no way that women can be separated from the rest of human kind. Most women are poor. But they can only be rescued from poverty by means which would help the poor in general. Even if women could be saved separately, leaving the men to drown, that would still be unjust and immoral.

The 'political' separatism of the women's movement is what distresses a pragmatist like me. I have long accepted the advisability of excluding men from women's centres and many women's gatherings . . . one good reason for which is not so much ideological as practical. There still are men who will pursue a battered wife into a women's refuge, or even attempt entry into a women's centre to find out addresses where she might be. There are still men, believing themselves to be fully sympathetic and well meaning, who will, given less than half a chance, dominate the discussion at any meeting. But women who are not prepared even to *try* to enter into meaningful and productive dialogue with men are really opting out of the struggle for equality. As Mary Midgley reminds us, they are as much half the human race as we are.

But separatism is not confined to the ban on male participation. The *London Women's Liberation Newsletter* has a list of prohibitions about the content and nature of articles on its inside front cover. They include: 'No entries which contravene the seven demands. No entries from men. No ageist, racist, classist entries. No anti-lesbian, anti-semitic, imperialist, fascist entries. No entries from other political parties/groups unless the women's caucus or an individual wants to inform other women about their activities.' To me the most interesting word in this list is 'classist' – a new word for an old, old preoccupation. It indicates that the young theorists of the women's movement are trying to define what they mean by 'class' in their own milieu . . . a well worthwhile task.

One of the librarians at the Feminist Library Information Centre told me that she had got together a group of women to discuss what they meant by 'working class' after advertising in the *London Women's Liberation Newsletter*. To her surprise, twenty-five women turned up at the inaugural meeting, all anxious to move away from traditional definitions. There was a good range of family backgrounds and of expectations in which the women had been brought up. The group's founder had been motivated to explore the issue of class with others because she felt that it was being raised 'in an extremely unproductive way', especially by a group of working-class women who saw middle-class women as the enemy. In a radical feminist journal

Trouble and Strife of this period I found an article which was illuminating about what seems to me an obsessive concern with class difference. The writer was of the opinion that the feeling of inferiority which some women put down to their working-class background probably springs from a cultural difference: the middle-class woman has 'the luxury of words which spring to mind in an argument or debate; an articulateness with the whole of the English language. . . . We at times,' she said, speaking for the working-class majority, 'experience the English language as alien, full of nuances and subtleties which are available to the middle classes. Certain words are totally out of our experience.'

In the early days of Women in Media we were often, to our sorrow and bewilderment, called 'elitist'. Now I begin to think that this may have resulted from our easy command of words – after all, were we not all writers and broadcasters? And so I wonder if some of the anger of women who regard themselves as working class may not be due to the difficult, technical language of political analyses which form a large part of the mandatory reading for would-be feminists. It is wholly a good thing that women's studies courses should proliferate in universities and polytechnics, but they tend to be devised by academics for academics. I have often felt 'excluded' myself, not having been reared on *Das Kapital* or Freud.

The spate of books on women's subjects in the last few years has been extraordinary. Too many, in my view, have been inaccessible to me, who left my grammar school at seventeen, and to the girls who leave their comprehensives at sixteen – not to mention the many others in between. I think it is time to concentrate more attention on the writing, on the simple, comprehensible exposition of ideas rather than on the bibliography. On the other hand, I think there can hardly be too many well-written books about our foremothers which rescue all the thinkers and campaigners, all the women scientists, painters, composers, travellers and philanthropists, to say nothing of all the writers of tracts and pamphlets as well as of plays and novels. Shouldn't schoolchildren be encouraged to do projects on these women rescued from oblivion, as well as on women of the renown of Florence Nightingale and Octavia Hill and Elizabeth Fry?

Does what I have written so far about The Cause seem depressing? I myself see hopeful portents. One of these is the fact that the British electorate not only voted into power a party led by a woman, but also returned that party with an overwhelming majority four years later when she had, so to speak, been tried and tested. The sardonic laughter with which many feminists will greet that statement is, I think, somewhat misguided . . . Margaret Thatcher's politics are anathema to me. She is not a feminist, by any standards, but the fact that she has twice been the head of H.M. Government is a tremendous reinforcement of a claim made by Barbara Castle some years ago: 'Women have conquered the credibility gap', something which I never thought to see in my lifetime. If a woman can be prime minister and a woman can be Lord Mayor of London, that entrenched male enclave, is there any reason why in the lifetime of my daughter, if not in my own, there should not be a woman chairman of the Bank of England, a woman Lord Chancellor, and even a woman Archbishop of Canterbury? The newspapers have stopped referring to the prime minister as a woman, stopped describing her hair-do or her clothes. They are for her or they are against her, but they never, never say, 'What can you expect from a woman?'

If women's liberation groups no longer come together nationally and the membership of some older women's organisations has declined, other soundly based groups of women with common interests are increasing all the time, notably the 'networking' groups like women in the manual trades, women in computing, women in libraries, women in management, women in the civil service, women executive secretaries, the National Organisation for Women's Management

Education (NOWME). Then there are the self-help and caring organisations, largely run by women, like Gingerbread, Cruse, the National Association of Widows, the Pre-school Playgroups Association, the National Association for the Welfare of Children in Hospital, the Association for the Improvement of the Maternity Services. They are not feminist, but they make it shiningly clear how women can and do initiate, organise and maintain voluntary organisations of top-class value to the community.

The National Housewives' Register is a particularly interesting example of the 'new look' women's organisations because it began in the same kind of way as consciousness-raising groups – it started from a letter written to the *Guardian* by a young mother who felt isolated from contact with her own kind, and it was for many years run by volunteer national organisers from their own homes. Individuals were put in touch with each other; local groups were formed to provide stimulating discussion and like-minded friends. Most housebound women feel the need for adult contact of this kind, particularly when, like many NHR members, they are married to men whose jobs take them to different parts of the country. A husband makes his new friends at work, but for the housebound wife tied by young children contacts with potential friends are few indeed. Latterly, of course, as its membership has moved upwards towards 30,000, NHR has had to evolve a structure and to elect (not appoint) a national organiser and provide her with an office and office equipment. The organiser and a 'national group', elected by postal ballot, keep NHR branches informed by means of a quarterly newsletter and necessary communications about activities. But that is the limit of its structure. It seems to work well, although national organisers are not usually willing to serve more than three years and the problem arises of whether the office can be moved around the country as a new organiser is elected. However, the success of the pattern so far is a tribute to the ingenuity of women in working out methods to suit their needs.

A majority of young feminists, I guess, are atheists, humanists or agnostics, and would regard the ordination of women as of a peripheral importance to the status of women in society. I doubt if they are altogether right, and no one could deny that the persistent work of the Movement for the Ordination of Women to the Historic Ministry of the Church, which campaigned for fifty years before handing on its torch to MOW (the Movement for the Ordination of Women), was in the true tradition of feminist action. Basic to many men's thinking though they may be scarcely if at all aware of it, is the concept that man was made by God in His image, to be the superior being, the master, the provider of the rib from which the lesser being, Eve, was created. Once these gallant campaigners, the Anglican deaconesses and the women priests ordained in Anglican communions overseas, have persuaded the Church of England – and they will – to admit women to the full ministry of the church we can wave goodbye to St Paul. In our traditionally Christian culture something of the church's change of stance will inevitably come to influence the thinking of non-church-going men (and women) once women are accepted even theologically as fully adult human beings.

One more remarkable little organisation, to lead me back towards constitutional campaigning for The Cause, is the 300 Group, set up by a 'loner', Lesley Abdela, a brilliant publicist and exceptionally imaginative organiser, to encourage and help women to stand for Parliament. Lesley instituted 'study cruises' across the North Sea, debates on topical subjects in House of Commons committee rooms and celebrations of notable anniversaries, like the entry of Viscountess Astor into the House of Commons, the first woman to take her seat there. Members of the 300 Group are entirely, I would guess, well-educated, middle-class women, but they have drawn support from many of the best-known women in public life and are bound, I think, to have an influence on the political party headquarters in recommending women candidates. But alas, their influence on the 1983 general election was virtually nil. The number of women returned to Parliament was lower than to almost any Parliament since women won the vote, and in 400 of the 650 constituencies throughout the country there was not one woman candidate of any party for whom electors could vote. I can only say that I believe that through the efforts of the 300 Group, the Fawcett Society, the Women in Public Life Group and others, all party headquarters have now been made to feel rather ashamed of their poor showing in the matter of women candidates. It is now up to women in the constituency parties – and to ordinary women voters, whether Trad or Lib or unaligned – to take it into their consciousness that a woman may be at least as good an MP as a man . . . and perhaps better in relation to the matters that affect women personally and politically.

Is there hope for an effective attack on discrimination against women in education, employment and other areas by the Equal Opportunities Commission as many of us, rather sceptically, hoped in 1975? Not very much. The EOC has produced excellent research documents, and has brought together the women's voluntary organisations at a number of enlightening conferences. But this is not all we hoped for. Because it is a quango under the Home Office, the EOC has never entered into direct confrontation with the government on issues of the day, even when the representatives at its consultative conferences have wished it. Concerned, conscientious and hardworking as she was, the first chairman of the Commission, Lady Lockwood, seldom entered the fray to fight discrimination on the shop floor or in the classroom. Her successor, Lady Platt, has seemed even less likely to do so. What many of us had hoped for when the EOC was established was the setting up of centres in every town and city to which women who felt they were discriminated against in pay or opportunity, or in educational opportunity, could go for advice and help.

We ought to have known better. The commissioners (all part-time now) are appointed by the Home Office. The TUC and the CBI are represented, as it were, statutorily. When groups like Women in Media suggested that women with experience of the women's movement should be appointed they were actually told that they had no 'constituency'! Surely even women's groups not drawn to involvement in 'constitutional' procedures should be lobbying Lady Platt and her fellow commissioners and staff to institute more investigations into discriminatory practices. In its first seven years the EOC initiated only seven investigations.

I see rather more encouragement in the initiative begun by Lady (Trixie) Gardner, an Australian dentist, now a member of the House of Lords, who is currently the United Kingdom representative to the United Nations' Status of Women Commission which is due to hold its 'end of decade' session on discrimination against women in Nairobi in 1985. Lady Gardner is the first British representative to the Commission to have set about finding out what the women's NGOs (non-governmental organisations) wanted H.M. Government to put before the UN. I understand that it was that determined young internationalist and feminist, Georgina Ashworth, founder of the Decade Network and the 'Change' pamphlets on women's progress around the world, who suggested the idea, and it was the Women's National Commission which organised it.

The 'soundings' started in 1983 at a packed meeting in a House of Lords committee room of members of a great range of organisations, but apart from the Women's Rights and Resources Centre (now the Feminist Library Information Service) I do not think any of the liberation movement groups were represented. Did the Women's National Commission not have their addresses, did they not invite them, or were the women's liberation groups not interested? Surely women from these groups would have been glad to put forward their strongly held views on, for instance, violence against women, the legal status of women, health, the social services and social security? It is interesting that the women's groups present gave top priority, as a subject for representations by our government to the UN, to education – followed next by health and then international action and employment.

Ever since I began to participate actively in the women's movement I have been motivated predominantly by a longing to be a bridge-builder – between all kinds of women's associations and groups. I do believe that women's consciousness has been raised, and I know from experiences like the 1980 Women's Action Day that a high degree of sisterly co-operation, and even a substantial degree of agreement on policy, can be achieved. Some of the Trad organisations are a bit stuck in their 'anti-political' views and have been conditioned by the media to think every feminist is a shrill, man-hating virago. Similarly, members of some of the newer feminist groups think that members of the Women's Institutes are still interested only in 'jam and Jerusalem' and that most of the rest of the 'organisation women' are Tories. It seems to me that it is this sort of 'political' divide that is proving so hard to cross.

Looking back over the dozen or so years since I began to devote a large part of my time and thought to The Cause, I swing between exhilaration and depression, between fear and hope. The exhilaration of our successes does not fade. There was the passing of the Sex Discrimination Act which, for all its limitations, was a vindication of the effectiveness of the campaign to which Women in Media contributed so much enthusiasm and hard work. There was the moment in Radio Four's 'Today' studio when I was being interviewed by John Timpson, looked across the table at his co-presenter Libby Purves and said, 'If it hadn't been for women like me you wouldn't be there.' There was that torchlight march up Whitehall. There was the heartfelt singing of Ethel Smyth's 'The March of the Women' at the close of Women's Action

Day, linking us with our suffragette foremothers.

Why depression, then? Because as I grow old and less able to kick myself into vigorous action I see groups in which I have been deeply involved flagging and even folding. The one I grieve most over is WIPL (the Women in Public Life sub-group of the Women's Action Group set up as a result of our Women's Action Day in 1980). It brought together stalwarts of all parties, like Ethel Chipchase, former women's officer of the TUC, and former Labour MP Joyce Butler; Lady Banks and Nelia Perman for the Liberals and Lady Gardner for the Tories, as well as a variety of keen, much younger women. (Never scorn the idea of having a life peer on your committee – she can provide a room in the House of Lords which is far more comfortable than an office or a pub . . . and is free!) This happy and energetic group went on deputations to party political headquarters, to a number of government departments and to the Public Appointments Unit which maintains a list of people which government ministers can draw on to fill places on quangos and so on. (Would it were consulted more often.) I think we made a small dent in the thinking of the men we lobbied, but when our grant from the EOC ran out we could no longer pay our part-time co-ordinator – or find anyone with time to do all the work, or any means of paying for stationery, stamps and photocopying. And there is so very much more to be done.

Another source of profound sadness is the failure of all the women working for The Cause to persuade more than a handful of men to *listen* to us. Most of those amiable men we meet in Parliament, industry, business, the professions, in our work, in our play and even in our own homes, look at us quite kindly, but even if they do not tease us – amiably or not so amiably – about our preoccupation with the limitations on women's activities, even if they accept our right to choose our own way of life, few think it is any of their business, and hardly any of them do anything to help.

I am very well aware that organisations come and organisations go. I can remember when the Rechabites, the Oddfellows, the Buffaloes and similar Friendly Societies were at the heart of our 'social security' system and when the maternity and child welfare service was almost entirely run by volunteers. If women's liberation groups and even large and influential women's societies close down, it does not necessarily mean that they have stopped caring or abandoned their involvement. They may well have moved into new involvements. Sad though I am that there seems now no network to bring liberation groups throughout the country together in inspiring, invigorating conferences, I know that the commitment is still there. The fact that there is such a large and enthusiastic readership for feminist books proves it. (Books and publications are now probably the most effective 'glue' bonding feminists together.) If evidence of this were needed, it was provided by the amazingly large turn-out of women for the first International Feminist Book Fair at Covent Garden in the summer of 1984.

When I go through these moments of depression, I remind myself that the Fawcett Society has survived as a 'focus for feminists' for well over 100 years and is still 'knocking on doors' and drawing in women who believe in *action* as the only justification for talk. And when I feel sad that there are so few women today giving a lifetime of service to The Cause, as Millicent Garrett Fawcett did from 1866 to 1928, I remind myself that she never had to earn a living for herself; she never had to rely on a widow's pension or social security; she probably never had to cook her husband's meals or care for her little daughter round the clock, and she certainly did not have to clean the kitchen floor or wash the bed linen.

Perhaps today's crusaders for The Cause who have so many duties, inside and outside the home, don't do too badly? What I am certain of, as certain as that grass is green and summer skies are blue, is that the movement towards the emancipation of women from dependence on and domination by men cannot be reversed. It may take decades to achieve fully that 'equality in law, custom and practice' which is the Fawcett Society's stated goal. One fears that in the Third World not very many women may live to see it. But it will come. As night follows day, it will come.

3

The Art of the Possible

There is no day, no month, no year when it would be exactly right to write about one's political stance or even one's experience of politics. Though one can trace the beginning of one's interest and involvement, and can chart the changes in political parties' ideologies over the years, one can never say: 'This is where I shall always stand; this is my firm and lasting conviction about the way a nation ought to manage its affairs.'

Perhaps the time of my writing this, 1984, is no bad time for *me* to make an assessment, or at least put my personal views and experience on paper. The general election of June 1983 was in some ways dramatic and, for some of us, traumatic. It was the first general election which the Social Democratic Party had fought. It was the first general election since 1934 at which the Labour Party had been routed. It was the first general election to make the public aware of the case for proportional representation, or 'fair votes', as we call it now.

For me it was the first general election since I was a schoolgirl – apart from Dr Una Kroll's campaign as a Women's Rights candidate in 1974 – in which I had involved myself in day-by-day campaigning. Because of this involvement I was more intensely aware of the political issues, the personalities, the campaign strategies and methods and the role of the media and the pollsters. So I must take a deep breath and try to sort out my political attitudes, principles, hopes, fears and convictions.

In *Forgetting's No Excuse* I wrote: 'I began life as a little Liberal. It seems that I shall end it as some kind of liberal.' I added that it had seemed to me, 'blow by blow, that Socialism had become a label for a political party rather than for an ideal or a crusade.' And then, 'There isn't really any label now to cover my kind of beliefs – social justice, government by consent, international brotherhood, and non-violence.' That was written in 1971. Ten years later, in 1981, when the Social Democratic Party was formed, I became a founder member, and when the Alliance with the Liberals was agreed, in the run-up to the 1983 election, I saw my prophecy fulfilled . . . 'some kind of a liberal'.

So I must begin my story by trying to explain my increasing unease in the Labour Party. It started, I think, with Labour's opposition to British membership of the European Economic Community. For as long as I can remember I had been an internationalist. My schoolgirl ambition before I was mysteriously 'called' to the profession, or trade, of journalism, was to become a secretary at the League of Nations headquarters in Geneva. This was a result of my pacifism which was widespread among the young people who had grown up in the 1920s and who were intensely aware of the horrifying slaughter of millions of young men of the European nations in the 1914-18 war. This horror remains a basic part of my political thinking. To my mind it is absolutely vital to the survival of the world as I have known it – a world which draws its political and legal systems, its belief in democracy and justice, its culture and philosophy, from Europe, including ancient Greece and Rome – that the nations of Europe should learn to co-operate and never again contemplate armed conflict, the one European nation against another. To think in rather more up-to-date terms, I believe it is vital that Europe should gradually become a viable entity so that it can truly be a balancing factor between Russia and the Eastern bloc and the United States.

I am not really touched by the arguments that membership of the Community has pushed up prices, especially of food. Equally, I am not touched by the argument that to quit Europe would cause the loss of many British jobs. I understand the alarm many good Labour supporters feel at the possible domination of the international cartels. I share the feeling that Britain is bearing an unfair proportion of the cost of the Community and can accept that French farmers are even more self-protective than British farmers. But I still think that we have to battle on steadfastly to make European co-operation *work*.

The United Kingdom is no longer the core and centre of a Commonwealth of Nations, let alone the possessor of an Empire, as it was for many years after I was born. So we need a new partnership, a new family, a new ambience, a new ideological power base. When you compare how much of the basic British way of life has been developed over the centuries through the influence of Greece, Rome, Italy, France and Germany with how much it owes either to Russia and the Eastern bloc or to the USA, you cannot doubt, it seems to me, where our natural 'home' is. So, surely, we have to plod on trying to plait together all the varied strands of European political thought and practice – and to persuade our fellow citizens that voting in elections for members of the European Parliament is no less important than for members of the Parliament at Westminster.

How can it have come about that the Labour Party – the party of international brotherhood, as I always assumed it to be – has seemed so often antagonistic to the European Connection? One can understand an Enoch Powell fiercely rejecting the slightest possibility of Britain giving up any grain of sovereignty over its own affairs, but not people who call themselves socialists. It was disconcerting to read quite recently the postscript to a letter my brother wrote to me in June 1950, not long before he died: 'What crazy world is this we live in, when the Leader of the Tory Party advocates a United States of Europe and the Leader of the Socialist Party says that he rejects out of hand any suggestion of supra-national control.'

The next thing that bothered me increasingly was unease over the doctrine that more and more nationalisation was the cure for all the nation's economic ills. Of course when I joined the ILP Guild of Youth, around 1927, that was exactly what I thought, and I still am appalled at the idea of 'privatising' any part of essential services like the Post Office, the health service and the transport system. For I can think back to the 1920s and remember that desperate fight to nationalise the mines and the railways and the plight of the working-class families, especially the women, who could not afford a doctor in the days before the National Health Service.

But nationalising the great industrial companies? Would it really be better for the economy? Would it really be better for the employees? Clearly the employees of the National Coal Board and British Rail are *not* notably happier in their employment than they were when their industries were in private hands – though the miners, particularly, are infinitely better off than they were, as anyone knows who can remember the General Strike of 1926 and A. J. Cook stumping the country with his demand: 'Not a penny off the pay, not a minute on the day.' Industries run by national boards tend to be at least as subject to strikes as those run by private companies. The nature of the management may be part of the reason for this, but one has sadly to admit that 'much does want more', and that few people are moved to sacrifice their own interest for the common good. A quite common cause of strikes, though seldom admitted, is determination to maintain the differential between the strikers' pay and that of other jobs. I do remember, in the Depression of the thirties, journalists voluntarily giving up Saturday and other freelance work so that it could be given to men and women who were otherwise unemployed, but that is a fairly rare example, I think, of 'one for all and all for one'.

The older I grow the more I dislike the idea of 'the bigger the better'. That companies with quite different interests should amalgamate just because it gives them more financial clout is repellent to me. I incline to the view that the bigger the *less* efficient (especially in human terms). And if this is so in private companies, it must surely also be so in the state-run industries. The bigger the organisation the more remote is its central control point from the peripheral human being, whether employee or customer. The same thinking must apply to local authorities, and indeed ultimately to the running of the EEC.

The reason for the Thatcher Government's onslaught on the Greater London Council and other metropolitan authorities seemed to be more to curb what Conservatives called 'socialist profligacy' than to strengthen the voters' interest in and responsibility for the way their services are run. It is obvious that if there are not to be very large authorities like the GLC, the Greater Manchester Council and so on, there has to be close co-operation between all smaller authorities over services as vital as transport. But we can see from the nationalised gas and electricity industries, now run day-to-day by regional boards, how wide is the gap between the boards and the consumers. This separation has led to the implementation of such nonsensical policies as the Conservative Government's instruction to the Gas Board to put up its prices so that British Electricity could compete. All connected with the gas industry were naturally opposed to such a step at a time when their trading profits were healthy.

It seemed odd indeed that a Conservative Government should insist on 'competition' of this kind – protecting the weaker against the stronger; it seemed even odder that this concealed tax, inevitably falling most heavily on the poorest section of the community, should have been regarded as good fiscal policy. But the gas and electricity consumer bodies are not nearly powerful enough to influence their regional boards to any material extent, let alone the Government. Nor is POUNC, the Post Office Users National Council, which can raise scarcely a cheep against rising postal charges and reduced services. Once upon a time a letter posted early in the morning would reach a local destination the same afternoon. Often enough now a letter posted with a first-class stamp will take up to four days to reach an address less then twenty miles away. In our area, if a postman falls sick or goes on leave, he is replaced by a colleague on overtime, so that even a letter posted locally with a first-class stamp may reach its destination with the 'first delivery' at 1 p.m. to 2 p.m. When the quest for 'economy' is pursued to such lengths it seems to me to be verging on fraud.

Nationalisation only makes sense in human terms if it is operated for the consumers' (as well as the employees') good and is monitored by potentially powerful, democratically elected councils or committees representing the consumer interest. The story of the declining co-operative movement well illustrates this point – that bigger is not necessarily better. The co-operative movement's stated aim, at the time of writing, is to cover the country with only twenty-five retail societies, and to rationalise at every level, cutting out the smaller shops and any stores which are not profitable. The result is that thousands of older members without cars are now quite unable to 'shop at the Co-op'. The last general secretary of the Co-operative Women's Guild told me, just before she retired: 'I have half an hour's walk from the Guild office to the nearest co-op, and you can't get there other than by walking. From my home you can add another fifteen minutes, so it means dragging a trolley for three-quarters of an hour there and back through a crowded street market.'

Laurie Pavitt, Co-operative and Labour MP for Brent South, who grew up in the co-operative movement (his mother was a leading Guild member), wrote in the *Co-operative News* at the time of the last general election: 'I am now a Co-op MP, with no co-ops. More than twenty co-op shops previously displayed a poster saying "Send this co-operator to Parliament". Now? No shops, no windows, no publicity.' – and, I would add, no feeling among those co-op members who do still have a co-op hypermarket at which they can shop that they are in any sense members of a movement that belongs to them. 'Caring and Sharing' is the Co-op slogan. Much sense that makes to people like me who not only haven't had any kind of a co-op store within walking distance for more than ten years but also now (since a large co-operative department store was closed) have none within range of one bus journey. The co-operative managerial leadership has been working on the principle that bigger *is* more efficient and better. The decline in co-operative trade has, however, become noticeable, and doubts about policy are quite often expressed in letters to the *Co-operative News*. The message of 'nationalisation' often also seems to be 'rationalise', 'streamline', 'computerise', even though its stated aim is to remove the power from private individuals to 'the people'. But how, now, do 'the people' influence the control and development of the mines, the railways, gas and electricity? How would 'the people' control the banks, the favourite target of the nationalisers?

This scepticism about nationalisation was an important ingredient in my decision to join the SDP. The third factor was the divisions in the Labour Party and the jettisoning of long-standing, conscientious MPs in re-selection processes stagemanaged by ardent Leftists. No doubt there have been and still are Labour Members of Parliament whose activity in the House of Commons seems to have been minimal, whose views have grown steadily less radical and whose concern for their constituents has not been notable. But this certainly does not apply to all Labours MPs nor to all the prospective Parliamentary candidates turned down by constituency caucuses of left-wing socialists. The autocratic use of power by some trade union officials and executives to support or reject this or that candidate for Labour leadership or parliamentary candidature is deeply offensive to me — as is every aspect of the ruthless pursuit of power and the deliberate personal denigration of an opposing candidate by foul means rather than fair.

So I joined 'the nice people's party'. Does 'nice' mean 'wet'? When I took the chair at an SDP rally in Manchester not long after having been elected to its national committee, I made a plea for 'niceness'. I don't think it went down particularly well. People don't like newspaper and TV gibes about being 'nice', for they fear that it implies they are 'wet', woolly-minded and amiable political novices. I don't mean that 'nice' does necessarily mean being soft in the head, just as I don't believe that being determined necessarily means being ruthless and kicking one's adversaries in their vitals. If this were how the SDP came to operate on its way to power I fear I should have to leave it, as I had to leave the Labour Party.

However did I, at the age of seventy-five, come to offer myself as a candidate for the SDP's national committee? Not surprisingly to people who know my involvement in the women's movement, it was at a meeting of Women for Social Democracy that the suggestion was made to me by fellow-members in Blackheath, where I live now, and in Greater Manchester, where I used to live. I was flattered, of course, but dubious. Too old? Not sufficiently politically well informed? I talked to *Guardian* colleague and friend Polly Toynbee, and let her persuade me to allow my name to go forward. I should be an 'independent' kind of candidate, she said — having no ambition at all for Parliamentary candidature. So I did stand for election and thoroughly enjoyed the process of collecting support in a wide variety of constituencies from friends with whom I had worked in the Fawcett Society and Women in Media, as well as in the SDP. My oldest supporter, Gertrude Boyd, was then ninety-eight; the youngest was not more than thirty. The carefully constructed democratic nature of the SDP constitution meant that I needed to be nominated by not more than two members of any one constituency party but must have

supporters from at least ten parties. It was, you might say, a
bobby's job for me, my name being quite well known through
my *Guardian* writings and my Fawcett activities, and my friends
being very well spread over the London area and the north-
west.

I was on a painting holiday in Massa Lubrense, Bay of
Naples, when I learned that I had come fourth in the ballot
among the nationally elected women candidates and was therefore elected. My companions celebrated heartily with me under
a clear night sky, overlooking the Mediterranean, and I mom-
entarily felt a Very Important Person. But not for very long.
When I began to attend the monthly meetings of the national
committee in the boardroom of the SDP's Cowley Street
headquarters, I began to think my earlier doubts were justified.

Had I, tacitly exploiting my *Guardian* connection, been right
to stand for this central decision-making body against women
who were so much more politically experienced, had given so
much more service for the party and were so much younger and
more energetic than I? I certainly was a learner rather than a
contributor and I was sometimes dispirited by the long
discussion of tactics within the constituencies and *vis-à-vis* the
Liberals. Was this what politics is all about? I am afraid a lot of
it inevitably is, and it takes a very strong and politically
idealistic spirit to survive bickering over procedural hassles.
Procedure has to be sorted out, but perhaps the political
novices, 'the nice people', the 'wets', have a role in indicating
now and then, when we can summon courage to challenge the
tacticians, that 'ends' are really what matter and what keep
enthusiasm alive, and, even, that means can corrupt ends.
Sometimes I fear that the more 'political' one becomes, the
more one is likely to lose sight of the goal that made one join a
party in the first place. Sometimes I think that many women
hesitate to enter the political battle because of a revulsion
against 'tactics' and 'confrontation'.

The only contribution I was hopeful of making to the work

of the national committee was attending its communications committee along with high-powered professionals in advertising, public relations, opinion-poll analysis and statistics. Perhaps I imagined that my female viewpoint was not very seriously regarded by the largely masculine committee; perhaps my knowledge of the women's side of newspapers and magazines might have been useful in time − but in fact all the sub-committees were suspended on the eve of the 1983 general election and the communications committee was not re-convened in my time on the national committee. I was sorry, but I learned quite a lot from these experts, even if they learned nothing from me.

My anxiety about the influence of the media on politics today was intensified. Even before the general election of 1983 there was disturbing evidence of this. When I was young I used to talk to co-operative women's groups about the influence of Lord Beaverbrook's *Daily Express* on the attitude of the British people towards international peace initiatives, and we were well aware that Lord Rothermere's *Daily Mail* took a pro-Fascist, pro-Nazi line in the years leading up to the war. But this was a different sort of influence from that of the media today. It was direct, overt and clearly dictated by the political views of the newspaper proprietors.

Today when we talk of the media (often assumed to be a singular noun, though in every sense it is plural!) we are talking of a conglomeration of a great many *people* − newspaper proprietors, editors, reporters, columnists and sub-editors; BBC governors, heads of departments, producers, reporters, interviewers, commentators; ITV directors and their teams of men and women at various levels of command and on the ground. All these are in some way involved in the job not only of reporting what is happening in an election but also of interpreting − and, many would say, influencing it.

The dictum of C. P. Scott, great editor of the *Manchester Guardian*, is always being quoted: 'Comment is free; fact is sacred.' But in any situation, particularly any political situation, there are many facts. For reasons of time and space a selection of facts has to be made and it is in that selection that the inbuilt, perhaps unconscious bias of the reporter/ interviewer/commentator/sub-editor/producer is liable to show – as well as, and perhaps more than, the bias of the editor or proprietor. A grossly biased selection of facts results in such a distorted picture that even the political ignoramus is likely to recognise it. But two by-elections of 1983 produced voting results which quite clearly had been influenced by media coverage. The newspaper press's picture of the left-wing Labour candidate Peter Tatchell was smeared over with hints about his homosexuality and his advocacy of extra-Parliamentary political activity. This smear tactic sickened many people who would in no way have voted for a candidate so far to the Left as he was, but it made it quite certain he would lose his fight.

The by-election at Darlington shortly after was almost certainly lost for the SDP by the media's handling of their candidate, Tony Cooke. He was not an experienced politician; he had been a prospective Parliamentary candidate for only a very short time; he was certainly not a match for the very experienced and sharp-witted TV reporter Vincent Hanna whose questioning made him look a fool. Perhaps Tony Cooke might not have won the seat in any case. Perhaps he did not deserve to win it and the SDP should have taken care to select a tougher and more adroit candidate. But it is worth bearing in mind that Mr Hanna is known in the National Union of Journalists as a convinced left-winger. Can he honestly claim that he would have pinpointed the weak places in the armoury of a novice *left-wing* Labour candidate in the same fashion? I hope he has tried, or will try, to answer this question.

Every political commentator must have 'bias' in the sense of an honestly held viewpoint. A political reporter would scarcely be human if he or she did not have a personal point of view, even a set of profound convictions. Is there not a case for men and women with acknowledged political allegiances to be assigned to other duties during the period of elections? The SDP's Darlington by-election flop must have alerted many political groups apart from the SDP's own national committee to the fearful burden carried by every by-election candidate in a seat which is 'marginal'. Candidates of all parties now are likely to have 'minders', not just to see that the candidate appears at the right place at the right time but that they say the right things to the right people and are briefed on up-to-the-minute issues. Crash courses in political strategy as well as political theory are advocated.

One can hardly suppose that good nature and good intentions are enough to fit a candidate of any party for membership of the House of Commons. But sometimes one fears that basic conviction, sincerity, firmness of purpose and altruistic desire to serve one's fellows are coming to be of minimal value compared with a quick tongue, a facility for dealing with interviewers' questions and a charismatic television personality. Party leaders now are evaluated to such an extent on their television impact that one is driven to wonder whether any candidate is as nice, as well informed, as sincere, as firm of purpose and as capable of leadership as he or she appears to be on the Box? The Liberal leader David Steel made such a notable impact on television during the 1983 election campaign that millions of voters would probably have been pleased to see him in Downing Street, even though he had never — through no fault of his own, of course — held even the most junior government office. On the other hand, the other Alliance leader, Roy Jenkins, a former Home Secretary, Chancellor of the Exchequer and president of the EEC, was talked down by the media, on the strength of his TV appearances, as 'worthy but dull'.

One could not help feeling when that sincere, able and most likeable man Michael Foot stood down from the Labour Party leadership that the choice of his successor was bound to be greatly influenced by the TV factor. And so Neil Kinnock triumphed, not totally because he was more able, more energetic, closer in his views to the majority of Labour supporters or of trade unionists, but to some extent at least because in front of the cameras he had a pleasing, impish smile, and is ready-witted in dealing with even such 'hard-line' question masters as Sir Robin Day. When I repine about this, my older friends remind me that the leaders of long ago rose to power and influence because of their powerful oratory – David Lloyd George, Aneurin Bevan and even Winston Churchill. But I doubt if this was true of the Liberal leader H. H. Asquith or the Tory leader Neville Chamberlain. And can anyone picture that admirable Labour prime minister who presided over the introduction of the Welfare State, Clement Attlee, being a runaway success on the Box?

So I asked myself how much Margaret Thatcher owed her immense success to media support. Initially one must, in all honesty, admit, scarcely at all. When she emerged as leader of the Conservative Party it was an astonishment to many, if not a majority of, members of her own party. She owed her success in the leadership contest partly to her own courage and determination, partly to luck, and partly to the gentlemanly attitudes of some of her party colleagues who did not want to be seen as wishing to ditch the former prime minister, Edward Heath. Margaret Thatcher, it seemed to me then, was regarded as a useful diversion. If Willie Whitelaw, now Lord Whitelaw, had accepted nomination he would very probably have been elected, and the picture of British politics for the next decade would have been considerably different. Margaret Thatcher stood firm and was elected.

Disliking almost everything about her policies as I do, I am still glad that a member of the 'second sex' achieved the premiership of the United Kingdom in my lifetime. Perhaps in a way I am a little glad that the first woman prime minister is a

Tory. One is free to express dislike not only of her politics, her economic fanaticism, her passion for privatisation and total incomprehension of the plight of the unemployed, but also of her apparent indifference to specifically women's issues. If our first woman prime minister had been Shirley Williams or any woman leader of the Alliance or of the Labour party, how miserable it would have been to hear people say 'she is no friend to women'. And it probably would be said by ardent feminists even of a *feminist* prime minister ... if one can imagine such a person . . . for she would be driven, I believe, to concentrate her thinking and her activities in Cabinet and out of it on matters of life-and-death importance like nuclear disarmament, before giving time to working out policies to secure equality between the sexes.

The psychologist Anthony Clare's analysis of Margaret Thatcher offered some penetrating insights into the way her 1983 election campaign was fought as well as into the nature of the chief protagonist. In 1983 he wrote in *The Listener:* 'The Labour Party's failure to acknowledge the Madison Avenue realities of the modern television election is a striking indication of the way this country, or a powerful element within it, resolutely insists on remaining "quaint"'. Was it 'quaint' then to feel a little sick at the way Margaret Thatcher's election campaign was master-minded by Christopher Lawson, previously in charge of a Mars Bar company called Vendapak which sold pre-cooked meals for automatic vending machines? Christopher Lawson was appointed by the Conservative Party chairman as Director of Marketing. Marketing Mars Bars was evidently an excellent preparation for marketing Margaret Thatcher. When this remarkably skilful man went to the Conservative Party central office in 1981, the Conservatives were third in the opinion polls, behind both Labour and the new SDP/Liberal Alliance. Michael Cockerill, who prepared a programme on the Tories' election campaign, wrote in *The Listener* also in 1983 that 'one right-wing journalist wrote at the time that if Lawson succeeded in selling Mrs Thatcher to an unwilling electorate it would be an advertising triumph that would make selling ice-cubes to Eskimos seem like kids' stuff'.

He did succeed . . . partly by the most sophisticated technique of analysing voters' views and popular and unpopular issues ever seen in Europe. He also initiated the use of the 'head-up' device (first used in Britain by President Reagan) at a razzmatazz rally of 5,000 young Conservatives. It is a device which projects a prepared speech onto a pair of screens in front of the speaker which only he or she can see, and which enables him or her to look directly at the audience, from the right of the hall to the left. It is called, with a cynicism that repels and unnerves me, 'the sincerity machine'. I think that even I, with a scripted speech on a desk in front of me, can talk to an audience and make them feel I am involved with them, and they with me, without the need of artificial aids. Winston Churchill learned by heart all those magnificent war-time orations by which he raised the courage and strengthened the determination of British people and their friends across Europe during the Second World War. Is it 'quaint' to question whether the impact would have been so powerful if he had had the use, in the Commons or elsewhere, of a pair of 'sincerity screens'?

Perhaps it *is* – but I do not think it is 'quaint' to ask whether democracy is best served by public relations and marketing techniques which are based on the rule that the more often you repeat a political argument the more acceptable it will become and the more the electorate will come to believe it . . . For these techniques are operated by people who are paid enormous fees for their work, whether or not they have any loyalty to the doctrines of the party which is paying them, and the party with the most money will be able to afford the widest and most sophisticated coverage. It strikes me as an extraordinary gap in our control of electoral expenditure that though in the constituencies every penny has to be accounted for to the Returning Officer, nationally parties can spend million upon million without any limit except the willingness of supporters to subscribe. The solid financial base of the party of big business and the party of the trade unions obviously gives them an immense advantage. The other parties, even those with as many adherents nationwide as the SDP-Liberal Alliance, are inevitably and permanently at a disadvantage . . . at a very honourable disadvantage, since their support rests solely upon the convictions of their members.

'Quaint' it may be, but I am convinced that in politics sincerity is what matters and that in the long run a synthetic appearance of sincerity is not convincing. Or if it is, I want no part in it.

Even some of the SDP's pre-election poster advertising was, I thought, 'too clever by half', appealing more to fellow public relations and advertising experts than to the ordinary man and woman walking by. The one moment in the party's pre-election television party political broadcast that made me sit tense in my chair was the summing up by party president Shirley Williams – simple, direct, utterly sincere. Shirley does not need to be worked over by anyone – as Margaret Thatcher was – as to voice, appearance or manner. She speaks as she thinks, as she is, and her voice is a gift of nature, not of some speech therapist.

The two things that most bothered most electors in the 1983 election – and will very probably bother them in the next election, whenever that may be – were unemployment and defence. To me it was almost beyond belief that the Conservative Party evidenced so little concern for the unemployed and had only miniscule plans for job creation. With three million men and women without jobs and nightly reports on TV of more factories closing down, one would have expected that the electorate would angrily reject a party which had no more to say about unemployment than that it was a product of world-wide recession. The reason I myself felt so

bitter about this aspect of Tory 'policy' was that I lived
through the traumatic Depression of the thirties in the
Lancashire cotton town of Bolton.

Having come from the relative prosperity of Leicester I was
horrified not only by the 'deadness' of Bolton and the other
cotton towns but also by the number of men hanging about on
the street corners and waiting in the dole queue. The evidence
of poverty and misery was all about me. This was the time of
that heart-breaking play *Love on the Dole* and the time of the
hunger marchers. It was also, as we who are old vividly
remember, the time of President Roosevelt's New Deal, which
gave all of us an inspiration as to what might be done for the
workless by the setting up of great public works – needed in
the USA then and much needed in the UK today.

There was a deep and heartfelt sympathy right through the
nation for the men thrown out of work. (The problems of the
employed women were not appreciated. Woman were thought
to be abominably selfish if they held on to a job which a man
might do.) Good people like the members of the almost
obsessively 'non-political' Townswomen's Guilds had fund-
raising efforts to buy coal for the unemployed, collected seeds
for their allotments and clothes for their children, had
'unemployment boxes' into which members put what they
could spare and ran raffles for 'six pots of marmalade'. Today
there is Social Security and the children of the unemployed are
not, thank goodness, in danger of developing rickets or having
to stay off school for lack of a pair of watertight shoes.
(Though things can be bad for the families of striking miners,
and their sympathisers lend support in much the same way
Townswomen did in the thirties for the great mass of the
unemployed.)

But in the eighties Mrs Thatcher's own constituents and the
electors of the prosperous counties of the south-east seem
unable to imagine the shock of receiving a redundancy notice
in a pay packet, let alone what long-term unemployment

feels like. There are other ways of starving than being short of food. You can starve for lack of occupation, self-respect and the companionship of your fellows. A Sheffield steel worker told a *Guardian* reporter that after two years' 'redundancy' he was not glad to be done with his hot, dirty and dangerous job. 'I miss the lads at work,' he said. And isn't it even worse that not only middle-aged men but also youngsters gradually get used to being 'kept' by the community? Unable to contribute anything to their own maintenance or the maintenance and servicing of their fellow citizens, they can but fritter away their lives, not standing on street corners like their grandfathers, but in watching the telly or listening to Radio 1 on their trannies.

During the 1983 general election Tony Benn claimed that eight and a half million people had voted for 'an openly socialist policy'. This made me ask myself, with a keenness I had never felt before, 'But what is socialism?' In his vivacious *Intelligent Woman's Guide to Socialism and Capitalism* (which I first read aboard an eight-day boat to Boston, Massachusetts, in 1929), George Bernard Shaw declared that 'Socialism means equality of income and nothing else.' If only it did. If only it could. If only we could all stand on a level footing for ever more. But socialism can't be as simple as that. It must not only mean the wish and the will to abolish poverty and social injustice, but also an agreed strategy for doing it. This is where virtually irreconcilable differences arise between people like me and some of those who think of themselves as socialists. There are, I understand, people who would close down British Leyland and other vast industrial enterprises by industrial action in the hope and belief that this would bring about the total collapse of the capitalist system and leave the way open for the establishment of a socialist state. We ought to know by now that this would inevitably lead to a period of frightful and probably violent chaos before any replacement sytstem could be established and stabilised.

From my late teens onwards I always thought of myself as a

socialist. What did I mean by socialism? Only, I think, that I
passionately believed in social justice. Longman's *Modern
English Dictionary* (1976) gives a definition which I certainly
would have accepted: 'A political and economic theory
advocating collective ownership of the means of production and
the control of distribution . . . it is based on the belief that all,
while contributing to the good of the community are equally
entitled to the care and protection which the community can
provide.' I should *not* have accepted socialism in the sense my
Concise Oxford Dictionary (1934) defines it: 'Principle that
individual freedom should be completely subordinated to
interests of community, with any deductions that may correctly
or incorrectly be drawn from it e.g. substitution of co-operative
for competitive production, national ownership of land and
capital, state distribution of produce, free education and feeding
of children and abolition of inheritance.' Take your pick.

I suppose the only economic strategy I have ever fully and
totally endorsed is that of the consumer co-operative
movement. (I actually wrote a best-selling pamphlet for the Co-
operative Press called *The People in Business*.) But the immensely
successful tactic which the Rochdale Pioneers instituted in the
Toad Lane store, Rochdale, Lancashire, in 1844 – dividend on
purchases rather than on share capital – has now long been
abandoned by the movement, and the control of retail,
wholesale and productive enterprises by directors elected by
retail society members has been so diluted as to be scarcely
meaningful. The educational sections of the movement are also
losing the battle for existence *vis-à-vis* the drive for economic
survival in the war with the great supermarket chains.

My political thinking, such as it is, has been coloured for
years by F. D. Roosevelt's dictum 'politics is the art of the
possible' – another way of putting the Fabians' 'inevitability of
gradualness'. That is to say that I believe that if you work away
long enough and with sufficient conviction and determination
you can prepare the ground – that is, public opinion – for

change. Changes imposed without fairly general assent will at best be bypassed by all sorts of dodges and fiddles and 'moonlighting' types of private enterprise, and at worst will be resisted by widespread 'industrial' action, by the flight of capital, or even by violence. I am totally opposed, by nature and by conviction, to the use of violence, personal or political, but one has to recognise that sincere campaigners up against an impregnable blank wall are likely to resort to violent methods when they are denied access to the ballot box . . . like the suffragettes in the early years of this century; like the 25 million Blacks in South Africa today.

When Bennite socialists say that 'the right to free speech is meaningless without the right to be heard by others' I applaud. But when they argue against the right of inheritance I am apt to look woebegone and say, 'But I wish to leave my small estate to my beloved granddaughters.' I feel the same about rights of ownership. If you say to a dustman who wants to buy his council flat that this is anti-social, he may well look at you first with incredulity and then with resentment. 'I've worked hard to be able to afford it, haven't I? Why shouldn't I buy my flat, then? Better investment than National Savings, innit? Keeps pace with inflation, dunnit?' It would, I think, take longer than the lifetime of a Parliament or two to convince the ordinary voter that he or she is not entitled to own his or her own home. I think it may be a natural human impulse to own things, to work to own things and to love and fight for what we own. And if not inborn, this concept is so deeply embedded in our conditioned thinking that it would take much more than one generation to make the concept 'all property is theft' even superficially acceptable.

The whole concept of class warfare seems to me out of date. One reason I am in the SDP is that it has an 'anti-class' image. I do not seem able to find anyone who will provide me with a definition of 'working class' which seems applicable to the way we live now. I have been an employed person, a member of a trade union affiliated to the TUC since I was seventeen. That doesn't make me working class. I have been made redundant and lived on unemployment pay. That didn't make me working class. I don't believe anyone, and certainly not Viscount Stansgate, Anthony Wedgwood Benn, can *become* working class by renouncing his title and becoming plain, hail-fellow-well-met Tony Benn.

Who *is* working class then, in society today? And why? Are our pleasant and efficient dustmen working class? Or the friendly members of the NUR who staff our local British Rail station? Or the printers, members of the toughest unions in the TUC, who set into type and print what I write? The crews of the buses I ride on? Or only the men who work in the steel foundries, the car industry and the mines? I don't care a scrap if queries like this make me sound naïve to my younger friends. I really want to know who is regarded by them as working class and why. Even the difference between poor and comfortably off has been blurred. Even being poor, like many unsupported mothers and pensioners, does not make you working class.

I believe that the economic difference between employers and employed needs to be worked at hard and steadfastly. We have a very long way to go in developing employee participation and responsibility, in control of industrial monopolies (especially the soulless international cartels) and in devising and operating curbs on the activities of exploitive tycoons. But I now feel that the sharpest divisions in our society are cultural rather than financial, and that the greatest area of underprivilege is in education. We should not, of course, forget how much progress has been made during this century. I have a photograph in one of my mother's snapshot albums of me, aged six or seven, on the back row of a class of sixty children at an elementary school where my father was then a teacher. Almost all those children, some of whom are noticeably ragged and unkempt, would have left school at fourteen. Their older brothers and sisters also probably left at thirteen, or were 'part-timers'. Hardly one of them had the slightest chance of higher education.

I was one of the lucky ones, getting a scholarship at the age of ten to one of the earliest girls' grammar schools, established in the 1870s. Probably, had I wished it, my father would have managed to send me with the aid of a small bursary or scholarship to a university or teacher training college. But even from this very good, academic school only a handful of girls went on each year to higher education. We forget how few universities and colleges there were then. Today a youngster from a disadvantaged background can, if he or she has an extra share of brains and determination, get to the top of the educational tree. I met one such in a 'staff and delegates' coach' going to a SDP conference. He was not only the first person in his large family ever to go to university, but also the very first pupil in his London comprehensive school to do so, and he was on his way the following autumn to Oriel College, Oxford. Happily, I met him again at another SDP conference . . . he looked a new man, very nicely dressed and groomed, and quietly, happily confident. He was on his way. If there are only a few hundred boys and girls like him, able to make the most of their natural endowment with the aid of state support, I would think it a blessed improvement on things as they were when I was young.

But educational opportunities are not equal all over the country — not equal for boys and girls, and not equal for all sections of the community — and until we can find some answer to the disadvantages suffered by the children of the poor and the culturally backward and by immigrant families we have a great deal of thinking to do. In education as in health care, the *best* should be available for everyone, not just what cheeseparing governments and local authorities may decide is 'adequate'. But I cannot quite bring myself to accept that no one should ever be allowed to opt out of the state system, either in the case of a serious illness or a serious need for special education. My husband had admirable care, beyond all criticism, under the National Health Service. But would I not have struggled to pay any fees, even extortionate fees, if it had seemed necessary to save his life? Our daughter made her own way through the state system to an excellent academic 'direct grant' school, but when she was facing the 'eleven plus' we did pay a private tutor a modest fee to sort out her problems in maths. I think most parents would be inclined to do the same if they could.

The educational system has to have some degree of flexibility, not just because parents will always tend to seek out the best they can find and can afford for their young (though of course it would often be better if we would engage in the battle to improve what is available for all), but also so that educational pioneers like A. S. Neill and Dora Russell are not barred from trying out new ideas. I know very well that if I had had an exceptionally musical child I would have fought tooth and nail and made any kind of sacrifice to get him or her into a specialised music school.

I have left until last the political question that troubles us all most deeply . . . nuclear disarmament and defence. Often I have felt deeply ashamed of having opted out of participation in the peace movement in which I was so much involved in my youth since I became active in the SDP. Why was I not phoning round my friends and acquaintances saying, 'Please can I cadge a lift to Greenham Common?' How could I leave the Labour Party which has — more or less — committed itself to a policy of unilateral disarmament and join a party which takes its stand very positively on the multilateral approach? I find it difficult to explain to myself, let alone to my friends. I know that I myself am still a pacifist, in the sense of denying categorically that it is better to be dead than red. I deny it for myself and I deny it for my granddaughters. I remember a German Social Democratic refugee from Nazism saying to me during the Second World War: 'The river always finds its way to the sea, even if it has to go underground.' And I believe that however many decades it took, the spirit of democracy in this country would never die, even under a Communist or Fascist dictatorship. But if you are dead you are dead, and in the event of a nuclear war so are your children and your grandchildren and all your friends, relations and your dear cats and dogs – in the most hideous imaginable fashion.

I profoundly believe that there is no defence against the nuclear bomb, and that no kind of 'shelter' could protect us against either the bomb or the post-bomb destruction of our fellow citizens and our environment. I cannot see how any member of any government could think otherwise. But what can pacifists do today? When I joined the Peace Pledge Union in the late 1930s, many of us believed we should go to wherever there was an area of armed conflict and lie down in front of the tanks, the guns, the poison gas shells. What can any of us do now, physically, to prevent the finger being placed on the button that would set off the bomb which would ensure the destruction of civilisation as we know it? The Greenham Common women have courageously persisted, amidst all hostility, all ridicule, all media misrepresentation and all physical discomfort and harassment, in their campaign against the presence of American Cruise missiles on British soil, often with powerfully moving demonstrations of sisterly solidarity like linking arms right round the perimeter of the base. I would never oppose, much less deride, their campaign. But I have come to think that there is a great deal that has to be done by dedicated politicians and their supporters to foster also the idea of multilateral disarmament.

Somehow we have to insist that the Pentagon and the Kremlin talk about 'no first use', about 'no further stockpiling of nuclear weapons' . . . For heaven's sake, two or three nuclear bombs exploded by either side could totally devastate the civilised world. What can possibly be said to justify the stockpiling of thousands or even hundreds of these abominable weapons? Has the whole 'civilised' world gone mad? I often think so. But I remember . . . in 1939 when we knew almost for certain that war was coming, we were almost as terrified of gas as we are now of the nuclear bomb. And it didn't happen. I still have a hope, amounting almost to a conviction, that mankind will draw back from the brink. And I believe that it is our job, and women's job, particularly, as the childbearers, to go on telling the politicians and the defence ministries that it is completely idiotic to suppose that they would survive the nuclear holocaust any better than the most humble of our citizens. Even more importantly, we have to insist through the ballot box and by every other means possible that they go on talking and refuse to be put off even by rather aggressive noises from the Soviet bloc or the USA. It is ludicrous to suppose that human beings of *any* nationality, *any* political complexion, are seriously preparing to launch the nuclear weapons.

Why then do we not nag them, in season and out of season, every day in every way, to renounce nuclear weapons, first by bargaining on the limitation of stockpiling, and then to start getting rid of them? Has any political party begun publicly to discuss *how* we get rid of them? And isn't it time we all did?

4

Communicating

What most alarms me about Breakfast Television is that it will
increasingly isolate me from my fellow citizens. The first
morning I switched on BBC TV and saw the amiable and
experienced Frank Bough sitting at ease in his chair, dispensing
news and pleasantries, I said to myself, 'Don't be daft. You can
read all that while you have breakfast and then get on with
your work.' So I switched off, never to switch on at that hour
again. But how ignorant I must seem to avid telly watchers.
Already I am almost completely ignorant of the world of youth
because at best pop bores me and at worst it hurts my ears. I
don't even know the stars' names; I don't know the characters
in 'Dallas'; I never watch 'Coronation Street' or 'Crossroads'.
And now I shall seem more of a 'wally' to them than ever
because I don't know half the leading telly presenters or the
'personalities' they coax into their studios to comment, off the
cuff, on the events of the day.

When cable television becomes part of the scene, there will
be still more programmes around the clock. Isn't it becoming a
crazy sort of world we live in? If you feel a sense of
responsibility to know what is going on in the world around
you, or even if you wish to be known as a well-informed sort
of person, you are almost driven to switch from programme to
programme, to listen to this social problem being analysed, that
situation probed, that cause elucidated. But perhaps it is an
illusion of our times that the more television you watch, the

better informed you are? The *quality* of the comment, the analysis, even the reporting, must surely be debased by having to spread it over so many hours? Can there possibly be enough really well-informed men and women to be talking heads on every subject that seems to be newsworthy? 'News' *must* be a fabricated mock-up at times, mustn't it – when there are no strikes, no sit-ins, no terrorist bombs, no rapes, no scandals in high places?

Or are we becoming so conditioned that *anything* photographed for TV is automatically assumed to be newsworthy, simply because it is televised – just as every person seen to be talking also *must* be important? (Three minutes on TV does infinitely more for your reputation than a 1,000-word article in a serious newspaper over which you may have laboured for a week.) So of course almost everyone invited to spout on TV grabs at the chance, and many campaigning groups set up courses to instruct their enthusiasts on how to cope with the camera. (Sometimes I think the best piece of advice *I* could give to aspirants would be, 'Take your knitting.' All that time spent sitting around and waiting for something to happen while producers and television crew communicate with one another – silently as far as you are concerned – is calculated to reduce you to a state of either nervous tension or furious irritation; and in neither case are you likely to be able to make a balanced but incisive contribution). As the number of channels and programmes increases isn't it getting to be a ridiculous situation with more and more of the population gawping at one another?

What is the *point* of more and more TV? A latter-day Karl Marx might well call it 'the opium of the people', to keep us quietly in our homes as ever-increasing hundreds of thousands of us have no paid occupation, no means of earning a livelihood. I don't believe it is possible for any human being to sit in front of the Box from breakfast to bedtime and take in all that is happening. So TV is becoming, as radio long ago became, just a bit of company in the house. I have been in quite a few households where people talk through the TV programme, even if it is a play, then go out of the room and return not at all disconcerted to have lost the thread of what is happening, if indeed they ever grasped it.

Does it not seem strange that television is one of the notable growth industries, employing ever-increasing numbers of people not only in writing and presenting plays, documentaries, news and comment features, but in all sorts of other rather mysterious ways? The list of credits at the end of any 'important' feature programme or play grows longer and longer. How many musicians, graphic designers, visualisers, and so on, are employed not only in presenting the programme but also in devising its preliminary publicity? Do programmes need to be 'advertised' and introduced by all those star-spangled devices? Should we not watch if we had a plain announcement? Should we switch to another channel if we didn't have all the jazzy, come-on stuff?

Television is a great and growing threat to the newspaper press. That alarms me, of course, because I am a newspaper-woman, almost by birth and certainly by conditioning and lifetime experience. For some time newspapers have been faced with the threat that advertising revenue could be soaked up by the more popular modern medium. (This does not yet apply to local advertising, though who knows, if cable TV becomes established all over the country, what may happen to the free sheets that in many areas have replaced the old independent weeklies and are financed by pages and pages of 'smalls' – local advertisements for jobs, houses, cars, services, miscell-aneous wants and goods for sale.) Not only the competition for advertising revenue, but also the competition of 'immediacy' threatens newspapers. More and more of the people who turn on the TV while they have breakfast and again as they return home from work are likely to stop buying newspapers. The circulation of all the popular newspapers is tending to fall. The circulations that are holding up well or even increasing are for papers like the *Guardian, The Times* and *Financial Times,* whose readers actually like to *read.*

I doubt if enough attention has yet been paid to the psychology of the fact that our methods of communication are so radically changing. Our children now are continuing the *aural* comprehension of words right up into adult life. A baby learns to speak in part by mimicking . . . 'Mumm-a', 'Dadd-a', 'dinn-a'. When schooltime arrives he or she learns to associate these sounds with printed symbols – the letters of the alphabet. By whatever method you learn to read – the old-fashioned 'C-A-T says cat' or the less precise 'look and say' method – you learn to 'spell' . . . that is to say, to translate sounds into letters and letters into sounds. A majority of adults are still, I should say, better able to spell a word by writing it than by saying it and for them it is the *appearance* of the word that fixes it in the memory. I myself find that names of places and people heard on radio news do not fix themselves in my mind until I have seen them in print.

But a great many of today's children do not read either books or newspapers. Their knowledge of words, as well as of the world they live in, is based on what they see and hear on television. This may be a perfectly efficient way of acquiring knowledge. I don't know. It may be that the newspapers of the future will be on our TV screens. If so, we shall have to develop a different kind of technique for storing information in our minds and for retrieving it if we cannot refer to books or days-old newspapers.

Newspapers, half aware that they are fighting a losing battle, are increasingly parasitic on television. They not only regard it as essential to print television programmes in full, but also to treat the happenings of TV soap operas not to mention the doings of the soap-opera stars, as front-page news. A large-circulation tabloid newspaper not so long ago led its front page with a large headline, 'Deirdre seals it with a kiss', perfectly confident in the assumption that all its readers would know that Deirdre, a leading figure in 'Coronation Street', had been estranged from her husband and had decided to make it up.

If spoken English is likely to become so much more important to us than written English, isn't it perhaps time that we gave more thought to the simplification of written English? Simplified spelling has never had many influential advocates. Even George Bernard Shaw's support of it was almost completely ignored. Written English has twenty-six letters to indicate, separately and in combination, thousands of different sounds. The different sounds the same letters make, and the different letters that are required by our traditional spelling to make the same sounds, have to be learnt, for there are remarkably few rules. 'Ough' may, in different words be pronounced 'owe' (though), 'uff' (rough), 'off' (cough), 'oo' (through), 'aw' (ought), 'ow' (bough) and 'uh' (Middlesbrough).

Shall we be able to go on placing this burden of learning to spell a rule-less language on a multi-racial society whose children have been conditioned since they were born to hear words rather than see them? Far into the foreseeable future we must retain a written language, for documents, records, contracts, rules, pension and other order books, signposts, transport information (buses and tubes and railways), and so on. But is it really right that we should forever follow the historical pattern just because for linguists, etymologists, philologists, lexicographers and poets the spelling not only indicates the history of each word but also is in some way a part of its meaning? Perhaps the day will come when we shall, like the Chinese, have some kind of demotic English and some kind of Mandarin? But if that means two separate cultures in our society wouldn't it be even worse than the disease of illiteracy one wants to cure?

To some of us our written language is as precious as our musical heritage. You can't explain why, to someone who hasn't the same delight in words, it is a vital part of our cultural history. You can't make reasonable, religious persons see why you wince at 'When I was a child, my speech, my outlook and my thoughts were all childish. When I grew up I had finished with childish things.' It is not simply, I think, that it has lost the patina of the King James Bible version: 'When I was a child I spake as a child, I understood as a child, but when I became a man I put away childish things.' Not only the words we use for our thoughts but also the pattern they make, the ebb and flow of a sentence, make the thought memorable. The original function of poetry was, I am sure, to make a pattern of words that would keep the thought, the sentiment, in the mind. In this sense the beautiful, the sonorous sentences of the Authorised Version and the Church of England prayer book are poetry not to be cast aside lightly ... but on the charm and historical value of words, enuf is enuf.

What supremely matters, of course, especially in an island like ours, crowded with people of different tongues and accents, is communication ... language, written, spoken or heard, that is readily understood. How can anyone doubt that endless time is wasted, endless misunderstandings caused, by incomprehensible documentese? Two remarkable people, Chrissie Maher and Martin Cutts, living in Salford, Greater Manchester, have done an admirable job in alerting Authority to the menace of what they call 'gobbledegook', and since their 'Plain English' campaign was fostered by the National Consumer Council it has made a noticeable impact on local councils, business houses, welfare organisations and many others. Which is more than can be said for that great and good man Sir Ernest Gowers, whose *Plain Words: A Guide to the Use of English* was published in 1948. It was intended not only for 'those commonly called civil servants but also for members of the Navy, Army and Air Force, local government officials and the staffs of public bodies such as the railways'. If he had anywhere nearly achieved his aim the Plain English campaign would hardly have been needed.

On the writing of 'official' letters, Sir Ernest said: 'Good English can be defined simply as English which is readily understood by the reader. To be clear is to be efficient.' What would Sir Ernest have said to this masterpiece of non-communication from an official of a Benefits Appeals Tribunal in Yorkshire to a man whose appeal was being turned down?

The requirements of Regulations 2(1), 5, 14, 15 and 19 of the Supplementary Benefit (Requirement) Regulations as amended and where appropriate from 22:11:82 or further amended by Regulations 1(2), 2(11), 2(2), 2(4), 2(9), 2(10) and 2(12) of the Supplementary Benefit (Housing Benefits Requirements and Resources) Consequential Amendments Regulations 1982 (S1 1982/1126) and S1 1982/1124 of the Housing Regulations 1982, have been correctly applied.

The official who sent this treasure (quoted in the *Guardian*'s 'Diary' column in February 1983) cannot possibly have been so stupid as to imagine that the man who received it would understand it. So he must either have been too arrogant or too insensitive to feel that it *mattered* that the recipient understood what he was saying, or he was too lazy to bother to translate the relevant statutes and amendments into comprehensible terms. He had done his duty, hadn't he, citing the relevant authority?

This sort of thing really won't do. The Plain English campaign deserves everyone's support. Its awards and its 'booby prizes', which it calls Golden Bull Awards, must surely have had some impact. When Lord Denning presented the awards in 1982 he explained that much of the trouble with lawyers' jargon derives from the fact that courts interpret statutes and commercial documents by the letter and not by the intention. 'The lawyers,' he said, 'seek for certainty and try to cover every contingency but in doing so they get lost in obscurity.' As in this Golden Bull:

An enactment in which Section 31/6 and (7) of the Criminal Law Act 1977 (pre-1949 enactments) produced the same fine or maximum fine for different convictions shall be treated for purposes of this section as if there were omitted from it so much of it as before 29th July 1977 had the effect of a person guilty of an offence under it was liable on summary conviction to a fine or maximum fine less than the highest fine or maximum fine to which he would have been liable if the conviction had satisfied the conditions required for the imposition of the highest fine or maximum fine.

It is to be hoped that not many of us will come up against that particular Golden Bull, but we are all at the mercy of commercial firms which employ the most pompous (or nervous) kind of lawyer to protect their interests *vis-à-vis* the customer — as in this letter, sent by Thorn EMI Domestic Electrical Appliances to people who order spare parts:

Certain of the components comprising our electrical appliances have inherent characteristics, the effect of which, whether before or after such components have been introduced into appliances or during such introduction, make it desirable in the interests of safety for the introduction of spare components to be carried out by a competent person.

It seems a common human weakness to assume that the more complicated the sentences we write, the more impressive they will be and the more respect we will earn and receive. Sociologists are particularly prone to this weakness, and have an extraordinary jargon of their own, which would seem to me to cut them off completely from their 'customers', 'clients' or whatever you call the human beings with whom it is their business to deal. Doesn't the way we put our thoughts into words tend to condition the way we think? Here is a sentence from an essay on the significance of friendship for women in later life: 'Ageing people look to friends for direct aid in the form of behaviour clues and sanctions and indirect aid which consists of support and permissiveness in trial and error learning, validation of self ritual observance.' Later in the same essay comes this remarkable sentence: 'Most studies of friend-ships among older people focus on the scope of networks and the structural characteristics of the members of the dyad pair, rather than the quality of the dyad friendship.' Not being familiar with the word 'dyad', I looked it up in my dictionary. It means 'group of two. Couple.' So we are reading about pair-pairs, two-twos, couple-couples. Really!

Lawyers have some excuse for their special kind of jargon language. It will be understood very precisely by other lawyers, and carelessness in drafting might mean life or death for a person accused of murder or the loss of thousands of pounds in a commercial case. It is necessary, too, for many scientists to use terms which the lay person may not understand but which have only one possible meaning for other scientists working in the same discipline. But most people – and I include sociologists – use the jargon of their profession in either a lazy or an ego-building way. I think, too, that some trade unionists, and some industrialists and businessmen, rely on the stock phrases of the 'at this point in time' kind because they feel safe with them. Often the jargon phrases muffle meaning rather than make it too dangerously obvious.

All sorts of accusations can be made against journalists – and I have to make some myself – but obscuring meaning is not often one of them. No journalists worthy of the name fancy up their prose for fame's sake, and if they do, there is 'Pseuds Corner' in *Private Eye* to cut them down to size. The journalist's job is to be read, to hold the reader's attention from the first sentence to the last, whether it be in a news story, a feature article or an editorial ... and the fewer words he or she can use to make the meaning plain the better. Technically, I guess British newspapers are as well written as any in the world. They have to be, for no one is going to pay up to 23p a copy for a paper he or she doesn't understand or is bored by. Competition for an inevitably shrinking readership is now intense.

We journalists may claim truly to write clear and comprehensible English, and wish we could teach lawyers, parliamentary draughtsmen, insurance companies and the DHSS a thing or two, but who of us could honestly deny that the *content* of newspapers has seriously deteriorated in the last ten years or so? The tabloids – and these comprise all the national dailies except the *The Times,* and *Guardian,* the *Daily Telegraph* and the *Financial Times* – have now degenerated into daily gossip magazines. Unless there is some tale of horror, like multiple murders in a south London surburb, or unusual drama, like the 'kidnapping' of a race horse worth a king's ransom, the tabloids' front-page lead may range from the Princess of Wales's new hair style to a vicar's row with his parishioners. On a day when nearly 700 deaths were reported in Australian bush fires, the *Daily Mail*'s front-page splash heading was 'Tatchell Tumbling' – this was about a left-wing Labour candidate standing in a by-election in the East London constituency of Bermondsey. Not only the sort of gross Tory bias which all left-of-centre politicians and party members complain about continually, but also a gross trivialisation of the news itself.

Trivialisation makes one wince, but the deadly competition between the popular dailies and against the encroachment of television on newspapers' news reporting rationale, has intensified the search for sensational sex/violence/royalty stories and gossip paragraphs to a quite nauseating degree. The Press Council accepted as true the allegations of 'cheque book journalism' in the case of Peter Sutcliffe, known as 'the Yorkshire Ripper', during the months when he raped and murdered at least twelve women. Even more roundly the Press Council condemned offers of large payments to Sutcliffe's relations and to the parents of his victims. More importantly still, it censured 'the shiftiness, foot-shuffling and deceit' of some editors in answering its questions about these unpleasant transactions. The Press Council's judgment on the *Daily Mail*'s behaviour in relation to the Ripper case concluded that 'a group of senior executives not only set out to deceive Mrs Sutcliffe but their conduct had the effect of artificially creating and sustaining a cheque book market in her story'. The paper's explanation amounted to 'a confession that the *Daily Mail* was guilty of gross misconduct'. Its gallant editor was knighted during Mrs Thatcher's first government.

When I was a very young reporter, a colleague amused us greatly by keeping going for days a totally fictitious story about a well-known violinist's war-time exploits. It was irresponsible, you might say — but it did no one any harm. In February 1983 an *Observer* columnist challenged the *Sun* for having printed a fabricated interview with the widow of a Falklands hero. The widow claimed that she had never spoken to the *Sun*. The *Observer* columnist phoned her and she reiterated her statement. The *Sun* never offered a shred of proof for its story, and in spite of the *Observer*'s blunt accusation, and the judgment of the Press Council, it gave the lamest of excuses about 'shortage of time to check'. So the three million readers of the *Sun* will probably never know that they are addicted to a newspaper which makes up news to suit itself. If they knew, how much would they care, I ask myself. Enough to change to another newspaper?

What most sickens me personally about the behaviour and attitudes of today's newspapers is the hypocrisy. There are so many fine, handsome defences for grubbing about in the mire. 'We must protect the freedom of the press at all costs.' Indeed, the freedom to investigate, to report, to print, is precious. But to report on what? The fact that a vicar goes off with his (married) lady organist? That a character in a TV soap opera has lost his licence for drunken driving? That a minor member of the royal family has been seen in a pub with a telly starlet? 'Well but,' continue the defenders of the freedom of the press, 'if we didn't give the public what it wants to read, they would stop buying our newspapers and there wouldn't be any possibility of printing the news that you believe really matters.' In a sense, yes — but it *is* possible to be half a step ahead of the lowest denominator. I know I should not want to work for the largest-circulation daily in the world if I thought it had reached its mammoth sales by debasing the currency of popular journalism.

Then there is the defence that when people in the public eye involve themselves in some scandalous situation the newspapers have 'a duty' to tell their readers about it. To which I say firmly, 'rubbish'. The duty arises only if the scandal directly affects the guilty party's public duties. The chairman of a company who is fiddling the books deserves to be shown up. The chairman of a company who is maintaining a discreet separate establishment does not. His private life is irrelevant. The defence of 'public duty' is almost always put forward by the gossip columnists, and I despise them for it. They purvey titillating or scandalous gossip about well-known persons not because it is their duty but because it attracts readers and enhances their reputation. And I know and shamefacedly admit *how* I came to know that their methods of tracking down titillating gossip can be pretty despicable. A few years ago I answered the phone to a stranger.

'Could you let me have Babs Todd's address?' the voice inquired.

'Who is it speaking?' I asked.

'Oh, a friend of Babs,' said the voice. 'I understand she has moved, and would like to call.'

Babs Todd is a friend of Maureen Colhoun, formerly MP for Northampton, whose defeat at the following general election resulted very largely from the fact that she had admitted she had a lesbian relationship with Babs.

'I think I can find you the telephone number,' I told the caller.

'Oh, I'd really like her address, so that I can call round.'

Innocent idiot that I was, I let the caller have it ... with the result that my friends were persecuted by press photographers driving up and down the street outside their new home, and a detailed story about their relationship appeared a few days later in Nigel Dempster's *Daily Mail* Diary. So sick did I feel about being used in this way by one of the diarist's assistants that, covered in embarrassment and confusion, I was driven to say to my fellow judges on the British Press Awards Panel that if they decided to make an award to this particular columnist I should have to resign from the panel in protest. They did not make the award. Possibly they would not have done so in any case.

Some readers of this book may remember, I think, that Nigel Dempster was interviewed on a television programme about remarks he had made on American television about Princess Diana and the way in which she was making Prince Charles's life a misery. If so, they may be rather taken aback to read what Nigel Dempster wrote in a 'guest column' in *The Journalist*, organ of the National Union of Journalists, in January, 1983: 'The idea that any journalist, especially from the *Sun* can telephone Balmoral or Sandringham and elicit a quote from a guest is risible. Yet this is what the *Sun* gaily prints, sure in the knowledge that the royal family can only deny and even surer that they do not even have to carry that denial.' Can the Palace, then, find any way of denying publicly Dempster's allegation about the Princess of Wales? Obviously not, and it seems to me quite extraordinary that a columnist who in his Diary has so often embarrassed at best, and hounded at worst, public figures from royalty to a hard-working Labour MP should have the gall to attack other reporters and gossipmongers from other tabloid newspapers.

If the Princess of Wales, young, shy and inexperienced in fending off media pressures, did – as some newspaper hacks predicted was likely – suffer a nervous collapse, would any of the newspaper leeches have suffered a pang of conscience? I doubt it. They would without any exception have said they were acting under editor's orders or in the public interest. Just as the Peeping Tom photographers taking sneak shots of the royals on holiday convince themselves they are acting in the public interest. Does the public *really* think so? Perhaps the general public ought to be reminded now and again that newspaper proprietors' private lives are not held up for the titillation of their readers. Sauce for the royal goose is not sauce for the newspaper gander.

About ten years ago a distinguished ex-editor of the *Daily Mail*, Michael Randall, wrote an article in the *Sunday Times* under the heading: 'A sickening week in the life of Fleet Street'. It began: 'I know an intimate secret about the Hon. Vere Harmsworth, chairman of an alleged newspaper, the *Daily Mail*. I learned it on the lowest authority and have no intention of revealing it.' Mike Randall's protest was about the way the Fleet Street gossip writers had handled the divorce case of Harold Pinter, in which Lady Antonia Fraser, now Pinter's wife, was cited. Nigel Dempster announced: 'Her name figures glaringly in a divorce scandal — and suddenly her past life has come into sharp focus.' Who but Mr Nigel Dempster, asked Mike Randall, suddenly brings her past life into 'sharp focus'?

Alas, to the gossip columnists of Fleet Street have now been added the legions of television and radio commentators, sucking every last drop of juice from the break-up of the liaison between a Conservative minister, Cecil Parkinson, and Miss Sara Keays when she was expecting his child. Because he had very recently been Chairman of the Conservative Party, because he was a member of Mrs Thatcher's government, and because the prime minister felt obliged to ask for Mr Parkinson's resignation, the affair obviously had to be reported openly, but only a debased set of values could justify the day-by-day chewing over of Mr Parkinson's 'disgrace' or Miss Keays's determination to justify herself. Telescopic lenses were focused on the Parkinsons' young daughters, and a photograph of them even appeared in the *Guardian* only a few days after their columnist Jill Tweedie had been saying that the *Guardian* was not like those pop papers that 'make one so angry and ashamed'. The girls looked to me so woebegone that I was moved to write to the editor, Peter Preston, who has young daughters himself: 'You know the worst thing you could do to them would be to become a by-word and have everyone talking about how awful their Dad is. And their friends and schoolmates gawping at a photograph of them in the newspaper.' In reply, Peter Preston told me that the Parkinsons 'made themselves available for a variety of photocalls. They sheltered the press in their garage when it rained.' He added, 'I am suggesting, from complete knowledge, that the relationships were not those that a casual reader or, more relevantly, a casual TV viewer might have supposed. There has been a considerable degree of orchestration on all sides by people experienced in that orchestration. That doesn't make the overall position particularly palatable . . . but it does, I think, alter the perception of a sorrowing family being intruded upon. It wasn't like that and I think that makes a difference.'

The difference this letter made to me was that I grieved still more for the corruption of standards of behaviour which could apparently allow the Parkinson parents to let their daughters be so publicly involved. I asked Peter Preston whether the *Guardian* really had to go along with the slide into the gutter – and have a reporter in the crowd outside Sara Keays' house. But I had to acknowledge that the *Guardian* was just reflecting what I consider an ugly decline in moral values – not *sexual* morals, so much as kindness and concern and a decent respect for human beings. These scandals seem to hit our British public way of life from time to time. Twenty years earlier it was the Profumo affair that titillated us (then, almost entirely through the medium of the popular press). The call girls Christine Keeler and Mandy Rice-Davies who were at the heart of the scandal did very nicely out of it, financially. Mandy Rice-Davies was reported as saying, 'Every person in this case is under contract to some newspaper.' The *Guardian* took a very different stance then, and one or two sentences in a leading article are worth quoting. I doubt very much if anything like them would appear today:

Other things have been discussed in this case than the prostitution of the bodies of a few young girls. One of them, not discussed much because it is so personal is the idea of a genuine and durable relationship which includes a physical relationship but is not circumscribed by it; another is the function of the press. The immense publicity focused on the girls and their clients, and on the tawdry high living they enjoy, has served to glorify a way of life which is without any truth or beauty or any of the depth of fellowship and understanding which men and women are able to share. The girls concerned were in the news for so many weeks that some of their juniors must be asking whether this is not the life for them . . .

If Miss Keeler and Miss Rice-Davies are still proud of their profession, many a journalist must be ashamed of his . . . The *Daily Mirror* and *Sunday Mirror* and the *News of the World* have deliberately debased values which a civilised society cannot afford to be without.

That *Guardian* leader named Sir William Carr, Chairman of the *News of the World*, and Mr Cecil King, Chairman of the *Mirror* group, as newspaper proprietors who 'competed for the privilege of purveying pornography', and therefore were in 1963 the contemporary newspaper bogeymen. Ever since I became a newspaperwoman, in 1925, we have had our bogeymen. In those far-off days it was Northcliffe, of course. He was the real creator of the popular penny daily, and his *Daily Mail* would, in my view, put today's *Daily Mail* to shame. He was undoubtedly a newspaper genius, and his later mental collapse has obscured the virtues that he undoubtedly had, despite his autocratic view of his role *vis-à-vis* the nation as well as his staff.

Then there was Beaverbrook, the dominant influence on the newspaper press throughout my younger days. He too was a newspaper genius, and he had the immense good fortune to recruit an editor of equal genius, Arthur Christianson. Every young journalist in those days before the Second World War regarded the *Daily Express* as the supreme example of popular journalism. Its politics may have been abhorrent to most of us, but its technical excellence was beyond compare. I am inclined to think that the *Daily Express* was the newspaper that really elevated the sub-editor – the person who handles and shapes the news, rather than the person who digs out the facts and reports on them – to the status he or she held for very many years in the newspaper hierarchy.

Beaverbrook was the prime example of the *political* newspaper baron. The *Daily Express* still carries on its front page the red Crusader which was Beaverbrook's symbol for his Empire Free Trade Campaign. To people of my political stance, the *Daily Express* seemed quite shockingly biased. Beaverbrook was totally opposed to the Co-operative Movement, for whose publications I worked so long in my younger days. It was, I think, to Beaverbrook's newspapers that Stanley Baldwin referred in his comment that, in the years leading up to the Second World War, the popular press was 'like a harlot who, down the ages, exercised power without responsibility'. Beaverbrook could be compared with our present newspaper 'bogeyman' Rupert Murdoch in that he was omnipresent in his newspaper kingdom. He knew not only everything that was happening in his newspaper office but also everything that his newspaper executives were doing. I remember my old friend of Co-operative Press days, Sydney Elliott (editor of the Co-operative Press Sunday newspaper *Reynolds News* and later of Beaverbrook's *Evening Standard*), telling me that Beaverbrook would track him down and phone him wherever he happened to be having dinner. But it should not be forgotten that Beaverbrook, for all his buccaneering, autocratic methods, brought to prominence some remarkable journalists – Michael Foot, for example, later Leader of the Opposition and a former editor of the *Evening Standard*.

Cecil King, a Harmsworth nephew, was only briefly a

bogeyman – partly because he then owned the apparently insuperable *Daily Mirror*, and partly because he was given to very confident, alarmist public statements about the future of the national press and the predicted steady decline in titles. Lord Thomson of Fleet, who after building up a large newspaper chain in Canada started in this country with the *Scotsman*, took over the Kemsley empire and ended up with both *The Times* and the *Sunday Times*, was a very different sort of tycoon. He was known to journalists, disparagingly but not altogether venomously, as 'the Grocer', because he bought and sold and ran newspapers as if they were just another kind of merchandise. He was quoted as having said, no doubt jokingly, that editorial matter was the stuff that went between the advertisements, but in fact he seems to have left his editors to run their own show and it was in his time that the *Sunday Times*, under Harold Evans, gained such a splendid reputation for courage and independence in its investigative journalism.

As I write, the bogeyman who frightens and fascinates us all is the Australian newspaper tycoon Rupert Murdoch. The story of his takeover of *The Times* and *Sunday Times* has been vividly told by the editor he sacked, Harold Evans, who alleges some fairly nasty skulduggery in the way that John Biffen, the then Trade Secretary, was convinced that there was no need to refer the purchase to the Monopolies Commission, despite the fact that Murdoch already owned two mass-circulation national papers, the top seller, the *Sun,* and the Sunday *News of the World*. It is impossible for someone like me, sitting on the sidelines, to establish where the truth lies. Murdoch does not need to defend himself. He retains the papers and the power. What seems strange to me is that Harry Evans should ever have thought he could trust Murdoch, and perhaps 'handle' him. He was taken with Murdoch's charm and vitality, and the invitation to edit *The Times* was exceedingly hard to resist, especially as his own gallant effort to set up a consortium to buy the paper had come to nothing. But he surely must have remembered a letter in the *Guardian* from a previous Murdoch victim, Stafford Somerfield, who edited the *News of the World* from 1956 to 1970. In it he told very bluntly the transactions by which Murdoch removed all authority from the then Chairman of the *News of the World*, Sir William Carr; how he made changes in the staff, layout and content of the paper without consultation, and finally sent for Somerfield and said, 'I want your resignation.' The interview, said Mr Somerfield, lasted three minutes, 'which led to a telegram from another ex-editor, "Why three minutes, you talkative bastard?"' Harry Evans had been warned.

The state of the British newspaper press is parlous. The national dailies and Sundays are practically all in the hands of very wealthy tycoons. Not all are equally deeply concerned in the day-to-day running of their newspapers; not all are equally politically involved. But they have a power over the public mind from which they cannot be dislodged. There seems no possibility of a consortium with genuine newspaper expertise that could raise the necessary millions to finance an operation of this size. Politicians of the left and even of the centre may complain from hell to breakfast about bias in the press, but how is it to be prevented? (Actually, some of their complaints of *deliberate* manipulation of news do not hold water. Journalists tend to go along with the prevailing policy of the paper they serve without much self-questioning, unless it becomes too blatantly biased for them to tolerate.)

The spate of very serious strikes during the last two or three years is a symptom of a threatened industry. The man or woman in the street wonders how members of the National Graphical Association, Sogat 82 or any of the big print unions could bring the newspaper press to a halt when this is such a threat to the continued existence of many papers. The real cause of the strikes and strike threats is the coming of a new technology which is in process of destroying an ancient and honourable craft job — the job of the printer. I think fearfully of a

time, not so very long distant, when all our morning and
evening news will be printed not on paper, but on the
television screen.

And since all the television corporations and companies (not
only the BBC) operate under licence and cannot be manipulated
by any wealthy tycoon owner, should that remove the
bitterness that so many campaigners and politicians feel against
the purveyors of news and comment? Not at all. The greatest
bitterness, I fear, is expressed towards the broadcasters; it is
now they who seem to have 'power without responsibility, the
prerogative of the harlot'. It seems to most of us lay people
that the technique of the interview is now based on
confrontation. The newspaper interview is quite a different
technique — one of leading on the 'subject' gradually to
explain himself, expound his views and tell his story. There
have been, and still are, some tough newspaper interviewers,
but if the interviewee shuts his mouth and refuses to answer a
question, he cannot be *seen* doing so. If the interview is read,
the reader has time to think, 'Well, I don't see why he should
answer that question if he doesn't want to.' On the screen, the
interviewee is in a quandary. He will look either foolish or
obstinate. The interviewer is almost bound to win. I have only
once myself been in a position of being asked questions which I
would have preferred not to answer (some aspect of widowhood) and I am afraid I just fudged it, as amiably as I could.

Of course, no one *has* to submit himself to ordeal by
television . . . but natural vanity apart, the campaigner feels he
has a duty to publicise his cause. Causes can seem boring to
hardened interviewers and commentators, so they are under a
strong temptation to 'stir it up' for the benefit of viewers by
asking some needling question which will be answered with
some feeling. Indeed, I think this technique must be part of
their 'training'. The perfect answer to the embarrassing
question was provided by Lord Snowdon, when Michael
Parkinson asked him something about his relationship with

Princess Margaret. Lord Snowdon just smiled . . . and smiled . . . and smiled. We are not all so ready-witted or perhaps so well prepared or so experienced.

I do not go along with the campaigners who attribute conscious bias to every interviewer. It is an undeniable fact that we all, inevitably, have a point of view. We see things from a certain angle, and for the most part we are unaware that our view is slanted – because of our temperament, our life experience, our conditioning, the parameters of our job. I don't doubt that 90 per cent of interviewers and commentators aim sincerely to be impartial; equally I have no doubt that this is in practice well nigh impossible. I don't know what is to be done about it. I believe that it is a good thing that powerful persons like Sir Robin Day, who masterminds 'Question Time' with such vigour and aplomb, should be keenly challenged by a campaigner of the stature of E. P. Thompson, the guru of the nuclear disarmers, who confronted him in a letter to the *Guardian*. He wrote of his conviction that 'all of Sir Robin Day's programmes are carefully crafted: the selection of performers; the differing degrees of deference or abrasiveness displayed towards them; the sifting of incoming phone calls; the editing of tapes.' Mr Thompson told the story of an experience on Sir Robin's 'World at One' programme when, after he had 'slipped in a comment that at least one of the British warships lying sunken in the Falklands Sound might have nuclear weapons,' one of Sir Robin's assistants who was interviewing him jumped up and switched off the tape-recorder. This action may have been mistaken, may have been altogether 'unfair' – but if time presses in a newspaper office, it rushes at gale force speed in broadcasting studios. I know about battling frantically against the clock from my sub-editing days in the *Manchester Evening News*, but there every *minute* was vital. In broadcasting it is every *second*. There is no criticism implied either of E. P. Thompson's sincerity or of the value of his contribution to the nuclear arms debate when I say that he would find it very difficult to chair a session of 'Question Time', giving all the opinionated panellists and the 'viewy' members of the audience a fair hearing and never letting his own 'bias' show. *Of course* Sir Robin Day sounds abrasive. He has one of the most difficult jobs on the TV screen, and handles it pretty well.

My point of view, my bias, if you like, is much nearer to Mr Thompson's than to Robin Day's. But I still think that critics of the media should beware the temptation to assume that deliberate manipulation is rife throughout all broadcasting organisations and all the newspaper and magazine press. Mary Whitehouse seems to think that the BBC is staffed with semi-pornographers; others seem to think that the BBC is staffed by rightists; still others that it is under the orders of Moscow. I once carried on quite a long argument by post with a humanist who was convinced that the *Guardian* was run by embattled Anglicans. There isn't *time* for checking over every piece of copy, every report or interview to be broadcast to see that it conforms to some arbitrary standard imposed by the powers that be.

So I think it is right that powerful television and radio presenters or interviewers should be challenged. The presenters, the interviewers, especially on television, acquire great power over public opinion. They should strive to use it humbly and generously, as should all people who have power over the minds and lives of their fellow citizens. Perhaps if radio and television interviewers were not taught from scratch that the best way to produce a good, lively interview is to confront, even to 'accuse' the interviewee so as to needle him or her into forceful assertions or denials, we should be less likely to feel the urge to protest against 'bias'? How hard it must be to remain humble when the whole nation knows your name, your face and your voice. But it *is* up to the Robin Days, the David Frosts, the Fred Emerys and so on to try, isn't it?

5

Family Matters

Without a family I feel I should stand naked to the four winds
. . . I *feel* that, but is it really so? What *is* my family? Of my
own generation there remain only one brother, Guy, a few
cousins, only two of whom I ever see nowadays, and my
brother Ralph's widow Ella; then there are assorted nieces and
nephews and my own daughter and her two daughters. No
contact at all for many years with any of my father's family.
Very friendly relations (but little opportunity for visiting) with
my husband's family. Not much of a buttress against the chill
night air, would you say?

But the living evidence of being part of a family is far from
being the whole story. The family provided the soil for my
growth, the map on which my path can be traced. It shaped
the nature and scope of my thinking. I have been Mary Stott
'officially' for nearly fifty years, but to myself I am about two-
thirds Bates, one-third Waddington, and not a Stott at all, in
my inner being. My mother, Amalie Bates, was the eldest of
seven clever, charming, enterprising brothers and sisters, and
was herself a real 'organisation woman'. She was also
affectionate and warm-hearted and needed friends every bit as
much as most of us do. But where was she to find them? In the
early years of this century (she died in 1931) women did not
have men friends, and the women she met, even in the
Women's Liberal Federation or the War Seals Committee or
any other of her organisations, talked chiefly, she used to say,

about their children and their chars. So her need for friendship was met by her brothers and sisters. Wherever they were she kept in touch. Charlie went off to America when he was not much more than a lad. Harry and Frank went, at different times, to India. Leo became an artist and lived a Bohemian kind of life in London. Frieda and her family were closest to us, and her two daughters are still my friends. Poor Florrie married a man named Bastard whose nature matched his name. She was always having to be rescued from awful situations.

So they, the family, were my mother's close friends on whom she expended her love and concern and with whom she shared a delicious giggling sense of humour. It has not been the same for me. Yet I feel the blood tie very strongly still. Even though friends have filled up so much of my life, the sense of responsibility to the close family remains. When Ralph contracted tuberculosis it was automatic for Guy and me to do all we could to help finance his stay in a Swiss sanatorium. Would there have been such an overriding sense of obligation to help a friend as to help a brother? Do siblings feel that way about one another today? I don't know.

What I do know, and what everyone knows who grew up before the Second World War is that family patterns have changed so much that it is pointless now to pontificate about the 'normal' family. There is no normal family. What was thought to be the norm – father, stay-at-home mother and two dependent children – accounts for only five per cent of British households. Judges and magistrates and MPs and ministers and social workers and some psychologists may orate as they will about the function of the family in maintaining 'traditional values', but the groupings that now regard themselves as a family vary almost as widely as the household groupings in Trinidad and Tehran. There were in 1979 no fewer than 840,000 single-parent households, of which all but 100,000 were headed by women. Fifty per cent of all mothers with dependent children had paid jobs, full or part time. Some of the single parents were widowed, some divorced, some deserted and some lone parents by choice. In some families wives were still body servants to their husbands; in some the husband was the stay-at-home parent while the wife earned the family income. In some, as in the home of my dear friend Anne Armitage, a polio victim who lives by the grace of an 'iron lung', the husband for many years has been 'mother' not only to the children but also to his wife.

People still pontificate about the family as if all the ways in which we live together in groups, adults and children together, were cut to one pattern. Ferdinand Mount, in *The Subversive Family*, claimed that 'the nuclear family is universally a basic co-operative in human society which stands as a bulwark of free enterprise against the encroachment of socialist bureaucracy.' Edmund Leach wrote that 'far from being the basis of the good society, the family, with its narrow privacy and tawdry secrets, is the source of all our discontents.' He also predicted that come what may 'the English will continue to rear most of their children cooped up in boxes like battery hens. They have no choice.' And Katharine Whitehorn engagingly wrote: 'What I mean by family is what you find behind your own front door. Whether it is two people or ten what it has to offer is *known* . . . I may bound up the steps thinking, "At last", or crawl up with my arms dragged from their sockets by the shopping, but when I get in it is my private territory; my private refuge from the jungle outside . . . family is you, me and the teapot . . . and it works.'

Of course the family began as a co-operative, mutual support unit. Before our primitive ancestors grasped the connection between copulation and pregnancy, instinct made the woman hold the baby to her breast and instinct made the baby suck. There was no place for men in this basic activity, but perhaps our fiercest separatist feminists should accept that men have always done something for women other than just impregnate them? Such as bringing home the food and fighting off large fierce animals? It isn't likely that our earliest ancestors were monogamous or formed pair bonds, but some kind of 'rules' and taboos must have evolved pretty early, so as to preserve some kind of formal pattern – not that those patterns would necessarily suit our notions of family life. In her *Travels in West Africa* (1897), that intrepid, humorous and altogether delightful Victorian traveller, Mary Kingsley, observed that the African lady often took the view, 'the more wives, the less work'. She added, 'I have known men who would rather have had one wife and spent the rest of the money in a civilised way, driven into polygamy by the women. Of course this state of affairs is most common in slave-owning tribes like the Fans' (who were cannibals, with whom Mary Kingsley got on surprisingly well).

Because of the very strong family pattern which shaped K Stott's life as well as mine, and which we tried to continue in our own married life, I am uneasy and often very anxious about the variants which are replacing it. I don't believe that in any aspect of life, social, political, psychological, we can turn the clock back – but should we not refer to the past now and then for guidelines? What was good about the nineteenth-century and early twentieth-century family pattern was that it offered stability and emotional security. What was bad was that it was constricting, leading to sickening hypocrisy in the rule-dodgers and often appalling cruelty to the 'weaker sex', as women then undoubtedly were. But now that all of us are reasonably free to make our own pattern of family life, how much happier are we? How much better off are the 'products' of the family, the children? How much more satisfying are the lives of adult men and women?

We can choose to marry or not marry. I understand the idea of marriage as a sacrament, indissoluble, a lifelong commitment, but by the time I married I had become an agnostic. I could not with a good conscience have married in church. I still feel hostile to the idea of marrying in church largely for the sake of a public show which makes the white-gowned bride the cynosure of eyes for an hour or two, even if she has been more or less publicly living with her bridegroom for months. K and I were, in fact, married in a registrar's office, but I would have preferred not to go through any kind of ceremony if it had not been for the fear of offending the susceptibilities of our relations, especially of my in-laws. I feel even more strongly now than I did then that people should not commit themselves to marriage unless they have discovered that they are physically as well as mentally compatible.

So you commit yourself to a union you think of hopefully as permanent; anything less than that hardly qualifies as 'family'. There are nowadays many couples who are childless by choice (they even have an organisation to support their interests). In the days of my youth childlessness was thought to be the height of selfishness – childless couples were 'spending their money on a car, continental holidays and every kind of trendy luxury'. I found that attitude very offensive, for it tended to pressurise into having children couples who might well have been totally unsuited to parenthood. Parenthood should indeed be by choice. What sort of future is there for a child born to a reluctant mother and father who continue to resent (as, of course, all 'reluctant' parents do not) the intrusion of the child into their lives? (The anti-abortion fanatics who think they are protecting the interests of the unborn child seem oblivious to the fact that the unwanted child might well have preferred, if choice were possible for the baby in the womb, not to be born.)

But now I do think that the childless who take the view that responsibility for the well-being of the coming generation rests solely on parents, and that they should not have to contribute through rates and taxes to their maintenance and education, are certainly selfish. If they have no children of their own, who will care for them in their old age, or during any incapacitating illness, but other people's children? I deplore, too, the insensitive attitude of a few of the 'childless by choice' women who denigrate or even deny the validity of the 'maternal instinct' – that drive towards child-bearing which is so powerful in some women.

I fully support the right to be childless by choice . . . yet looking round the childless women I know in their thirties, I feel sad. Some are truly 'unparental' and even in their old age will probably not regret the lack of grandchildren. But some simply do not know what they are missing. Some men – surely a minority? – yearn for children, even if only to inherit a title or an estate. But most men give very little thought to child-rearing until the first baby arrives. My observation suggests that many then are entranced by the tiny newcomer and thereafter devote much of their thinking and caring to its well-being. Isn't the present generation of young professional and business women rather like this? How do they know that they are not made for motherhood without having known the inescapable responsibility of an infant born of their own body, suckled at their own breasts? How do they know that they will not ache for the love of children or grandchildren when it is too late to do anything about it?

When I was young it was often said that so far from strengthening a marriage, the coming of children threatened it. More men then than now were apt to resent the demands the young family made on their mother for attention, time and love. Today starting a family is more a deliberate joint decision, and many more fathers are present at the birth of the babies and involve themselves from their earliest days in their care. When Robert Lacey took over the 'Look' pages of the *Sunday Times* for a while in 1973 he started off with a series of interviews with husbands. 'The married man,' he asserted, 'works harder for his wife and family in 1973 than ever before.' The evidence for this statement was not all that strong. Tommy Steele did try changing his daughter's nappies but gave up because he was afraid of sticking a pin in her. James Burke, TV journalist, said that when his wife went away he never did a stroke of work. Joe Bugner, the boxer, said, 'Every man has the instinct to rule and say "I'm the breadwinner".' Geoffrey Godfrey Smith MP said, 'I wash my pants and socks when I travel abroad but as soon as I come home I expect them done for me.' But Robert Lacey himself declared that 'Modern men don't feel desexed by making the bed or doing the shopping.' Today many men think like him, rather than like James Burke. Ten years later the 'serious' women's pages all quite commonly have articles and letters from 'house husbands'. Working wife, stay-at-home husband is a pattern that can and should work well. It may have to be put into practice quite often if modern technology and a world economic depression continue to reduce the number of jobs available to men. I wish it had been acceptable to my husband when he developed a heart condition. If he had been willing to let me be the sole breadwinner, he might have lived longer . . . and he was a very good house husband, as cook, shopper and general handyman.

But this pattern, which can be so rewarding, does not always work out any better than the other patterns we are now trying out. If such a marriage does break down, the man may feel even more bitter than the sort of man who expects his wife to attend to all family chores. After a 'Woman's Hour' broadcast in 1978 I had a letter from a male listener who wrote: 'I bottle fed my kids, bathed them, read to them at bedtime, got up to them during the night, and when they woke in the morning it was Daddy they called for.' But when he left his wife, she was awarded custody and only with the greatest difficulty did he manage to maintain a relationship with his daughters. There are harrowing stories of deprived Dads, as well as of deprived Mums. Not infrequently custody is awarded to the mother without reference to the care she is likely to give to her children compared with the care the father offers. The case was widely reported in 1979 of a security guard who had cared for his little daughter from the time she was nine months old, when her mother had left her. He lost his application for custody because the High Court judge, Mr Justice Payne, believed 'a man ought not to give up work and turn himself into a mother figure or a nanny and devote himself to the bringing up of a little girl at the expense of the state. His brain should be used in work' – a comment which shows what Mr Justice Payne thinks of the 'work' that women normally do in the home. Mr Justice Ormrod, a few days later, expressed himself more kindly: 'No one can read this case without sympathy for the father and without understanding how this order will strike him.' Yet he added: 'but the fact is that one has to look at these things from the best interests of the children . . . And in general a father has to rely on neighbours, give up his job or find another woman to look after the children.'

Well-known journalist Wilfred De'Ath has described movingly the anguish and anger of a father struggling for access to his children. When he had to hand them back to their mother 'feelings of anger, bitterness, guilt, remorse and resentment all combined into the worst pain I have ever known'. He did not continue to blame his wife. 'She was obviously unhappy and she had the right to end it. Since then she has had to live constantly, as I have not, with the pain of children deprived of a father whom they deeply love.' But on balance, at the time he wrote this article, he felt that it would have been better for his wife and him 'to have stayed together and sacrificed our own happiness and independence for the sake of our children'.

These stories of deprived fathers are no more than a reminder that it is not always the wives who suffer intolerably from the loss of their children. One has to bear in mind that not all judges favour the mother at the expense even of an outstandingly devoted father. But Scottish judges have been noted for harshness to the mother who leaves her husband for another man, even though the husband might have kidnapped the child – not an indication, one would have thought, of a tender and gentle parent. And though mothers do from time to time snatch their children it is most often from fathers who have denied them access. Kidnapping fathers are more likely to act out of vindictive anger at the mother's preference for another man. The case of Caroline Desramault, in 1972, was followed with fascinated interest by the great British public as her mother fought for two years to win her back when her father defied all court orders to hand her over. To regain the custody of a child who is taken abroad is agonisingly difficult.

Guardian columnist Jill Tweedie related after the Desramault case that in 1961 her own four-year-old daughter and two-year-old son were taken from their home by their Hungarian father, and for *three years* she did not know where they were, despite following up every possible line of enquiry. 'My husband,' Jill wrote, 'took a particular view of fatherhood that had dimensions over and above simple love for his children. He saw himself as the head of the family and his wife and children were, among other things, irrefutably his possessions. When a possession rejects its owner, as I did him, a desire for vengeance is not least among the motives.'

There was another aspect of the situation which all women in the same position will endorse. 'I knew that my husband's conviction of right . . . was something that gave him formidable strength . . . the very faintly insane ability of one human being to convince another that there are no rules he will not break, no legal barriers he will not crash, no ethic he will not ignore, no lengths to which he will not go, to attain his ends.' Patriarchy's grip is still strong. But as strong as ever? I have often been astonished in recent years to note how often I am told by acquaintances of men walking out on their wives and children without warning. It is the wives I am likely to know, and they have all seemed to me charming, sensible and potentially lovable – though in the privacy of the home they could, I suppose, be the reverse. Most of these deserted wives seem to me to make a good job of managing on their own with the child or children – and that, I suppose, is the explanation for their deserting husbands' apparent irresponsibility. Women *can* cope, nowadays, even though the living may not be good for them, especially on social security. They *can* be economically independent; they *can* run a household without male support if they need to. This, I presume, is how the departing husband reasons to himself: 'They will be far better off without me.' A pretty poor excuse for callous behaviour, I would say.

It is still my absolute conviction that the best thing we can do for our daughters is to give them the ability to maintain themselves and, if need be, their children. I stick to that even though I know that it lets too many men off the hook of responsibility and makes others feel that they have been deprived of their traditional role as family providers and cherishers. I look back with horror to the letters we printed in the *Guardian* following an article of mine on marriage and money, around 1964. A few quotes may reveal how much attitudes needed to change only twenty years ago, and may also prompt us to ask ourselves whether they have yet changed enough:

Often my husband, apparently extremely generous, provides me with a blank cheque and tells me to buy 'that' dress. He forgets that the night before he spent telling me in detail that over the last year he spent 1s 8½d more than he earned. That life is hard and that we cannot afford anything as, after all, he is the only earner.

I have asked on occasion of a rise in my husband's salary if I could have a personal allowance, however small. His reply has always been that we have a joint bank account and that is all that is necessary. But I find I am emotionally unable to use this account as I might if I had any of it. I wish I could explain the sense of non-worth and impotence which I feel vis-à-vis money matters.

Another woman who admitted that she was never any good with money said that after thirteen years of marriage and the birth of two children she never had more than £1 in her purse – 'and even that is searched in case I may have purloined an extra 10s and may be tempted into a wild orgy of spending.'

The most remarkable letter in this compilation was from a woman with an exceptionally strong social conscience. It illustrates for me how financial dependence can lead to subjection over a far wider area than shopping and household management. Because her husband disagreed with this woman's desire to help people socially disadvantaged either by class or by colour, she wrote:

I salved my conscience by working secretly for a year on a six-hour home-help job, and the 24s I earned I felt was mine to give away to a young coloured couple in need. I have now come up against it again with a young mother and baby deserted by the husband because the baby is not his. I helped her with the baby milk and shillings for the gas until I could get her to the National Assistance Board, but my own children objected that I was using 'Daddy's money'. Happily last week I managed to get a night duty job at an old people's home for Saturday nights . . . Fortunately on night duty I am not even using my housekeeping hours to gain my 'charity' 30 shillings, so my conscience is now at peace.

I have often wondered if one of my favourite characters among regular *Guardian* correspondents is still alive and active. She once signed herself 'Five-bob-a-week wife', for that was all her husband, a quite well-paid local government official, allowed her for her private spending . . . for bus fares to her pottery classes, reading matter, stamps, and so on. We corresponded quite often, and she assured me emphatically that she was not alone in her predicament, for there were even teachers of her acquaintance who accepted that the father of the family took charge of the allocation of his wife's earnings, as well as his own. This was all the more astonishing to me because when I moved from Leicester to Bolton, Lancashire, in 1931, I found that the custom was for the mother of the family to receive the unopened wage packets of all members of the family and to dole out 'spends' – to her husband, as well as to her grown sons and daughters. I suspect that Lancashire matriarchs like my splendid mother-in-law would have made mincemeat of any attempt by their menfolk to enforce patriarchal domination in the home, though society at large was then still firmly founded on the assumption that the man was the head of the household and responsible in law for everything that went on within it.

And yet, and yet . . . those Lancashire matriarchs could have ruled the community as they ruled their families, I am sure. And though their regime was rigid and in some senses harsh, it seemed to me to produce first class citizens with a strong sense of duty. Father-in-law, a sweet-tempered amiable man, was deprived of his favourite relaxation, playing the piano, until after his wife died – the piano was parked on an upper landing and no one touched it. In our home, in later years, he happily pottered through 'The Geisha Girl' and 'The Gondoliers' whenever he felt like it. Perhaps my sensitive, musical husband also suffered as a boy from artistic deprivation. But Bertha Stott brought up three sons and one daughter who had a profound sense of their duty to their family, their employers and society at large. None of them could conceivably have gone off and left wife or child to struggle on their own. This freedom that we have won from the traditional constrictions of family life, how much happier does it make us?

I think of children I know whose parents fight over them as fiercely as dogs over a bone. Even after years of separation and perhaps remarriage, ex-partners may still be vindictive towards each other. I think of children 'playing up' at school or even truanting because they are so desperately unhappy over their parents' behaviour. At least in years gone by children were kept in ignorance of their fathers' extramarital affairs or their mothers' 'misbehaviour'. Now if the parent with the roving eye does not tell all to the offspring, the other partner may do so, perhaps out of spite or perhaps to build himself or herself up in the child's estimation. What are parents like these doing to their children by making them feel both ashamed and hurt, both angry and unloved? Unloved? Well, certainly less loved than the parent's new partner.

Despite some published evidence to the contrary, I tend to think, with Wilfred De'Ath, that most children would opt for their parents, even warring parents, to stay together, unless one of them is physically or mentally cruel or alcoholic. The child may often think Daddy is a pig, but he is Daddy. Mummy may be beastly mean, but she is Mummy. I don't believe that this attitude towards parents is just acquired from the romantic 'happy ever after' stories children read or watch on TV. 'Mum, Dad and the children' is still the pattern most children accept as 'normal'. And what most children most hate is *not* being normal. I believe we *have* a hope of giving children emotional security outside the framework of our present nuclear family pattern, but it needs a lot more effort, concern, generosity and imagination than many parents seem prepared to put into it.

Even while this chapter was being written, I was invited to the home of friends in which the mother and her second partner, her first husband and their two teenage children, and the mother's baby daughter by her second husband, all lived together, apparently in amity. Not only the teenage daughter but also the ex-husband was clearly attached to the baby. I have been told since that this unusual joint household was set up very largely for financial reasons, because neither the newly weds nor the ex-husband could afford new homes. It may be so, but it could not possibly persist unless the first husband and his children were willing to make a go of it. If modern permissiveness led to a reduction in sexual jealousy, I would be very thankful, for that might open the door to extended families in which half-sisters and brothers might sustain one another in the way that siblings did in the large families of our grandparents' time. Too often the deserted wife or the 'betrayed' husband will go to fantastic lengths to keep the children of new unions apart. Why? Lest the second family should 'corrupt' the first? Or simply out of anger and hatred?

Desertion may be even harder to endure than the death of the beloved partner. I don't know. But I do know that time, even if it can never fully heal, can make most things bearable — at least for those who feel they have some responsibility to the living.

The newest family pattern of all is that of the single parent by choice. By no means all those one and a half million children in single-parent families come from homes broken by divorce, desertion or death. And increasing numbers of women, it seems, want children but not husbands. Outstandingly, and appropriately, Jane Streather, Director of the National Council for One Parent Families, is such a woman. In a *Guardian* interview she said that at the back of her mind she had always wanted to be a parent, but during her twenties 'my whole life became committed to work and to politics . . . and the years went flying by. Then suddenly I was in my early thirties. There had been a number of men in my life . . . but nothing had worked out on a permanent basis. I made the decision to have a baby, and then it became a matter of choosing the right man and the right time.' Ms Streather chose her man very carefully. 'When it came to the decision, Tom's father was the only one I wanted to have a child by. It wasn't an intense relationship and I was extremely fond of him and I respected him. I talked to him only once and that was "pillow talk". His first response was, "What rights do I have?" and I thought that was a good start because I believe a child has a right to know his father.' But, I wonder, how great a part do these coolly selected fathers play in the lives of the children they have begotten? Enough?

Irma Kurtz, *Cosmopolitan* agony aunt, is another single parent by choice who, in her position of advice giver, has obviously had to think out her attitudes very carefully. Usually she advises *against* single parenthood. Always she advises great caution and self-awareness. 'It is never advisable for a single woman to have a baby until she is perfectly sure that she herself

is ready to stop being a child in search of a grown-up of her
own to give her protection, financial support, or anything else
her baby will need and demand from her alone.'

Rita Craft, in a letter to the *Guardian* in 1981, made the life
of the single mother vivid: 'A typical single parent does it all
alone, single-handed, tends every night to a wakeful child,
never catches up the lost sleep, stays upright through illness of
her own, goes to work, cooks all the meals, does the laundry,
paints the house, tends the car and spares what is left of her
time from this to sing, play and talk to her child.' Some truly
married women with unco-operative husbands might tell exactly
the same story, surely? Another difficulty of which Irma Kurtz
reminds her readers is that the unmarried mother 'needs to be
comfortable in her single state because she is going to be
reminded of it more than ever she was before . . . Having a
child restricts a single woman's social life for obvious practical
reasons, and also because the activities of motherhood, from
ante-natal clinic to parent-teacher meetings will keep her in the
company of married people' – and, one might add, of married
people who tend to ask, 'What does your husband do? Does he
help you with the baby?'

In my long life one of the most radical changes in social
attitudes has been the attitude to the illegitimate child and its
mother. Think of Tess of the D'Urbervilles and Adam Bede's
poor tragic love, Hetty Sorrel, who was hung for infanticide
because she could not bear the shame of her 'fall' and the
lifelong brand on her offspring. You don't need to go back to
Tess and Hetty to recall the outcast mother and her 'shameful
bundle'. It isn't so very long ago that unmarried girls who
found themselves pregnant would put their head in a gas oven,
jump off a high bridge or slash their wrists. Even in 1961 when
Margaret Bramall became director of the National Council for
the Unmarried Mother and her Child (now the National
Council for One-Parent Families) girls used to arrive on the
council's doorstep from all over the country. 'They were in

terror,' Margaret Bramall told me, when I talked with her on her retirement. 'They walked up and down the street before they could face coming into the office, because they were so ashamed.' Even in recent times there are cases of newborn babies left on doorsteps. I suspect that these are usually the children of schoolgirls who may not be so much ashamed as terrified of their total inadequacy to cope with parenthood.

In the fifties and sixties there was still a strong need for mother and baby homes, though many of them were pretty hellish. In 1965, the NCUMC published a survey of mother and baby homes by Jill Nicholson, who claimed: 'Society is no longer obsessed by sexual sin and the desire to punish it.' But her researches showed that 'there can be few groups who suffer so much condemnation and receive so little help' as the unmarried mothers. She found that any help for these women was frequently regarded as encouragement to immorality and promiscuity – an accusation levelled at Margaret Bramall right up to her retirement. Most of the girls who spent the last weeks before the birth of their child in a mother and baby home felt they were in prison. The rules were positively punitive – no visits from boyfriends, even the baby's acknowledged father; very limited visiting hours even for parents.

During the sixties there was a network of young mothers in Lancashire (and probably in many other areas) who took pregnant girls into their homes in the later months of their pregnancy. The girls gave what domestic help they could and their hostesses gave them support, saw them into the maternity hospital and helped them on their way to their new life. It is my recollection that all tended to advise the young mothers to have their babies adopted. One of them whom I knew always said to her charges: 'You think of the baby as a cuddly little armful but you must remember that one day he or she will be an awkward and probably difficult teenager, for whom you will still be solely responsible.'

There are not many babies for adoption now. 'Accidental' pregnancies are fewer since the coming of the Pill; abortion is acceptable and safe among a large sector of women, though the anti-abortionists campaign ceaselessly (and to my view often unscrupulously) against it, and being a single mother is now, as I have said, no shame. Now many good couples are deciding to adopt children of mixed parentage. In the society in which such parents move, the black, brown and yellow children they adopt will probably be fully accepted both by other children and by their parents. I hope with all my heart that they will be as fully accepted when they are teenagers, and that none of them will be 'warned off' when it comes to dating and, even more, to prospects of serious love affairs and marriage. I am incurably optimistic about this. Why a charming, cultivated young person with the same sort of background and education as one's own offspring should be unacceptable because his or her skin is a different colour is so completely beyond my understanding that I have to believe that other people cannot long continue in the certainty of their own superiority and the inferiority of the others.

One further development in family patterns which is causing much interest and concern as I write is the artificial insemination by donor of women whose husbands are infertile. There are, for example, 'host mothers' (said to be popular in the United States) who, for a consideration, will allow themselves to be impregnated by the husband of an infertile woman. Some of these 'host mothers' regard it as a service to less fortunate women; some husbands of the host mothers apparently feel no hostility or even embarrassment. We have a lot of thinking to do on this development as the findings of the 1984 Warnock Report indicate. Shall we in time see host mothers bearing children for single, homosexual men who are unable to accept the idea of heterosexual partnerships? Such men are often potentially devoted fathers, and could be excellent single parents.

It is not just the composition of families that has changed so much in the last few decades but attitudes towards child rearing. The little darlings who are welcomed with such joy and whose every new word, every new skill is delighted in, can turn all too soon into rampageous teenagers, often hostile, often ill-mannered, often exceedingly odd in appearance and quite foul-mouthed! Even though one knows that this is almost certainly a passing phase, part of the strange pop culture of our times, it is hard to cope with. Today, thank goodness, the use of 'the strap' to punish bad and rebellious behaviour is not approved of and is, I believe (though how can one be certain?), uncommon. Are there still parents who dock pocket money for bad behaviour or actually lock up their daughters, as once they used to? Even if there were, I doubt if even the fiercest parents could triumph. Teenagers know their rights nowadays. At sixteen they can run away from home and not be escorted back by the police. (Alas, some under-sixteens run off, and are obviously greatly in danger since they dare not risk discovery.) At eighteen, young persons become adult. Was it wise, I wonder, to reduce the age of majority by three years, even though young men become liable for national service at eighteen in time of war? Is a person still at school really adult? Is he or she mature enough to marry without parental consent and approval?

I do not know any woman of my own generation who does not feel sorry for and anxious about today's teenagers. *We* were never 'teenagers'; we were not even categorised as 'adolescents'; we were just schoolchildren on our way towards becoming adults. Most of us went on living at home, boys and girls alike, until we married. *Of course* we were not always happy. Is any immature person? But the pressures on us were far less when there was no commercially inspired 'youth culture'. We dressed no differently from adults. None of us, I feel sure, could have accepted Punk fashion. Has any earlier generation in this country deliberately uglified itself? White-washed faces, glued-up spikes of hair in the harshest colours, red gashes like clowns' mouths . . . what could have been the appeal of this outrage to youthful beauty except rebellion? Of course, many of these fierce-looking young people were and are as amiable and generous-hearted as any pigtailed miss of my day – possibly sometimes more so, because today's teenagers feel free to behave as it suits them and are not compelled by convention to a politeness that could become wholly artificial and pointless. And many work heart and soul in various good causes.

But how do we ensure that freedom doesn't lead into glue-sniffing, marijuana-smoking, heroin injection, alcoholism and mindless promiscuity? No loving parent or grandparent could read without deep concern Rosie Boycott's horrendous account, in *A Nice Girl Like Me,* of her ten years from the founding of the feminist magazine *Spare Rib* at the age of twenty-one to her taking refuge in a clinic for alcoholics. Rosie, thank heaven, 'dried out', married and had a daughter. Not all her contemporaries were so lucky.

I truly do not know what more we can do to safeguard our precious children and grandchildren beyond encouraging open discussion (as often happens now between mothers and children) and beyond making it quite clear what kind of behaviour we think unsocial. Unsocial behaviour ranges from dropping litter all over the place to using coarse and obscene language in public, to nicking the odd trifle from the chain store and 'bunking off' from school. I cannot bring myself to believe that giving our youngsters freedom relieves us of the necessity to say what standards of behaviour we find acceptable and what are beyond the pale. The young will not necessarily come into line but I think there is far more chance that they will ultimately follow the worthy standards of parents if it is made quite clear what those standards are – by deed, of course, as well as by word.

I grieve with all parents and grandparents of children affected by family break-up. But I have to believe that many young people will survive this, and all the pressures of the teenage cult, and will become fine, stable people – perhaps almost saintly, like my friends Una Kroll (doctor and deaconness) and Phyllis Pearsall, head of the Geographers' A-Z Map Company, who both survived quite appalling childhoods and grew up to become founts of loving kindness and wisdom.

So here I am, an old woman now, powerless to secure the survival of the nuclear family and not quite sure that I would if I could . . . and certainly not the version that includes the automatic inclusion of Granny into a son's or daughter's household. Tory politicians may prate as they please but I ask myself if that strong-minded, powerful lady Margaret Thatcher would like to spend her last years in the home of either her daughter Carol or her son Mark? If she ever thinks of this possibility no doubt she brushes it aside as something that could never happen to her. Her husband is a wealthy man and she will have a handsome pension of her own. But supposing she were to develop arthritis or some other crippling disease? The odds, statistically, are heavily against Denis Thatcher's living to be a comfort and support to his wife in her great old age. The longer we women live, the greater is the likelihood that our last years will be as widows. But the women of my generation cannot easily bring themselves to move in with our sons or daughters, however dearly we may love them.

When I was a girl, my father's father came to live with us (he had been a widower for many years). He was a bit doddery and finally became so infirm that he was moved to a nursing home where, fairly soon after, he died. Later my mother's mother and father moved in. I wonder what that grand, fierce old man thought of his dependent state? Living with offspring was what everyone then expected to happen, but I cannot imagine that Grandfather Bates relished it. After his death Grandmother Bates stayed first with us and then with one of my mother's sisters. It may have been less difficult for her than for her husband, but she had brought up seven sons and daughters, entertained them all year after year at Christmas, had twice been Mayoress of Nuneaton, and had taken a continuing interest in all her grandchildren. Malie and Frieda were cut to her matriarchal pattern but did she not mind being the dowager for ever more?

My mother and father both died too young to be a burden to anyone, something which I accepted as a great blessing for my father, for after he died I found among some manuscripts of his a play based on the father of a family who shot himself rather than be in this situation of dependence. Mother Stott was in her way lucky, too. She and Papa Stott came to live with us while K was still in the Navy . . . but not as dependents. Granny was there to look after my baby daughter Catherine and was *de facto* head of the household for which I earned most of the money. Not very long after K returned home to us she had a massive stroke from which she died a fortnight later. I grieved over her loss, I grieved still more for her husband, and daughter and sons – but I did not grieve for her. She died in harness, splendidly useful, splendidly in command almost to the very end.

One of the most needed organisations I ever knew or helped to foster through the *Guardian* women's page was the National Council for the Single Woman and her Dependents (now the National Council for Carers and their Elderly Dependents). Started by the Reverend Mary Webster, its members were one of the saddest sections of the community – the women who lived on into middle age in their parents' home, often because Mum pressurised them, often because of a sensitive conscience. There used to be too many parents, often mothers, who made it plain that they 'needed' the beloved daughter at home and discouraged suitors. Often those self-sacrificing daughters longed for the day when they could retire from paid employment and have only one job to fulfil, the job of caring for a now very old, very frail and often very demanding parent.

Thank goodness the day of the self-sacrificing spinster seems to be passing — although it has not quite gone, and there are some bachelors, too, even in retirement, still caring for aged, incontinent, helpless mothers.

Is this an inevitable part of the price for the survival of the nuclear family? If so, I vow and declare we must find some other formula for a stable and supportive 'family unit'. It is also my heart-felt prayer never to become unable to care for myself.

6

Male and Female

How different, really, are men and women in the 'civilised' society of this last quarter of the twentieth century AD? Mothers say – mine did, having had two boys before me – that we come into the world different in behaviour and reactions, not just in the possession of penis or vagina. It doesn't seem possible to stand firm on the assertion that *all* the difference between the sexes is cultural, implanted in our consciousness from the moment the child's granny knits a blue jacket for the boy, a pink dress for the girl. And yet what I increasingly believe as I grow old is that the relative importance of the basic biological difference between the male human and the female human is shrinking in relation to the cultural and behavioural similarities between them, and that it will continue to do so until, some millennia ahead, the difference will be minimal. Ovaries are now fertilised outside the womb, babies may well be gestated in incubators, impregnation may well come to be divorced from the act of love. Who knows?

What we do know is that it is pure nonsense to say, 'You can't get away from nature.' You can. We have. Mother Nature's best device for securing the survival of mammal species is that the male's penis shall discharge semen into the female's vagina, thereby fertilising an ovary and producing a foetus, sheltered in the womb until it is able to emerge and draw nourishment from its female parent's breasts until it can find its own food. To ensure that this process should take place, Mother Nature provided that it should be as instinctive and at least as pleasurable to copulate as to eat and drink. What the 'You can't get away from nature' contenders won't admit is that in the millions of years that earth has been inhabited by anthropoids, hominids, naked apes and primitive humans, we have got further and further away from nature. Our far-distant ancestors, weaponless compared with tigers, lions, leopards, bears, poisonous snakes or spiders, invented weapons with which they could hold their own – the only species to do so.

Mother Nature did not provide us with the means to fly, so we invented aeroplanes. She did not provide us with the means to survive in or under the sea, so we invented ships and submarines. We have got so far from nature that a man has now walked on the moon and survived for months in the trackless wastes outside the orbit of Mother Earth. One day there will be a spaceship which will take the children of earth to some other habitable planet. You can't 'change nature'?

Male and female human beings are born with two eyes, two arms, two legs, two ears, two lungs, a nose, a mouth, liver, bladder, stomach and heart and, for heaven's sake, a brain and a nervous system. Are all these components of the human body of no importance at all compared with the sex organs? Many people still believe it, but I simply cannot agree.

A typical male fundamentalist view was expressed by Paul Ableman in a small book, *The Doomed Rebellion* (1983). 'Man is essentially a biological fertilising machine,' he said; 'A woman's body can almost be considered a biological factory for the initiation, gestation and ultimate delivery of new life.' I snatch a similar thought from a reply six years earlier to an article by the musicologist Hans Keller on segregation (in the form of a 'men only' room at the Reform Club): 'The spurious egalitarian ideology of complete sexual integration is proclaimed in defiance of the facts of man's nature, and many sociologists have warned and increasingly warn that man ignores such facts about himself, established over millennia of evolutionary history at his peril'. 'What sociologists?' I ask myself. 'And on what evidence?'

I cannot understand how in evaluating the contribution that we make for survival of the race, intelligent men (and some women, too) can think that this one essential function of reproduction should exclude all the other functions that men and women can and do perform. I like a thought put forward by Catherine Storr in her article 'What Separates the Sexes?' in the *Guardian* in 1968: 'Male and female have become two dangerous words. Originally used, innocently enough, to make a biological distinction between the sexes, they have become more than overweight; they cover a whole territory, strewn with theories, ideas, hypotheses and dogma.' I like even better the words used by Brigid Brophy as far back as 1966 – actually in reference to hostility to homosexuality on the grounds that it is 'unnatural'. They can be applied equally well to the 'You can't get away from nature' argument when applied to sex differences: 'I must get round to having my circular in reply printed,' wrote Brigid Brophy. 'Dear Sir, It is unnatural to wear clothes, create works of art and send rockets to the moon. You cannot judge whether something is good or bad by describing it as unnatural. You have to *think*. This is also unnatural. P.S. Your anatomy ordains that when your nose runs the discharge shall slide down a groove towards your mouth, but I pay you the compliment of assuming that you use a handkerchief.'

Completely 'unnatural' in many people's minds, of course, are the transsexuals. But they exist. It seems as if Nature has produced them – or so they themselves think – and now that there are medical techniques for changing the genital equipment they were born with, quite a considerable number of people who have had an overpowering conviction from quite an early age that they were born into the wrong sex have had themselves 'changed' from men into women or women into men. It is not possible for a person born with male genitalia to conceive or bear a child, or for a person born with female sexual organs to impregnate a female – though for all we know it may be, some day. But something drives these people to undergo this drastic experience and I gather that they feel deep satisfaction in having escaped from a physical frame into which their psyche could never comfortably fit. I wish that more transsexuals had written or spoken of the *basic* differences they found in the way society treated them in their two different guises.

Even the remarkably gifted James-into-Jan Morris does not fully answer the sort of question I long to ask. In *Conundrum* she wrote: 'Having . . . experienced life in both roles, there seems to me no moment of existence, no arrangement, no response which is not different for men and for women.'*How* different? What are the instinctive or automatic female responses and reactions that are different from a man's? What are the instinctive or automatic responses of the male *to* the female that are different, even in work situations? Transsexuals ought to be able to chart this muddy territory for us, but alas they don't. What Jan Morris wrote about was sadly superficial and almost all about *learned* behaviour. Indeed, she admits that being treated in a restaurant with a man 'with the conventional deference that a woman expects . . . is really deference of a lesser kind and the man behind me is the guest that counts . . . It soon came to feel only natural, so powerful are the effects of custom and environment.'

Ms Morris gives a side glance at 'the more preposterous handicaps of the female state, embodied in common law and in business prejudice,' but adds airily, 'they are clearly doomed. Nobody of sense can support them and they are mere impertinences left over from the past.' It does not seem to occur to her that she can cope with these prejudices and see that they are not part of the natural order, precisely because she did live for so many years as a man. If she had not lived as a man, would she necessarily have had such a keen appreciation of the fact that 'I am treated in many petty situations as a second-class citizen not because I lack brains or experience or character but because I wear the body of a woman'? I am glad to say that I know one transsexual who devotes most of her free time to the feminist cause. Would that Jan Morris did the same!

It is only a 'dullard' man 'who would want to brush aside or scorn a woman,' says Jan Morris. 'Intelligent men never do it.' But they do, alas, because they have been imprinted from early childhood with the belief that women are this and men are that, and that there is a whole range of things that women aren't quite up to. One recent quotation, from Rosalind Miles's book *Danger! Men at Work* (1984), must suffice. The head of a technical studies department, resisting the idea of admitting girls to his courses said, 'They couldn't do the work because their hands aren't big enough – or their brains.'

Often I wish that I could get even a few of the men who think that 'positive discrimination' in favour of women and girls is 'unfair' to listen a while to the tale of positive discrimination *against* women throughout the centuries. Oh yes, of course in various times and places *men* have been cruelly exploited and put down, as serfs, slaves, war victims, concentration camp internees. In some parts of the world they still are. But black men have not always been exploited and suppressed by white men; serfs have successfully revolted; the top dogs in one culture have been the underdogs in another. Throughout recorded history women, however, have been 'the second sex'. Men should really ask themselves how *they* would feel if women were the dominant sex and had decided that because men's part in the continuance of the race was so miniscule compared with women's *boy* babies should be quietly disposed of. Everyone knows that in many cultures it was the custom to expose girl babies at birth because they were regarded as a burden on their families. How many people know that female foeticide is still practised in India? According to a *Guardian* report, protests by Indian women's organisations and others resulted in a ban on the use of amniocentesis for sex determination, but apparently there were enough loopholes for selective abortion of female foetuses to continue. Indian doctors have described women coming to them desperately asking how they can avoid giving birth to daughters and have sons. Failure to produce a son results, they say, in ill-treatment from in-laws. It also seems to be well authenticated that young wives are 'accidentally' burned to death or otherwise removed from the scene if their families are unable to supplement the dowry with expensive consumer goods like washing machines, dishwashers, and perhaps, now, even video recorders, so that the husband can remarry and acquire a fresh dowry of money and goods.

How can women help being deeply resentful on behalf of their sex when they are told, as a little meeting of the United Nations Association was told not long ago, about women prisoners in Iran who, found guilty of capital offences, are raped before execution so they will not go to heaven as virgins? Or about female circumcision, or about chastity belts, or even about men of our times and our culture who think it 'normal' to bash up their wives when they are drunk or simply in a rage with life?

Deep down in the roots of the Jewish and Christian religions is the belief that all women are the daughters of Eve, the source of temptation to man to stray from the path of (celibate) virtue. That monastic celibacy was hard on men no one can deny, but that the response of the penis to the presence of the female was *her* fault and that *she* must be hidden from view at best and burnt at the stake at worst is something that men ought surely to be willing to feel collective guilt for. It was from Eva Figes's *Patriarchal Attitudes* (1971) that I learned first of Jacob Sprenger, 'hammer of the witches', who regarded woman as 'a useful tool of the devil', of the German philosopher, Fichte, who said that 'a woman's marriage utterly annuls her so far as the state is concerned', and of Otto Weininger's assertion that 'women have no existence and no essence; they are not, they are nothing . . . the meaning of women is to be meaningless.'

It was from Winifred Holtby's book, *Women* (1934), that I learnt that Tertullian cried out, 'The sentence of God is on this sex of yours in this generation. You are the devil's gateway. You destroy God's image in man'; that Mahomet said, 'I have not left any calamity more hurtful to man than women', and that there was a Russian proverb, 'A hen is not a bird nor a woman a human being.'

It was in *Not in God's Image,* an anthology compiled by Julia O'Faolain and Laura Martines (1973), that I read the horrendous life story of the fourteenth-century Florentine merchant, Gregorio Dati, who married four times, each wife bringing in a substantial dowry to help him in his business. Wife number one 'went to Paradise' after a nine-month illness started by a miscarriage. Three years later he married again, having meantime had an affair which produced an illegitimate child. This wife survived for nine years, during which she produced eight children, before she too 'passed on to Paradise'. His third wife died after bearing him eleven children, and wife number four produced four children, after which Dati apparently gave up writing his diary. Only 'about nine' of the twenty-three children survived – and none of the four young wives whose sole purpose in life was to produce them.

An almost more horrifying passage in *Not in God's Image* is the account of a judgment recorded in the Exchequer Chamber in 1663: 'If a woman who can have no goods of her own will depart from her husband against his will, and will not submit herself to him, let her live on charity or starve in the name of God, for in such case, the law says, her evil demeanour brought it upon her and her death might be attributed to her wilfulness.'

The fear of the sexual power of women may be the main reason why the Judeo-Christian religions are so strongly motivated towards constraining us, locking us up, covering us up, literally and metaphorically. But there is another aspect of the gender difference which is still powerful, though probably few men admit it . . . the fear of the menstrual flow of blood. Self-protectively, one imagines, since blood tends to be linked with magic in primitive cultures, men have convinced themselves that the menstruating woman is 'unclean'. To me it is quite horrifying that in this twentieth century the monthly 'cleansing' of the lining of the womb is regarded as ritually unclean and therefore a barrier to a woman entering any holy place or standing before the altar, a powerful argument against the ordination of women. A Swedish Lutheran priest, the Reverend Kerstin Bergland, told the *Guardian* in 1978: 'Greek women can't even go to church at that period, you know. And that's the whole issue in a nutshell. Deep in their hearts the opponents [of the ordination of women] say we are not clean. You can see that in all cultures, men have been afraid of women because they are not clean for five days a month. Can people go to Eucharist with a woman? Here many people think it is an act of very deep feeling, just because it is a woman.' I am afraid it is still true that many men who have come to accept cheerfully the service of a woman accountant, lawyer, dentist or even doctor feel revulsion at the idea of accepting the sacrament from the hand of a woman priest.

It is less than ten years since the Reverend Dr Cuthbert Keet, chaplain of an Anglo-Catholic organisation called Ecclesia, preached in Cambridge of 'strong forces who seek the creation of priestesses'. He went on: 'Their iniquitous campaign will continue, and those who value the apostolic ministry must maintain an eternal vigilance . . . and fierce and unyielding opposition.' I very much doubt whether the passion of Dr Keet's diatribe against 'priestesses' owed as much to his resentment that they, unworthy females, should presume to seek ordination as representatives here on earth of a male deity, 'God the Father', as to his unacknowledged obsession with the idea of women being 'unclean'.

It has often puzzled me that in these days when medical

marvels like heart transplants and micro-surgery proliferate, so little has been done to ease the life-long inconvenience of menstruation. I have been told by one young friend that so far from regarding menstruation as 'the curse', as all my contemporaries did, she looks on it as 'a nice token of femininity'. Tampons must greatly have reduced the inconvenience and embarrassment, and analgesics have, I hope, put an end to the sort of blinding pain that I used to suffer. But surely some women do still suffer pain? And we often read nowadays of the problem of pre-menstrual tension. If men had had to endure 'the curse' throughout the centuries, would not more have been done about it years ago, in the way, perhaps, of vacuum extraction? On their way up to the top all women experience the inconvenience, or worse, of menstruation and later the discomfort, if no worse, of the menopause. No woman who has experienced at least discomfort from these aspects of her femaleness can deny that there are days when they put her at a disadvantage in her working life. But the essential femaleness of Indira Gandhi, Golda Meir and Margaret Thatcher in no way detracted from their use of the power they achieved. My femaleness has certainly been entirely irrelevant to the way I – as with all other post-menopausal women – tackle whatever jobs I have had to do. I have certainly never regarded myself as a useless or dehumanised person because as a 'biological factory' I have long been on the scrap heap.

I think it is time that intelligent young men like Paul Ableman accepted that what men and women have in common in this twentieth century is more important than the ways in which they differ. If the biological differences between us were more important than the mental, psychological and behavioural similarities, you could say that a man had more in common with a male gorilla than with his sister or his wife – which is obviously nonsense.

I think we still need to remind ourselves – and to remind our brothers, our lovers, our friends and our colleagues – how men's (often very odd) view of gender differences has been used to women's detriment. There are some hilarious examples in Ehrenreich and English's *For Her Own Good* of, for example, the common advice of Victorian doctors to women 'to throw their weight behind the uterus and resist the temptations of the brain'. These authors quote Dr Edward H. Clarke's *Sex in Education, or a Fair Chance for the Girls,* published in 1873 and reissued in seventeen editions in the next few years, as saying that higher education would cause a woman's uterus to atrophy. Dr R. R. Coleman of Alabama warned young women: 'You have been incessantly stimulating your emotions with concerts and operas, with French plays and French novels; now you are exciting your understanding to learn Greek and solve propositions in Euclid. Beware!! Science pronounces that the woman who studies is lost!' (I am very happily reminded here of a story told me at a Fawcett Society party by an elderly lady who had known Philippa Fawcett, daughter of the great suffrage campaigner, Millicent Garrett Fawcett. Philippa's name is revered because in 1890 she was placed above the Senior Wrangler in the Cambridge Tripos – which meant that she must have had one of the best mathematical brains in Europe. The little-known story about Philippa is that at a Saturday evening party in Cambridge she was asked by a don to give her mind to a complicated mathematical problem. 'But,' he said, 'you must not work on this tomorrow. I do not approve of my students working on Sunday.' On Monday morning Miss Fawcett presented herself, and her solution to the problem, at her tutor's lodgings. He thanked her, but added sternly that she should not have worked on Sunday. 'Oh I didn't,' she said cheerfully. 'I worked it out in my head cycling home from the party.')

Give just a moment's thought to Florence Nightingale, who was thirty-two before she even began to emerge from the prison of upper-class young ladyhood which meant paying calls, doing the flowers and being read aloud to (which Florence described as 'lying on one's back and having liquid poured down one's throat'). We think of Florence, sentimentally, as 'the lady with a lamp', but in fact she was one of the great brains of the nineteenth century. 'What an archbishop she would have made,' said someone. Spare a thought for Clara Schumann, wife of the composer, Robert Schumann, distinguished pianist, close friend of Brahms. She actually thought it was 'presumptuous' of her to think that she, a woman, could compose music as well as play it. Spare a thought for Sophia Jex-Blake and all the other aspirants for medical qualifications who had such a rough time at Edinburgh University in the 1870s, being shouted at by foul-mouthed young men who sometimes used medical terms which the girls would understand but the police would not. There was, of course, a strong underlying sex hostility to women studying medicine. They were told by one medical professor that no decent woman would wish to study medicine, let alone any lady.

So deeply inbuilt into our view of society is the superior right of the male to inherit that no one seemed to think it odd that the late Duke of Norfolk could not be succeeded by any of his own children because they were all female; or that though by special remainder the daughters of Lord Curzon (Lady Ravensdale) and Lord Rhondda (Viscountess Rhondda, founder of the influential journal *Time and Tide*) had titles, they could not sit in the House of Lords until life peers were introduced in 1958. It is customary to offer a retiring prime minister an earldom. Will such a title be offered to Mrs Thatcher when she comes to retire? Will she take the equivalent female title 'Countess' and will she be able to pass it on to her twin daughter instead of her twin son?

Small matters, but useful indications of how our thinking has been conditioned over the centuries . . . What we are accustomed to seems 'natural' and what is natural is 'right'.

I have never had much stomach for a fight, and certainly not for 'the battle of the sexes', but in the fight to change the prejudices of men (and many women), it is only to be expected that there should sometimes be deep, dark anger. If you bond *for* something, the best adrenalin raiser is bonding *against* something – or some*one*. In the movement to set women free from second-class citizenship the 'enemy' has to be patriarchy – male assumptions that men know best what women are able to do, should do and even must do. Naturally this sometimes comes out as hostility not just to male values but to men, which grieves women like me who have had the utmost support from father and husband. Some women, indeed, are saying some exceedingly nasty things about men these days. The most horrific I ever had to listen to was at a Women in Media discussion on 'What has man hating to do with feminism?' One woman actually said that looking at her eight-year-old son she saw a potential rapist. I ended up at that meeting almost in tears, and had to be briskly reminded by younger colleagues that bitter experiences drive some feminists to get off their chests in this sort of way their anger at the way male-dominated society has treated them.

One should, of course, always aim to enter into dialogue with opponents. But how can one, with people who won't even listen? I have been acquiring books on 'the woman question' for more than fifty years, and cannot resist quoting a paragraph or two from a treatise on *Our Women* by Arnold Bennett, one of the outstanding British novelists of this century, published in 1920. I guess it was written for the readers of the popular newspapers to which he frequently contributed.

Intellectually and creatively man is the superior of woman.

Every man knows in his heart and every woman in her heart that the average man has more intellectual power than the average woman.

In creation, in synthesis, in pure intellect, women even the most exceptional and most favoured have never approached the accomplishment of men . . . it is a question of an overwhelming and constitutional difference, which stupendously remains, after every allowance has been made for inequality of opportunity. Therefore I am inclined to think that no amount of education and liberty will sensibly alter it.

Women as a sex love to be dominated. For some thousands of years, if not for ever they will love to be dominated. This . . . in itself is a proof of intellectual inferiority.

How could pontificating writers like Arnold Bennett *know* what they claimed to know, that the female intellect is intrinsically inferior? Even quite early in this century distinguished women writers were exploring the theme of what I call gynelethargia – the oblivion of women's history. In *A Room of One's Own,* compulsory reading for young women today as it was for me at the age of twenty-two, Virginia Woolf told the story of William Shakespeare's imaginary sister, Judith, also a poet, 'who scribbled some pages in an apple loft on the sly but was careful to hide them'. She followed her brother to London, was derided by the theatre manager who 'bellowed something about poodles dancing and women acting', was taken up by Nick Greene, had a child by him and 'killed herself and lies buried at some cross-roads where the omnibuses stop outside the Elephant and Castle'. And in Rose Macaulay's novel *They Were Defeated* (1932), which moved me even more deeply, there is Julian Conybeare, daughter of a friend of Robert Herrick, also a poet. Julian falls in love with the clever, arrogant John Cleveland and dies through striking her head violently on a table during a fight between him and her brother. Julian, for me, represents so much talent, so much grace of mind, lost for ever to posterity . . . not even the sigh which down the years has paid tribute to 'Chatterton, the marvellous boy'. I find gynelethargia quite heartbreaking.

The great international authority on gender differences in the fifties was Margaret Mead (now, like many 'authorities', questioned and attacked). Her *Male and Female* (1950) was particularly important to us in questioning the sort of gender role typing regarded then, as quite often now, as a sort of absolute. 'Surely,' she wrote, tongue in cheek no doubt, 'it cannot be true that women's heads are absolutely weaker – for carrying loads – than men's.' I have myself seen and photographed Greek women carrying huge blocks of stone on their heads, and on the Great Wall of China watched women heaving immense paving stones into place. One of my treasured memories is of our 'treasure', Mrs Higgins, a tall, well-built Salford Irishwoman, saying to the dustman who refused to lift a rubbish-filled old washtub because it had no handles, 'Oh you won't, won't you? Then I will.' And she heaved it up and walked with it to the garden gate. I expect that what he felt was anger, not admiration.

The really important thing that Margaret Mead said was this:

> We find no culture in which it has been thought that all identified traits – stupidity and brilliance, beauty and ugliness, friendliness and hostility, initiative and responsibility, courage and patience – are merely *human* traits. However differently, the traits have been assigned, some to one sex, some to the other, and although the division has been arbitrary, it has always been there, in every society of which we have any knowledge.

So the qualities ascribed to gender are variable, not absolute? Gentlemen, please note. But elsewhere Margaret Mead said that whatever characteristics and roles were assumed to be male they always had more prestige than those assumed to be female. Why, oh why?

In Elizabeth Gould Davis's *The First Sex* (1973) I enjoyed a great releasing laugh over her response to the question: 'On what is the assumption that woman's body was made for man's convenience based?' Ms Davis asserts that

> Proof that the penis is a much later development than the female vulva is found in the evidence that the male himself was a late mutation from an original female creature. For man is but an imperfect female. Geneticists tell us that the Y chromosome that

produces males is a deformed and broken X chromosome – the female chromosome. All women have two X chromosomes, while the male has one X derived from his mother and one Y from his father. It seems very logical that this small twisted Y chromosome is a genetic error – and that originally there was only one sex, the female.

Feminists are always being accused by men of totally lacking a sense of humour. I hope anti-feminists are not so lacking in a sense of the comic as to fail to understand what delicious mirth it causes us to read statements like that – whether or not the biology is sound or shaky. A nineteenth-century biologist, Frank Lester Ward, wrote, 'Women are the race itself . . . the strong, primary sex, and men the biological afterthought.' Oh shades of St Paul, of the early Christian Fathers, of Calvin, John Knox, of Freud, of male chauvinists of every age and every culture!

Another joy-giving book, perhaps the most endearing and imaginative of all writings on gender differences, is Elaine Morgan's *The Descent of Woman* (1972). Surely no one who reads it will be able to forget her description of a Miocene-type 'generalised, vegetarian, pre-hominid hairy ape who survived into the torrid Pliocene which scorched the African continent'. Life was tough for our remote female predecessors. 'The only food in plentiful supply was grass which her stomach wasn't designed to cope with. Everything in the vicinity (except the insects) was either larger, fiercer or faster. A lot of them were larger, fiercer *and* faster.' She found no escape route. 'She turned into a leopard's dinner. *That* generation of primates became extinct.' But, says Elaine Morgan,

There was another timid, undifferentiated Miocene-type ape who lived nearer the coast. She also couldn't digest grass; she also had a greedy and hectoring mate; she also lacked fighting canine teeth; she also was hampered by a clinging infant; and she also was chased by a carnivore and found there was no tree she could run up to escape. With piercing squeals of terror she ran straight into the sea. The carnivore was a species of cat and didn't like wetting his feet; and moreover though he was twice her body weight, she was accustomed to adopting an upright position, even though she used four legs for locomotion. She was thus able to go further into the water without drowning. She went right in up to her neck and waited there clutching her baby until the cat got fed up with waiting and went back to the grasslands.

And that was how the hominids learned to walk on two legs instead of run on four. Whenever this female ancestress of ours felt a need to go into the water she walked *upright*, because she could go further in and she could better protect her baby. Right through her book Elaine Morgan makes the point that the evolutionary process was always inevitably and essentially in aid of the survival of the baby – in whom lies the future of the species – and therefore that the *mother* was at least as much an initiator of new developments as the male.

Of course Elaine Morgan might be totally mistaken in her interpretation of how our hominid ancestors reacted to the great Pliocene drought. Her ideas, which she derives largely from Sir Alister Hardy's aquatic theory of human evolution, may for all I know be rubbish. I am no anthropologist or ethnologist. I am in no position to refute Desmond Morris, or Robert Ardrey or Konrad Lorenz. I do not know if any later writer has demolished Elaine Morgan's theories, or, indeed, Elizabeth Gould Davis's propositions. But I shall continue to enjoy their thinking – that the male is biologically inferior to the female, and that it was the female who taught the human race to stride the world on two legs.

It is our capacity for motherhood that typecasts us, of course, from puberty to the grave. I like very much a sentence of Harriet Taylor's in her essay on 'The Enchantment of Women', written in 1851 and recently republished with J. S. Mill's book *The Subjection of Women*: 'It is neither necessary nor just to make it imperative on women that they should either be mothers or nothing, or that if they have been mothers they should be nothing else during the whole remainder of their lives.' I am a mother, I always wanted to be a mother, and I believe that a majority of women do feel the biological urge to conceive. But we must be very careful neither to assume that *all* women feel this urge, nor to regard the non-maternal as 'unnatural' or in any way second class. Very many 'non-maternal' women are admirable, caring individuals. Devoted grandmother though I now am, I strongly resent the assumption that our capacity for childbearing and our natural inclination towards childcare and child rearing are the only reasons for our being here on earth.

This area of gender difference needs far more thought than it has yet been given. Most of *men's* thinking on gender difference seems absurdly superficial, ranging from, 'Wouldn't you be sorry to give up men's chivalry to women?' to dogmatic assertions that *of course* women are less intelligent and efficient I am truly sorry for the nice, sensitive men who feel they have lost the role they were educated to take on – the responsibility, financial and psychological, for maintaining wife and children – and who have not found the way towards genuine partnership with wives, friends, lovers. But why cannot they accept the inevitable, that roles in society are not now and cannot for ever be fixed by the biological difference between us? Why will they not *think*?

Women are often accused of concentrating on personal problems, their own and other people's, rather than on basic ideas and principles. No doubt this is true of some women, but I have found that it is certainly true of some men, perhaps a majority of men, in this field of gender difference. The men I know tend to base their view of the relationship of men and women on their experience in and out of marriage, of love affairs and of relationships at work. Women who have tasted freedom but not fully accepted its responsibilities may be partly to blame for this male obtuseness. But so are the men who laugh at the idea of 'women's studies', who jeer at 'the shrieking sisterhood', and who have never opened a book by even the most highly regarded writer which would open their minds to the disadvantages of being born female. They have not read J. S. Mill's book *The Subjection of Women,* Virginia Woolf's *A Room of One's Own,* Simone de Beauvoir's *The Seeond Sex* or Ray Strachey's *The Cause* – let alone any of the admirable studies by academic women of our own times. I think they should be ashamed to pontificate about women's roles without knowing what some of the most able people of our own and earlier times think about them.

But women have a lot of thinking to do, too, including feminist women. Mary Wollstonecraft wanted 'to see the distinction of sex confounded in society except where love animates the behaviour'. This, too, is my wish, as it is of a good many older feminists, I believe. But there are new-style feminists who emphasise 'the distinction of sex' as much as male chauvinists, because they glory in the belief that 'female is finer' and are convinced that only by establishing our own superior female values, as well as securing our economic independence, shall we throw off the yoke of men.

It is not uncommon to meet young women who regard any co-operation with men as contaminating. As Janet Radcliffe Richards says in her excellent book, *The Sceptical Feminist,* 'some feminists seem to slip into the idea that maleness can be used as a criterion for badness'. In London in recent years there has been a determination to keep men out of all 'women's places'. One can see the importance of this when the women's centres are refuges for battered wives and the like; one can see its importance in the case of advice centres like A Woman's Place, to which angry men might go in order to track down refuges to which their wives might have fled; one applauds all-women co-operatives, which run such services as taxis, as well as publishing houses like Virago. I also believe that a great many meetings on feminist issues, especially of a 'consciousness-raising' nature, are more helpful and constructive if men are excluded. But I don't think it can be denied that some hopeful projects like Women's City have broken down partly because the organisers were unwilling to admit any participation by men or even their presence on the premises. Among women in general there are too few 'isolationists', too many who are accustomed to the presence of men at home, at work and in leisure pursuits and too many who regard this as natural and desirable for any large-scale, women-only project to be really viable.

And why should it? For good or ill, there are almost as many men around as women. We can't just dispose of them. We can't exclude them from power as they for so many centuries have excluded us. So hadn't we better concentrate our thinking on 'meaningful dialogue'? There is so much to explore; perhaps, now that women are acquiring strength from working with one another, and are so much less dependent on the approval of men for their actions and ideas, we may venture, even if a little tentatively, to try to explore together. Janet Radcliffe Richards offers a fruitful line of thought in her examination of 'reason' versus 'intuition', logic versus feeling. I have always had a suspicion that 'intuition' is a phony concept, a sort of consolation prize for 'the little woman' who has never learned to reason, but that is not to deny that there are imaginative flashes of insight which illuminate the way to new 'truths'. Many scientific discoveries have been made in this sort of way, and 'intuition', if it exists, is certainly not confined to one sex.

I go back to the point from which I started. I do not believe that mind has a gender. I do not believe that human nature is totally male or totally female. I think one can get a good deal of help in understanding our true *human* nature from the Chinese concept of Yin and Yang. Yin does not equate with female, nor Yang with male. Both sexes contain the qualities of both Yin – receptivity, passivity and contemplation, and Yang – analysis, organisation and reason. It is the Yin in us that makes us support the Friends of the Earth, be protective of the environment and of rare species in the insect and animal world and link arms around the nuclear arms bases. It is the Yang in us that wants to get things done, to organise, to lobby, to make democracy work.

It is crystal clear, surely, that there is Yin and Yang in all of us, male and female both. But if you consider the long history of *homo sapiens* you perceive that Yang has always been the dominant quality. How could we have become the dominant species without the dominant quality we can call Yang? So Yang has, up to this very time, been more admired, more valued — and often more envied — even by women, than the gentle, contemplative Yin. Probably it is Yin that some present-day feminists want to elevate to prime importance. But surely we desperately need both? Doesn't the best hope for the future lie, as Sukie Colegrave suggests in *The Spirit of the Valley,* in androgyny? This is probably harder for men to accept than women. For a woman to be told that she thinks like a man has long ceased to be regarded as a compliment, but we can accept that the intention is to pay tribute to our logicality. But there is scarcely a man walking who would relish being told he thinks like a woman. 'Masculine' may not be a compliment when applied to a woman, but 'effeminate' or 'womanish' are the deadliest of insults when applied to a man.

If only we could acquire the best qualities of both Yin and Yang. If men could be less aggressive, less autocratic, more tender, more co-operative, and if women could become more independent-minded, more self-reliant, more confident, we might walk hand in hand down many public as well as private thoroughfares. I am perfectly convinced that androgyny should be the ideal, and I think it is possible, perhaps even likely, that we are moving towards it.

7

Loving?

There was a time, long since, when 'sex' meant for me and no doubt for many of my generation, simply male and female. 'Common are to either sex' we chanted in our Latin lessons, 'artifex and opifex'. When did sex come to have, predominantly, its other meaning of sexual relations? Now, I think, it is simpler to use 'gender' for the biological distinction, and 'sex' only for sexual intercourse. And now I feel driven to discuss how 'sex' in this sense seems to have taken over our lives.

Didn't it always dominate human behaviour? We are often told so, but I feel certain that sex did not dominate the conscious thinking of most women in the nineteenth century and the earlier part of this century. As for men, I can't possibly know, but George Bernard Shaw and Neville Cardus, the music critic, both admitted to being virgins until they were thirtyish. They were certainly not 'sex-starved'; the deprivation did not spoil their work and does not seem to have spoiled their lives. My father married my mother when he was a bachelor of thirty-six. (She was twenty-five.) I find it quite impossible to believe that during those long years before marriage he frequented brothels, and in the lower-middle-class, Nonconformist society in which they moved, he would have found it pretty well impossible to find partners in 'free love', either serious affairs, or one-night stands. Most unmarried young women lived at home and there were no motor cars with back seats available for cuddling and kissing.

I would stake everything I have and am on the certainty that my husband was a virgin when I met him (he was twenty-three) and that he never lay with any other woman, even during those painful war years when he was serving in the Mediterranean. I know he was exceptional, but I am very sure he was not unique. But since then one of the most remarkable revolutions in the history of the human race has taken place – the introduction and widespread use of the contraceptive pill. Since the early sixties, sex (copulation) has been divorced, for a very large section of the population of the 'civilised' world, from nature's essential purpose – the continuance of the species – and the fear, or expectation, of pregnancy has been removed. Fear, obviously, was the strongest deterrent to sex outside marriage. Now the whole ethos of sex has to be rethought. We are in a difficult and often painful transition period.

Sexual appetite is common to all living creatures. It must be, or the various species would die out. The human male had an urge to relieve himself in the body of the female; the human female had a vacuum between her legs which ached to be filled. This process was as natural as salivation at the sight of food, and was no more associated in primitive times with the female's swelling belly and later delivery of an infant than urinating and defecating were with eating and drinking. When did *love* enter in?

There must surely be a case for saying that in our far-distant ancestors the first emotion akin to what we think of as love was the feeling of a mother towards her infant, not the feeling of the male for the female or of her for him. Suckling goes on for months – in primitive societies probably until the toddler was pushed out to fend for himself or herself so that a new infant could be fed. There must have been some kind of bonding between mother and child, as well as something we would recognise as tenderness?

These, for me, are the essence of love.

How much bonding was there between male and female, in primitive times? Not much, one gathers from mythology. The Greek and Roman gods pursued female humans for their beauty not their qualities of mind and heart, and some nasty, dirty tricks they used, too, as when Zeus took on the form of a swan to seduce Leda, or the bull was sent by Poseidon to rape Persephone, resulting in the monstrous Minotaur. (Females did not always fall into the arms of unlikely divine messengers – Daphne, for example, fled from the amorous Apollo and escaped him by being changed into a very pretty bush. Even in mythology some nymphs were choosy and some wives, like Penelope, were faithful.) If the Greeks felt romantic love (in the sense in which William Morris wrote of 'my dear, my darling and my speech friend') they felt it, we read (as in books like Mary Renault's moving novels) chiefly for men and boys. (No one knows whether any women other than Sappho felt it for girls and other women, because women were seen only through the eyes of male poets, dramatists and philosophers, who didn't care, even if they knew!)

What was the germ of romantic love as we think of it? Whence came Heloise, or Juliet? The idea of romantic love must have gone alongside the crudest and most possessive kind of passion. The Crusaders, we are told, put their wives into chastity belts before they sailed off for the Holy Land. They did not, for certain, put their own sexual equipment out of action for the duration. One of the most striking aspects of the history of sexual morals is that men have regarded females of a lower social order, or a conquered race, as being as readily and properly available for their physical needs as food and drink. This belief was quite astonishingly prevalent among many men in the nineteenth century, during the reign of the highly moralistic Queen Victoria. One has only to read a life of Josephine Butler to appreciate the passion with which some men defended their right to the bodies of females and the hypocrisy that permitted even clerics and men holding public office to visit brothels where young girls were the commodity on offer.

There seems little doubt that at all times and in all places some restrictions have been placed on sexual behaviour, some taboos accepted or enforced. Puberty and marriage have both been marked with ceremonies; limits have been placed on who may marry whom. And once the link was established in the mind of man between copulation and conception, the question of 'property' entered in. The child was 'my property', 'my heir', and the fear that a wife, also 'my property', might cuckold him was a threat to his manhood and his sexual dominance. Women also, of course, were angered by the faithlessness of a husband, but they were conditioned (or even obliged) to accept it, partly at least because they were seldom confronted with the evidence of an adulterous relationship, in the way husbands inevitably were – by the existence of an illegitimate child.

Jealousy exists in both sexes, but in men tends to be more violent because of the property concept of marriage. The woman may be fiercely revengeful if her husband or lover deserts her for another – she is driven by the pain of rejection to hit back. The man suffers pain, too, but also outrage at the theft of his 'honour', the debasing of his manhood. I once wrote of 'the foul toad syndrome', having just watched a performance of *Othello*. Othello smothered Desdemona because he saw her as 'a cistern for foul toads', not only an intolerable betrayal of him, but also a threat to the mores of the society in which they lived. One can only be thankful that in our time the concept that the beloved's body would be polluted and defiled by intercourse with another, and that adultery would somehow be a source of hideous infection in the community, has almost gone – though not entirely, and not, I fear, in some other cultures. The 'foul toad syndrome' is almost certainly responsible for revengeful kidnappings of children by fathers after marital break-up, and perhaps sometimes for wife battering. In our 'permissive society' jealousy may still be a powerful force, and if anyone claims 'I am one not easily jealous', let him or her remember that that is precisely what Othello said. Modern man may not fully realise that he regards his wife as his property, modern woman may not realise the extent to which she regards her husband as a status symbol, but these out-of-date concepts survive.

The young are trying to abolish some of the old ideas about sexual 'rights'. *Crimes passionels* are surely fairly rare now, and attract much less sympathy than once they did. I think there is a prevalent desire to get back to a state of innocence about sexual relationships. We have largely discarded shame and embarrassment about sexual intercourse and now that it has been largely freed from the risk of pregnancy it is possible for many people to enjoy it without hang-ups. The concept of chastity as a moral obligation has been widely discarded. The word 'adultery' is not very often used now for extramarital sex.

A recent novel by Gillian Tindall, *Looking Forward,* gave me, and must give many women of my generation, cause for thought about our attitudes to marital fidelity. Her admirable heroine, a doctor deeply involved in the establishment of birth-control clinics and truly fond of and attached to her husband, has an affair with an American journalist. 'She, who had believed herself middle-aged, sensible, prosaic and almost tediously responsible for right-thinking,' Dr Mary thinks to herself, 'was a woman in love, a woman having an affair, a woman capable of giving herself to more than one man at a time. How horrifying, even physically disgusting she would have thought it and would have dismissed it as something for her unthinkable.' But then, one day, it occurred to Dr Mary 'how odd it was, considering that loving and giving were basic tenets of Christianity ("to give, and not to count the cost; to fight and not to heed the wounds") that conventional sexual morality was so heavily biased in favour of the unloving, ungenerous, self-protective stance.'

If sexual intercourse should ever become mainly a matter of giving and receiving physical pleasure, what does the future hold? It has always seemed to me that men who frequent brothels and go with prostitutes must have little more satisfaction out of the sex act than out of emptying a full bladder or distended bowel. But today's prostitutes, no longer 'fallen women', of course argue that they perform a valuable social service. In the words of a self-appointed spokeswoman, Helen Buckingham, 'We act as sex therapists and answer a social need . . . There are no emotional problems with us. We stop men getting tangled up with their secretaries or their best friends' wives. The act of paying out money stops that.'

Well, there is commercial copulation sanitised. Sometimes I think that perhaps I ought to try harder to perceive that sexual intercourse is as vital to life as eating and drinking and therefore must be obtainable for a fee if not available for free. But you *can* live without sex. Hundreds of thousands of widows could tell you that however sad or painful it may be to be deprived of sexual love for years, it can be done. And is. When I wrote in a *Guardian* article 'Deaths from sexual starvation must be remarkably few', one or two 'Letters' correspondents challenged me. But I stand by it.

It was when Lady (Joan) Vickers sponsored a meeting at Central Hall, Westminster, to debate the Street Offences Act of 1969 and to discuss the campaign of the English Collective of Prostitutes to remove all legal restraints on their trade that I wrote very strongly on the subject. I support the prostitutes' case for an end to harassment by the police and an end to being labelled 'common prostitute', and I agree that they should be allowed to live together in pairs without being charged with running a brothel. But I must reiterate that I think prostitution is a social evil and agree with what Joyce Ansell, an ardent member of the Josephine Butler Society, said at that meeting:

'Prostitution is the ugliest manifestation of the inferior status in society of women.'

An admirable young woman from a Bristol group declared at Lady Vickers's meeting that she would rather go on the streets than earn her living cleaning out stinking lavatories. To which I replied in my article, with genuine passion, that I would a million times rather clean out stinking lavatories than let a stranger violate my body. I think now that it might have been better not to have pursued this comparison with lavatory cleaning because it could have led some people to think that I think prostitution 'dirty' – in the same way as the 'bad language' to which so many people object is labelled as 'dirty' whether it consists of blasphemies, like the use of 'Jesus' and 'Christ' as expletives, or of vulgar words for excretion, like 'piss' and 'shit', or of sex words like 'fuck' and 'cunt'. This use of 'dirty' as a label for 'bad' is something I wish we could sort out.

Not only would I prefer cleaning lavatories to prostitution, but I would also even rather work in a factory where battery chickens are gutted, cleaned, chilled, trussed and frozen, as described in Pat Barker's brilliant, unforgettable evocation of the Yorkshire Ripper terror. This novel, *Blow Your House Down,* which is mainly about prostitutes, confirms for me that there *is* a choice for women – even if your man cannot or will not support you, even if social security will not provide enough for your needs or if your children are deprived. In Pat Barker's wonderfully imaginative and sympathetic book Jan, Carol, Kath and others choose prostitution. Maggie chooses the chicken factory, sick-making as she found it. As would I, and as would the majority of the women I have talked with, both young and not so young – though not *all*, I must add in honesty.

I simply cannot bring myself to accept that our Welfare State is such a hollow sham, such a shameful betrayal of the ideals and dedicated campaigning of thousands of women –

working-class Co-operative Guildswomen and middle-class National Council of Women members alike — that unsupported women today are driven into prostitution to save themselves and their children from near starvation. If this were really true we should be campaigning twenty-four hours a day to make social security a reality as our foremothers believed it would be.

How do women come to accept the life of a prostitute? Is it true, as some young friends have said to me, that there are girls, little more than children, whose first experience of sex is in a back alley for a fee? I find that dreadfully hard to believe, just as I find it hard to believe that a young mother, short of cash for the electricity meter, would offer her body on the street if she had had no previous experience of extramarital sex. Isn't it more likely that the majority of those who take to the streets as a way of making money, especially money to pay for the goods they and their children need or want, have been 'desensitised' about sexual relations? They may have come to accept sex as payment for a night out, or as a quite enjoyable alternative to a visit to the *palais* or the cinema. Or they may have had a number of transient relationships. Surely in 'the life of shame', as it used long ago to be called, it is the first step which counts? And how does this first step happen?

To my 1978 protest article in the *Guardian* came an equally passionate protest from Helen Buckingham, speaking for the English Collective of Prostitutes. She accused me of 'creeping into the debate with my mind on the sort of salacious aspects which even the *News of the World* no longer insults people's intelligence with'. She went on: 'I would like you to know that I think you have a very dirty mind and are very ignorant when it comes to understanding what our work is actually about. You may be anxious to make your name in journalism. We are anxious to change laws which keep us as prostitutes and keep so many journalist women as sex objects in order to persuade men that they are innocuous. We lack our education but we will answer your latest self-opinionated pieces with facts, more self-control than I can muster just now.' It seemed useless to answer her and explain that I was no novice journalist, but I did wonder how Josephine Butler, who had so much tenderness for the prostitutes of her day, would have reacted.

Since 1978 attitudes, it seems to me, have softened, or broadened, or whatever one likes to call it. When in 1980 Cynthia Payne was brought to trial for running a brothel in the very respectable London suburb of Streatham, it was reported that when her home was raided one December afternoon clergymen as well as barristers, businessmen, an MP and a member of the House of Lords were all to be seen clutching their 'luncheon vouchers' (for a session with one of the resident prostitutes). 'My old boys use them to satisfy their appetites,' Ms Payne was reported to have said, which seemed to cause more mirth than anger at the fact that women's bodies should be regarded as a saleable convenience in this way. A novelist, Paul Bailey, proceeded to write a full-length book, *The English Madam*, about Cynthia Payne, 'the Freddie Laker of sex', and was photographed with her for an article in the *Observer*.

In May 1983 the *Dartford and Greenwich Mercury*, south-east London, led its front page with a story headed 'Cops raid on brothel is lashed', the 'lasher' being the woman manager of a sauna which offered 'sex' for £30 and 'a range of other services for between £10 and £20'. She said, 'There was absolutely nothing wrong going on at the sauna. It was just a place where men of all ages and backgrounds went for sex if they wanted it. Only about one in ten were having sexual extras.' Miss D. claimed: 'We have some very high-class customers. A man of eighty-two used to come in with a box of chocolates for one of the girls.' I was reminded of a letter that had come to Central Television's 'Getting On' programme, after I had spoken on 'Sex for the Sixties', from a man who said that about once a month he visited a prostitute but could not afford it more often. Should the cost of living index take into account fees for sexual intercourse, then? Or could it be 'a supplementary benefit'? When Miss D.'s 'sauna' was closed down she said, 'It's difficult to know what they will do now – child molest or rape? You just can't say.'

You just can't say whether, in fact, prostitution is more common today than in more secretive and less permissive times. 'Free' sex seems to be pretty widely available, but perhaps the fact that so many men regard it as a more or less necessary part of life means they may be more ready to seek it from prostitutes when the free variety happens not to be available. Impulse buying, as with many another commodity these days? And has this expectation of 'sex on tap' increased the prevalence of rape? It seems at least possible, but surely there are many murky strands to be untangled in the psychology of a man who can savage a woman to satisfy his sexual urge? I wish men would write more on this subject, for we need to try to understand – not only so as to be able to take self-protective measures, but also to help *men* to examine their own attitudes.

It seems to me that quite a high proportion of men manage to convince themselves that women, after initial resistance, actually enjoy being taken by force. Such men own quite freely to having rape fantasies and often claim that women have them too. This seems to me a very dangerous assumption. Men may fantasise about the enhanced sexual excitement of overcoming a woman's reluctance and women may fantasise about the 'Mr Rochester' whom she first fears and dislikes and then finds she passionately responds to, but such fantasies have precious little to do with the act of rape, which is essentially sadistic. So far from being able to think of rape in terms of 'love bites and bruises', as it were, most women regard it as the most hideous crime that can be committed against the person. It is this particular horror which leads some young women to take part in 'Castrate the Rapists' demonstrations and which has given impetus to groups like Women Against Rape and Women

Against Violence Against Women.

Unquestionably, the risk of being involved in a traffic accident is far higher than of being raped or mugged. So I think it possible that though the media's wider reporting of rape cases may have contributed to recent helpful anti-rape legislation and to increased mutual support among women, its sensational coverage of individual cases may now do more harm than good. Such reports certainly so frighten many women of all ages that they are reluctant to go out alone after dark, and they may well excite the inadequate, physically unattractive, friendless man to 'prove his manhood' in this way.

To say to women, as policemen, magistrates and even some women do, 'Never go out alone at night', is to make us less than citizens. We have as much right to walk along the Queen's highway as any man. When my friends say 'No, you mustn't walk home, I'll take you', my response is not simple gratitude. I do not intend to live the rest of my life in fear, or circumscribe my evening activities because I am car-less. I greatly applaud the 'Reclaim the Night' campaigns and wish more women, especially older women, would support them. But as women usually have less physical strength than men and are at a considerable disadvantage if 'jumped on', ought we not to look at the laws which prevent us from carrying any means of defence? Why should the Home Office be so cautious about legalising the carrying, let alone the use, of a non-toxic spray? Our mothers and grandmothers could have recourse to a hatpin if attacked — and so could we, legally, if we ever wore one. I believe one could legally use a hairspray if one just happened to have it in one's handbag. But why should it not be legal to carry a non-toxic spray incorporating a strong dye which would temporarily brand the attacker? Perhaps if these were widely carried and used, and their use publicised after any successful prosecution, men might be inclined to be more wary of attacking women?

All parents are afraid for their young daughters today, and

not just because of the attacker in the dark. They are afraid because the pressures are so prevalent and so persistent to sample 'sex' at an earlier and earlier age. When society imposes scarcely any sanctions, parents are almost powerless to impose their own. They cannot ban all television watching, all teenage magazine reading, all outings in mixed company, all visits to discos. If they did behave so dictatorially the youngsters would find ways of dodging the rules, with no twinge of guilt, for would they not be 'doing what everybody does'? And doesn't society implicitly tell them that sex is altogether desirable and good? Some parents bury their heads in the sand and some ensure that their daughters go on the Pill quite early in life, which certainly avoids the worst result of premature sexual adventure. Of those who endeavour to 'lock up their daughters', a few will succeed, but most will fail, even to the extent of having their daughters leave home and fend as best they can — for at sixteen youngsters cannot be forced to live in the parental home.

I cannot believe that 'young love' when consummated in the back of a car, under the bushes in a local park or on the floor in the parental home, always with the fear of discovery, can be idyllic. More likely it will be sordid for the boy, miserable, painful and scary for the girl. But that is the situation we are in: the contraceptive pill has removed the greatest safeguard of female chastity and girls may now 'sow their wild oats' just as bachelors were long thought entitled to do. I do not think, and have not thought for very many years, that either men or women should enter into the solemn contract of marriage without previous experience of sex. It is not easy to argue, even, that it should be limited to discovering whether an affianced couple are likely to be harmonious sexual partners. If you have nothing to compare this experience with, how do you know that it will suffice? But how much is enough? Can a line be drawn between experiencing freely and uninhibitedly the joy of sex and regarding it as just one form of 'leisure pursuit';

between enlightening experiment and more or less mindless promiscuity?

When Jill Tweedie wrote about promiscuity in the *Guardian* in 1978, readers' response must have been startling to women of an older generation. 'I feel the time will come when what we now call promiscuity will be acceptable,' wrote one, though she feared that this happy state of affairs was not imminent in the suburb where she lived. Another wrote: 'As a happy woman who enjoys a multitude of sexual relationships, the word 'promiscuity' shocks me . . . because good sex, even a one-night stand, is about loving . . . the conviction that I am wanted for my personality, my blessed ability to share, makes my saggy, boppy middle-aged body beautiful in my mind and in my mirror.'

Is this kind of freedom going to lead to a sunny, guilt-free society? I doubt it. Sex *without* the involvement of tender love is no great addition to the sum of human happiness, and offering love does not always mean receiving it – nor does being offered it necessarily mean being able to return it. The torment of unrequited love is not going to disappear because out of kindness, or even out of habit, the beloved will oblige the lovesick by sharing his or her bed now and then. Amid this *Guardian* correspondence I found a remarkably mature letter from a sixteen-year-old schoolgirl virgin: 'She [Jill Tweedie] assumes that in some far-off happy Eden everyone will be well-orientated beings all going to bed with each other, no complexes, no neuroses, no guilt, no envy.' 'A lot of naive rubbish,' this girl called it, and added, 'good sex isn't dependent solely on how many positions and techniques you know. I want to be part of a trusting, faithful relationship built strongly enough on love and concern to make it tough and tolerant. I may be hopelessly idealistic, but meanwhile I'll wait for Jill's paradise world of free sex to happen – but I don't expect anyone to be happier or more well adjusted when it does.' Rereading this letter, I wonder if it *could* have been written by an inexperienced sixteen-year-old, but if it really was I hope with all my heart that ten years later she may be of the same opinion still.

How *can* we see our youngsters safely through adolescence? Nature has her own little way: however 'open' the customs of the home in which she grew up, almost every teenage girl goes through a period of intense 'modesty', dressing and undressing in total privacy and locking the bathroom door. (Do boys go through a similar phase?) This surely must be Mother Nature's method of protecting young females at such a vulnerable time of their lives, but well-intentioned (as well as less well-intentioned) adults do not always take note. Explicit sex talks can also be an invasion of the adolescent's privacy. Does a fourteen-year-old relish being told that 'riding' on a farm gate is a form of masturbation and that the sensations experienced are similar to those experienced in the sex act? There is a case for taking the mystery out of the sex act by explicit description of the physical sensations experienced, but I greatly doubt whether this would damp down curiosity.

Is there no way we could cool it for our dear children and grandchildren, could ensure for them a breathing space between the onset of puberty and physical and emotional maturity? How devoutly I wish we could dilute the intense concentration on youth culture. When I was young, one *wanted* to be old enough to join in adult enterprises and interests – the adult drama, music, literary, even political societies one's parents belonged to. Now youngsters waste precious years because they are conditioned to believe that everything adult is *boring*. How much of this has happened in aid of building up a market for goods, programmes and services that will have teenage appeal and attract teenage (or parental) cash?

All this teenage sub-culture is programmed towards relationships between the sexes. What today's teenagers are missing out on is the same-sex relationship which in our day was the greatest bulwark against premature physical experience

with the opposite sex. We had *friends*; we had crushes on older
girls or members of the staff. I remember my best friend of the
day not washing her hand for a week because her adored gym
mistress had clasped it when assisting her to jump over the
vaulting horse! I remember walking after dark through the
square where my adored classics mistress lived, and gazing up
fondly at her lighted window. I remember composing a
sentimental ode or two to the maths mistress. This did us
absolutely no harm at all. In fact in my case it did me nothing
but good, for 'Sten' was a brilliant teacher who, if she did not
turn me into a mathematician, certainly developed my power of
logical thought, and 'Domina', the classics mistress, gave me a
lifelong interest in Greek culture.

Later we developed intense friendships – slightly sloppy, no
doubt, but based on genuine liking and esteem. The friend I
acquired in the sixth form is still my friend, after sixty years or
so. Would any boyfriend have lasted all that time through so
many vicissitudes? The emotion we felt in these same-sex
relationships protected us against premature relationships with
boys, yet it was also a preparation for them, providing us with
experience of giving and receiving love. In our day there was,
of course, no physical component beyond holding hands as we
walked along or enjoying the contact with one another's bodies
as we sat together in one large armchair.

Nowadays the probability is that a same-sex friendship would
have its overtly sexual component, because the young now
know so much more and expect so much more. But we in our
time had absolutely no inkling of what a lesbian relationship
involved. Indeed, I can remember in my middle years the wife
of a doctor asking me, 'But Mary, what do they *do*?' – and I
had no more idea than she had. No one I knew would ever
have heard of oral sex. Few had heard of the vaginal orgasm,
much less the clitoral orgasm. It is probable that generations of
married women scarcely ever, if indeed ever, experienced
orgasm, and if they did it was not something to be talked about

or consciously sought. Marriage could be companionable, tender and good, without the complete sexual fulfilment that young women today would think their right. I do wonder – and obviously do not know – how much the bliss of the orgasm has added to human happiness.

Even in one's seventies one can fill in many gaps in one's knowledge about sexual behaviour. Not having read (or wanted to read) Kinsey or Masters and Johnson, I really did not fully comprehend 'the myth' of the vaginal orgasm until I read the thoughts of my friends Anna Coote and Beatrix Campbell in their valuable book *Sweet Freedom* . . . Or at least I did not comprehend the influence that the recognition of the superior physical pleasure derived from stimulation of the clitoris compared with the satisfaction from the penetration of the vagina by the penis probably had on the new women's movement.

Coote and Campbell relate how 'ill-typed roneoed sheets of a paper by an American, Anna Koedt, began to circulate in this country in 1969' and had a great influence on many of the consciousness-raising groups then being set up. The basic message of this paper was that the pleasure of the clitoris made women independent of men for sexual satisfaction. A turning point in the relations of the sexes? A turning point in sexual behaviour? It seems to me more an argument for doing without *any* partner to achieve sexual satisfaction than for doing without a *male* partner. Brought up as I was in an age when sexual relations, even the processes involved in procreation, gestation and childbirth, were never openly discussed, I came to the consideration of masturbation with a totally innocent mind. I have never been able to see what is sinful, evil, or physically or psychologically dangerous about it.

One can see, of course, that in ages when the only licence for sex was procreation it might seem sinful for man to waste his god-given seed in pleasuring himself. (Probably the Holy Fathers never even suspected that a solitary female could similarly pleasure herself.) The idea of the precious nature of man's seed remains to this day. Andrea Dworkin, in her *Right Wing Women,* quotes Norman Mailer in his *Presidential Papers* as saying, 'It is better to commit rape than to masturbate.' But this is not a view held, surely, by any woman, or by any rational man?

The self-induced orgasm seems to me a rational and harmless way of achieving release from sexual tensions. If masturbation were the only result of 'blue' movies or 'video nasties', I would not think them a social evil. There is a terrible legacy of shame and fear about solitary sexual pleasure. I am quite unable to see any valid reason for condemning it and I think that for people who are unable to find sexual partners – the old, the physically unattractive or disabled, even the young, segregated from the opposite sex – it may have real therapeutic value. Nineteenth-century medical opinion tended to be that 'self-abuse' would lead to madness. We know now that that is nonsense. Could we not have some more 'open' thinking on this subject, which surely is of importance to consideration of relations *between* the sexes, as well as to the mental health of those who are likely to remain solitary?

And is it not time that we explored the reasons for the deep-seated hostility that persists towards homosexuality? The justification for its being regarded as the sin without a name was that in Christian teaching *all* sexual intercourse was thought wrong unless it was with the object of creating a child. The old baptism service used, horrifyingly, to refer to the baby as 'being conceived and begotten in sin' – which was the reason why my daughter was not baptised until she decided for herself that she wished to be. Now that sexual intercourse is almost always enjoyed with no intention to conceive, there seems no fundamental reason for outlawing intercourse between people of the same sex. I can understand, and indeed, share, a distaste for the idea of being personally involved in a lesbian relationship, just as some of us have a distaste for heterosexual relationships. I have always enjoyed the friendship of women. In my old age I enjoy it more than ever, and welcome the present-day freedom to exchange little caresses on meeting or parting, but the idea of further physical intimacy is entirely displeasing to me (as indeed, physical intimacy with most *men* would be!)

But why learned judges should decide that a lesbian is unfit to have the care of her child, or a board of governors decide that a homosexual teacher must inevitably corrupt his pupils, I really cannot understand. A lesbian woman may or may not be a good mother, as may a heterosexual woman. A gay man may or may not be a good teacher, as may a 'straight' man. What *I* call moral values are not solely linked to sexual orientation. They are, in fact, for me, firmly based on a feeling of responsibility about the effect of one's behaviour on other people. One's moral duty is to avoid inflicting pain or mental damage on one's partner, one's children, one's friends, or even on the community. The really immoral attitude surely is, 'I am not my brother's keeper.'

Few men feel any responsibility to protect women against what is now labelled 'sexual harassment'. Sex jokes have always been part of our way of life, they feel, along with a certain amount of bottom pinching and breast squeezing. Why should women suddenly start moaning – as indeed they do, even to the extent to getting up in the Trades Union Congress and complaining of fellow delegates' sex jokes; even to the extent of including provision for treating sexual harassment at work as 'unlawful sex discrimination' in a Sex Equality Bill presented to Parliament by Jo Richardson MP? *Is* this a fuss about nothing very much? I myself don't remember any really offensive behaviour of this kind during my long working life, chiefly spent alongside men. That may be, of course, because I never was exactly a sexual provocation to my colleagues. (In his book, *The Guardian Years*, Alastair Hetherington, editor in my time, wrote of me, 'Meeting her you might have thought she was an ascetic spinster.' Alastair admitted that that was not the whole truth about me, but perhaps it was a not uncommon reaction. Thank all the gods there be that it was not the reaction of K Stott!)

But harassment undoubtedly does exist, even to the extent of blackmail – 'No job prospects for you, dear, unless we can have a little fun together.' A conference organised by the National Council for Civil Liberties was told that a survey by a member of UMIST (University of Manchester Institute of Science and Technology) found that fifty-two per cent of women managers interviewed had received unwanted sexual attentions. A survey by the Alfred Marks employment bureau found that more than half the women questioned had been sexually harassed, and Bernard Marks told the *Guardian* that the survey had proved to him that harassment problems were *not* figments of feminist imagination. Bosses may think that asking a secretary or typist, 'Are you wearing a bra?' or 'What colour is your underwear today?' is all good clean fun, but it is likely to be at least distasteful, if not downright offensive to many women.

The coarseness and insensitivity of much male humour is certainly offensive, and to add insult to injury men defend themselves by assuring us that if we can't enjoy a joke we have no sense of humour. I had a nasty surprise in this field at an SDP national conference when an admirable woman delegate was speaking on a motion on corporal punishment in schools. 'These days,' she pointed out, 'a girl of thirteen who is caned might actually be pregnant.' Two perfectly respectable male delegates sitting behind me burst into guffaws of laughter. I suppose they thought me a prissy old prude when I turned round and said coldly I saw nothing funny in what the delegate had just said. But shouldn't men ask *themselves* why they find the link between pregnancy, sex and physical punishment so frightfully funny?

I am inclined to think that this 'harassment' will lessen, as it is increasingly brought into the open. Trade union men may regard it either as a joke or as a silly fuss by a few 'libbers', but they are likely nevertheless to feel a twinge of embarrassment and learn to be a little cautious of being caught at it. I feel sure that bringing the matter to the attention of trade unions and professional associations is the best way to deal with it.

Surely what is awry in society today is the idea of 'the more sex the better' because one can't have too much of a good thing. But of course one can. Fish and chips are very good when well cooked, but a daily diet of fish and chips might well lead to a longing to sample paella or moules marinières or bouillabaisse or some other exotic-sounding dish. Exotic sexual delights are, surely, what pornography purveys and is likely to create an appetite for. I have seen, in Lord Longford's office when he was collecting material for his report on pornography, a cyclostyled letter posted from Denmark to an address in the UK offering 'very hot' reels of film portraying 'sexy young girls having intercourse with a donkey', or 'two very pretty young girls being fucked and licked off by a very young dog'. I have myself seen in a public lavatory a scribble urging women to enjoy the pleasure of letting their dog lick their private parts. A great deal of pornographic material portrays children. Is it possible that a majority of us could ever think that because paedophiliacs prefer sex with young children and claim that the children also enjoy it, this practice might ever become acceptable?

The other possible result of a surfeit is revulsion, and here and there one sees signs that the trend towards more and more sex may be reversed. An article in *Cosmopolitan* in 1980 described the reactions of a woman of twenty-nine who after ten years on the Pill and a string of mostly casual affairs decided to become celibate until she had found a man 'with whom she could plan a future'. Another woman admitted:

After the pill took away the excuse of pregnancy and when

morality changed to encourage sex, I found myself sleeping with men I wasn't even attracted to . . . the other night I met a man at a party who attracted me, but not all that much. After a few drinks he suggested we go off together. Some vestige of the past made me almost automatically say "yes" but I steeled myself and said "no". I've simply wearied of one-night stands and am trying to be more discriminating about whom I go with, though that's harder than you'd think.

What seems to be left out of people's view of sexual satisfaction today is that it is at its deepest and finest when one loves the *whole person,* not just the physical shape – and how can one begin to know the whole person unless one has shared bed and board with him or her for a period of time? I find the idea that a man cannot successfully make love even to his dear wife after she has had a mastectomy quite horrifying. I simply cannot believe that if K had come home from the Mediterranean mutilated in some way it would have affected my loving, physical response to him, or that if I had lost a breast it would have affected his longing to find bliss in my arms.

Sexual union with a beloved mate is a sort of blessed homecoming to the place where one belongs; or sometimes one can escape from oneself into some new state of being. Could such transcendent joy be achieved by uncommitted partners? I feel that for physical joy, suckling a baby would rate higher than uncommitted sex, and that transcendence would be more likely to happen to me – though not infallibly, of course – when involved in some sublime musical experience, or on a sunlit mountaintop or some wild shore where one is suddenly, inexplicably aware of the oneness of all creation. What a little, brief, transient thing the orgasm is, compared with that.

8

Where the heart is

Since I was born, in 1907, I have lived in a dozen different homes of one kind and another. Nine were houses, three were flats. Three were family homes with my parents, three family homes with my husband. Two were lodgings; two were single-person flats before and during my marriage (while my husband was in the Navy), and two were as a widow. Considered as places to live (leaving aside the question of whom I lived with), which were the best? It may sound pretentious to say that the best were the big ones. But in all honesty, the three houses I dearly loved were, though not grand, all large, with lots of rooms, and lots of space.

The house which conditioned this attitude was 31 Highfield Street, Leicester, to which we moved when I was seven years old. I remember remarkably little of the house in which I was born, in Regent Road. I know it was double-fronted and had a long garden to the road. I don't remember anything about the kitchen, or even whether we had a bathroom. I think there must have been an indoor lavatory, because the back door opened directly on to the street. I remember the dining room, because that was where I crawled under the kindly cover of the chenille tablecloth when we played a card game called 'Old Maid' and I was left unhappily with the Queen of Spades, which made me 'Old Maid'. I remember the sitting room because that was where we had a splendid picnic when the weather was so bad that the planned picnic in the country had to be called off. But what I most clearly remember was the front garden – the gravel paths, where I was always falling over and grazing my knees; the creamy-white rose in the corner near the house; the 'blue snowdrops' (scillas) that I ran in to tell my mother about; the front gate in which my beloved brother Johnny trapped his finger and chopped off a little piece. I have a dim memory of creepy-crawlies in the cellar. What were they? My mental picture of them is of woodlice. Could they have been?

In the summer, I think, of 1914, I rode in the furniture van from Regent Road to the large Victorian terraced house in Highfield Street next to the Synagogue, where we lived until I was nineteen. It was a marvellous place for children – attics where Johnny could lay out his train set; cellars where we could develop our films and print our pictures; a 'music room' where I could, in my teens, sing away by myself, and Johnny's 'group' (which included a bass drum and a trombone, if I remember rightly) could have their sessions; Mother's writing-cum-sewing room where I cobbled up dolls' dresses from the 'bit bag' of dressmaking scraps in the cupboard. The marvellous thing about this house was that we were never on top of one another but could always escape.

So what I regard as essential to the happy home is space. When I was in my teens I quite often visited the home of my mother's sister, where there were two female cousins and one male. I used to be embarrassed by their constant bickering, and came to believe that one of the essential ingredients of a happy home life is the possibility of getting away from one another 'Open plan' housing was an awful mistake. From early adolescence onwards, you need to be able to shut the door. Parents need to be able to shut the door, too, against the sort of noise, 'musical' or otherwise, that tears their nerves to tatters.

I myself, conditioned by 31 Highfield Street, seem to feel a need for vertical as well as horizontal space. It is miserably oppressive to me to be long in a place where the ceiling seems to be pressing down on my head. When I first walked round the Barbican concert hall complex with some friends and they asked me, 'Don't you think it is marvellous?' I had to answer 'No', because nowhere did I feel I could lift up my eyes and nowhere were my spirits lifted up.

The moulded ceilings were the special elegance of the Highfield Street house. In Cliff House, Salford, it was the mantelpieces – the one in the sitting room was pure white marble. The great windows of this room looked over the cliff down to the River Irwell and across Manchester racecourse. It was very beautiful, our first marital home, even though a bit decrepit and rather scrappily furnished. I think we paid ten shillings a week for it, plus rates.

Our other lovely house, in Prince's Road, Stockport, was mock-Tudor outside (but as K always said, it was other people who had to look at that, not us). Inside it was definitely Edwardian with very large rooms and very high ceilings. Its chief 'design' features were *art nouveau* coloured-glass windows in the hall and panels in the front rooms. I dislike the Edwardian period, and dislike coloured glass anywhere but in churches, so as soon as we could afford it we got rid of it all. Probably these panels would be worth quite a lot of money now – odd how furnishing fads change as decisively, though not as quickly, as styles in dress. When I finally left Prince's Road it was a bitter grief to me that I practically had to pay the auctioneers to take away my precious oak sideboard, for which I had no room. Nobody wanted it, yet it was a fine craftsman's job and quite beautiful wood – a wedding present from my grandfather to my mother.

Of course *we* followed fashion in our home – notably the fashion for patterned ceiling papers and 'three walls plain, one patterned'. The sitting-room ceiling once had a most beautiful paper with white roses on a dark blue background. I thought it quite unkind of K to say it was getting grubby and must be replaced, for there never was a paper anything like it, ever again! We were hooked on 'Swedish' and saved up to buy a set a month of Gense stainless-steel place settings. Our glasses were Orrefors, our oven dishes were a beautiful cherry-red Rorstrand. Furnishing and stocking up the home was an endless pleasure.

I hope in these times young couples enjoy home-building as much as we did. But what seems to obsess many young women in public debate is the awfulness of looking after houses and their contents: 'shitwork', they inelegantly call it. So I think one ought to dredge up a few memories of past home-tending, to keep the record straight. How would I, let alone any much younger woman, have coped with keeping that so-much-loved Highfield Street house reasonably clean and decent? It was built, of course, at a time when even families on quite modest incomes had a least one servant, often two or three. It had in fact a 'servants' staircase' at the back of the house.

We almost always had at least one maid and a 'daily', but my mother hated being dependent on living-in maids and from time to time would try to manage without. I don't quite know why she found this relationship so difficult – probably it was just the lack of a common language, a common educational background. It must be difficult for today's young women to appreciate how wide the cultural gap was in the earlier years of this century.

Today only really rich families have living-in domestics, but quite a few, especially in London, have foreign *au pairs* while their children are little. They are usually treated as part of the family, sit at table with them and go on family outings. By no means all of them are expected to clean the oven or the loo or the kitchen floor. So who does do the cleaning, and how much of it is there to do, compared with fifty or sixty years ago? In the Highfield Street house the stairs were swept and dusted every day, as well as all the 'reception rooms', the stairs and hall and passage. Nothing we used was stainless, heat-resistant or wipeable. There were no washing machines, dishwashers, refrigerators, electric irons. The earliest vacuum cleaners were great heavy boxes with a handle, which certainly could not be humped upstairs.

Our mothers could certainly have complained of 'shitwork' – though they certainly would never have used such a vulgar and offensive expression – for so much of what they had to do was repulsively smelly in one way or another. In our four-storey home there was only one lavatory, down a flight of stairs from the main bedroom floor. So if you had to get up in the night you used a chamber pot. Up until comparatively recently every hotel bedroom had a chamber pot in a little cupboard by the bed. But someone had to empty them into a 'slop bucket' and carry it to the lavatory. In the home Mother did that, of course, failing the current skivvy. One of my most shame-making memories is of the chamber pot I positioned exactly at the corner of the carpet so that my feet could feel my way to it in the dark. One night, when I had what my granddaughter would call 'accident tummy', I left a dreadful smelly mess inches from the chamber pot. Mother cleared it up next morning, without comment. Of course.

And there were those dreadfully smelly sanitary towels – to me one of the most loathsome stinks in nature. They had to be soaked in a bucket and boiled to remove the stain and stench. Everything then, of course, was washed by hand, and you boiled your 'whites' in a great copper with a coal fire underneath. You had zinc tubs and a scrubbing board, perhaps a 'posser' to thump the dirt out of the clothes, and a wooden-rollered mangle to squeeze the water out. It was exceedingly hard work and of course in households like ours it was all done at home. There was not enough money for a commercial laundry, even for sheets and blankets.

In Lancashire in the early years of this century and indeed up to the time when I lived in Bolton (1931 to 1935), there were public washing houses, an invention, my mother told me, of a

Liverpool woman, Kitty Wilkinson. In 1932, when I was working on the *Bolton Evening News,* I did a trial wash in a public washhouse, and still have a cutting of the article I wrote for my women's page. I wrote with almost lyrical enthusiasm:

My modest attaché case full of underclothes and jumpers lasted me 2 hours 20 minutes, so that I had to contribute an extra penny when I left the building. (The rate for washing machines is one shilling for two hours and one penny for every 20 minutes over. For washing stalls, where the washing is done in the ordinary way, by hand, it is 3d an hour, and one penny extra per 20 minutes over.)

"Everything in the building is foolproof," the manager told me. "It has to be," he said, more cynically than unkindly. It was the first time I had ever seen an electric washing machine or dryer and I was very thankful that the attendant kept a kindly eye on me. While the first lot of clothes were having their "hot wash" and "hot rinse" I had a deep sink, with hot and cold water to wash through my coloured garments. "Have ye not been here before?" asked my neighbour at the next sink. She told me that "it used to take me two days to get through my washing at home, and that was without the bedding. I can get through it in four hours here. There are eight of us, you see."

I always associated public washhouses with the north, though no doubt there were some in the south, including London. Among my cuttings I found one from the *Leicester Mail* of the same period describing visits by the Leicester Baths Committee to washhouses in Nottingham and in Poplar, to help them to decide whether to start a similar service in Leicester. I have no idea if they did . . . perhaps there was less need. Leicester was always regarded as a 'clean' city. It was in Bolton that I first became familiar with the nauseating smell of soot and its all-pervading presence. Sitting at my desk in the *Bolton Evening News* one sunny morning I observed a large black dot on my writing paper. When I put my finger on to it it squelched into a black, oozy smudge. This was soot which had floated in through the open window.

Soot was part of our lives. Coming from that 'clean' city, I was dismayed to find that the hem of my underslip and the inside of the collar of my blouse were grey after a single day's wearing. I had never before known that sickening, sulphurous smell that hung about curtains left too long at the window before being washed. I had never before had to re-wash towels or sheets drenched by a sudden shower of soot-bearing rain. It had never before occurred to me that one had to wash very carefully the best china stored in a glass-fronted china cabinet before putting it on the table for guests because it had acquired a slightly greasy, grey film which had to be removed with very hot water and soap. Not long before writing this I heard a 'Question Time' discussion on BBC TV about the closure of coal mines and the future of nuclear power, which made me prick up my ears. One of the panel said we were perhaps too obsessed with the dangers of nuclear power. Of course nuclear power is a threat to *life* – but what about the known ill effects on the health of hundreds of thousands of people during the years of dependence on the burning of raw coal?

Well yes . . . I do remember something about that. I remember my mother-in-law gasping in a desperate struggle to breathe when a real Manchester fog came down. I remember the panic that made me beg my husband, who suffered from a heart condition, not to drive home from work on a foggy night. I remember being called for at a North Manchester friend's by my husband and his colleague Tom Baistow (later of the *New Statesman*). It was a filthy foggy night. Tom had had to walk in front of the car to guide the driver. When they appeared at the door, Tom's hair, normally a cheerful red, was *black!* Later, in our industry-free agreeable South Manchester suburb, we had a visiting baker who used to leave us a loaf on the sill of the hall window. Often when we picked it up it left a clean white oblong on a grey background.

I have never read any estimate of what the Clean Air Acts achieved in improved health and in lower cleaning bills. It must have been colossal. I was never in London during a 'pea-souper' or a 'London particular'. Now I have lived in London nearly fifteen years and have never seen a real fog — nothing in the least like the dense and stinking fogs which in my old days in Manchester used to stop all the buses and cars and made progress on foot terrifying for all but the blind who have to memorise somehow the exact place at which they must turn right or left and cross the road.

The old policy used to be to let the soot take over the exterior of all public buildings. Once at a public dinner in Manchester Town Hall I sat next to a young architect who told me he loved 'Manchester's black velvet'. It didn't seem to have occurred to him that our lungs were 'black-velvet' too, and that his mother and all his sisters and his cousins and his aunts were struggling day after day to remove that black patina from their homes and their contents. Many years later, after I had moved my home to London, I had occasion to walk down Oxford Road and came within sight of the Manchester University. I looked, blinked, I giggled. Instead of being sooty black it was a quite vivid pinky-orange! All over the country, from the Houses of Parliament and Westminster Abbey to the town halls and assembly rooms and other public buildings of every industrial town and city, the scaffolding is up and the great washdays are on, in the confidence that this will probably not be necessary again for at least another ten years.

It is too easy to forget what an immense amount of drudgery the Clean Air Acts have saved the housewife, since they first became law in 1956. I know I am a bit churlish sometimes about the way young women grumble at the amount of compulsory housework that seems to be imposed on them. But even in my own young day (and I could afford to pay for help) the amount of cleaning and laundering and sewing was minimal compared with what our foremothers had to do. In her excellent history *A Woman's Work is Never Done,* Caroline Davidson made some startling revelations. To me the most horrific was about the battle that Jane Welsh Carlyle waged against armies of bed bugs. Jane, the brilliant wife of Thomas Carlyle, lived for thirty-two years in Great Cheyne Row, Chelsea – not exactly, you would think, a slum. The house was infested with bugs. Jane tried to drown them; she threw out furniture and replaced it, but still the bugs came. There is something monstrous to any good feminist that any woman, whether of the intellectual distinction of Jane Carlyle or not, should have to spend so much of her life dealing with bed bugs, but Ms Davidson reckons that a great many women had to cope with bugs right up to the slum clearance and de-bugging campaigns of the fifties. The 1983-84 President of the Institute of Housing, Mrs Mary Smith, told me that in her early years as a housing manager she had to hand out anti-bug spray to council tenants – this would be in the 1940s and 1950s.

I totally agree with Caroline Davidson that the three great liberators of the housewife were piped water, gas and electricity. It is quite startling for us in the last quarter of the twentieth century to realise that in earlier times women not only carried all the water they needed, but also made their own soap and their own candles, the only form of lighting. Not many of the people who read this book will, I imagine, have lived in houses without electric lights, unless they were brought up in remote country villages where people used oil lamps. I am almost certain that the home in which I was born was lighted only by gas and certainly the upper floors of the Highfield Street house had gas jets when we moved there, and we went up to bed with a lighted taper to ignite them – a very scary business for a nervous child like me.

Almost all my adult life I have cooked with electricity, but in my later years I have been immensely thankful to have been able to install clean, trouble-free gas central heating. How I should hate now to have to clean out hearths, or to have to get my walls and ceilings redecorated every two years because of the discolouration from the coal fires. Or indeed to have to have the chimney sweep in. I can't remember how long it is since I saw one. Do all my neighbours also have central heating? Or is there some new, do-it-yourself way of cleaning the chimney? Or does smokeless fuel, compulsory now in most inner-city areas, leave no deposit at all?

It amuses me sometimes to list the things that were part of every home's equipment in my earlier years and now are quite unknown. Whoever now has a slop basin? Even a tea strainer is fairly rarely found on the tea table. But then afternoon tea is a vanishing feast in big towns and cities, so if you have your mother's cake forks in your cutlery drawer you probably only set them out at buffet parties to spear cocktail sausages. There are no sugar tongs any more. If people still use lump sugar, the hostess probably puts it in with her fingers. There are no doilies, because there are hardly any bread-and-butter plates or cake plates. No napkin rings, because linen napkins are put out only for special occasions. In most newer houses and flats there is a dining kitchen, so the teapot and coffeepot don't often sit on the table. I guess that before very long mugs will replace teacups and saucers everywhere, for as fewer and fewer people take sugar in their tea there is no need of a place to put the teaspoon when we have used it. When did you last see a hot-water jug on the table? Mine remains permanently in the china cupboard, for if I need to fill up the teapot it is only a step into the little kitchen.

Only quite elderly people now remember the hair tidies that used to sit on every dressing table, though we still comb our hair vigorously and have to dispose of the loose hairs somehow. I doubt if even the most addicted embroiderer now turns out chair backs or table runners – or embroiders pillowslips or sheets. Now we have no picture rails, no brass name plates on our doors, no Venetian blinds (except in chic modern houses). Soon, I think, many people like me will be able to send all our blankets to the victims of earthquakes and floods on the other side of the world, for we shall all have the simple comfort of the duvet. Where, oh where, do people still use cardinal red for their floor tiles, dolly blue for their 'white wash' and black lead for their hearths and cooking stoves?

Does anyone still 'spring clean'? This was one of the major events of the homemaker's year when I was young, and a great opportunity for pages of advice in the women's magazines. Doubtless it used to be necessary, for in those unconscionably dirty days the heavy sideboards, bookcases and sofas had to be pulled out sometimes, so that the accumulation of dust behind and under them could be removed. Carpets had to be taken up, hung over the washing line and batted with carpet beaters (fearfully hard and unpleasant work). The springclean usually took several days and paterfamilias and children coming home for midday dinner had to be content with a picnic. No doubt the children thought it was all rather fun. I doubt if their mothers did.

It is quite obvious that our mothers, grandmothers and great-grandmothers spent much more time cleaning their houses than we do, or need to do. I am also quite sure that their houses were basically much dirtier than ours — else why did they always choose dark brown paint in preference to the white, pale grey or biscuit that most of us would choose today? Many new surfaces now are mini-care and they can be cleaned in minutes with a damp sponge so the little darlings' grubby fingermarks are no longer an irritation. Who except women very attached to beautiful old pieces of furniture now spend a weekly hour or two in polishing? When I moved from a large house to a small flat my daughter took over from me a very beautiful large mahogany linen cupboard which our 'daily' had polished devotedly every 'bedrooms' day. I wonder how long it is now since it was polished? Or, come to that, my little mahogany sideboard and my large mahogany china cupboard, desk and chest of drawers? They don't really look much the worse for it . . . though I must say that if I had not far too many other things to do, I should rather enjoy giving them a good polish once in a while. I like the smell and I like the gleam.

How much house cleaning one does is nowadays often a matter of choice rather than necessity. A quick whizz round with the carpet sweeper will cope with crumbs and fluff. A feather duster will keep the tops of bookcases, sideboards, piano and mantelpiece from looking scruffy. Nearly all modern furniture is heat- and stain-resistant. Why is housework labelled shitwork? The term could be far more appropriately applied to much of the work that trained nurses do for very low pay.

Housework is, in fact, a term applied to various kinds of work in the home. Even that admirable and influential book of Ann Oakley's, *Housewife* (1974), does not clearly differentiate between all the different kinds of work done by the woman in the home. She keeps the house clean and decent, of course, which means a good deal of tidying, as well as attending to floors, sinks, washbowls, baths and loos. She also purchases, prepares, cooks and serves the family meals and clears up after them. She purchases and looks after most of the family's clothes, washing, mending and taking to the dry cleaners. She makes the beds and copes with washing sheets, towels, and so on. Listed like that, it sounds an awful lot, especially when it has to be done by a young mother with little children to tend. But it is not a fraction of what our mothers and grandmothers had to do.

The number of households which have not only a refrigerator and a washing machine (or easy access to a laundrette) but also a dishwasher steadily increases. The proliferation of supermarkets must indicate large numbers of women able to drive or be driven there to stock up on food and cleaning materials for the week. (On the other hand, of course, most grocers and butchers in my younger days had a delivery service.) That thought-provoking writer Gillian Tindall wrote trenchantly in an *Evening Standard* article in 1974 on the theme of the decreasing labour of housework:

In the days when water had to be carried, fires had to be laid and lit before anything could be cooked or washed, when bread was baked, clothes were made by hand, and if you wanted food in winter a bottling programme had to be carried out in summer – then one could reasonably speak of the good housewife as a skilled and dedicated person. But to insist that running a Council flat or small suburban house today is in the same class of occupation and can itself be made into a justification for living is a pretence which often leads to insidious depression.

I think it is right to insist that keeping a family fed and clothed today needs less skill and takes less time than it used to. Anyone can pop a bag of frozen kippers into a saucepan, straighten and pull up a duvet or wash a shirt and hang it over the bath – and 'anyone' includes husbands and older children. I firmly believe that both boys and girls should be brought up to service themselves to a high degree, and should not need or be provided with a body slave to do this kind of work. And neither do I believe that taxpayers should be asked to pay women to do housework in their own homes. I know that in some areas of the women's movement mine is an unpopular view, but I believe that in the modern world both the married man's allowance to help him to maintain a full-time houseworking wife and the demand for 'wages for housework' are becoming nonsensical. It is time that clever women like Selma James switched her Wages for Housewives demand to a campaign for something like the 'guaranteed maintenance payment' recommended ten years ago by the Finer Committee, to help parents to bring up the next generation of citizens in decent comfort. Actually, though, there are quite a few serious-minded citizens who see no reason why taxation should subsidise parenthood. 'You have children because you want them and love them and are prepared to make sacrifices,' they say. And I suppose we ought to remind ourselves that when Eleanor Rathbone MP and others were first campaigning for family allowances, opponents included many trade unionists, who feared that they would encourage employers to reduce wages. Neither the Labour Party nor the women's movement has fought for the GMP.

To me, the very word 'housewife' is an absurdity. You cannot, even if you should, be married to a house, only to a man. The German 'Hausfrau' is all right, because *frau* means both wife and woman. But in English the word 'housewoman' would make that repellent 'body slave' implication all too clear. Why do I find so much hostility to 'homemaker'? If you are making a home, you are caring for people. If you are a 'housewoman' you are, by implication, caring only for the house and the objects it contains.

Even thirty years or so ago housework appeared to many women to be a full-time job. I treasure an extract from *A Simple Guide to Housework*, published by the Institute of Houseworkers in 1960. I think it was already somewhat out-of-date, for the instructions read as if they were addressed to paid domestic workers (of which there were remarkably few by 1960). I think the implication of the *Guide* was that every properly conducted home had this kind of day-to-day maintenance. Here is the table of duties to be performed every day, in the area of the stairs and hall:

Sweep outside front door and porch
Brush stairs lightly, using a small hard brush and dustpan for the carpet and a small soft brush for the paint surrounds.
Sweep hall.
Polish outside brasses and dust the front door when required.
In muddy weather well mop or wash the tiled or stone floor and front door step and attend to scraper.
Dust banisters, furniture and any ledges.

Those were the 'every day' jobs. Each day of the week had also its allocation of jobs for sitting room, kitchen, bedrooms, bathroom and lavatory. It is almost comic now to recall that the woman who did not put out her washing on a Monday morning was regarded as a slattern and a slut. Nowadays most wives who work outside the home and do not take their washing to a laundrette put it out on Saturday or even Sunday (which would have been regarded as almost sinful in my young day – neighbours might actually complain).

I believe that we should aim for the simplification of housecare and for the greater availability of every kind of labour-saving material and gadget. Housework ought not to be exhausting. There is nothing, to me, desirable or virtuous in the expending of 'elbow grease'. And though most of us dislike some aspects of housecleaning, most of us quite like others. My mother quite liked washday, even though it meant quite hard labour (lifting things out of a great copper and pushing them through a wooden-rollered mangle), and I rather enjoy it myself on a sunny, blowy day. There are, as surely everyone will agree, far worse ways of spending your days than doing housework, unless you are unfortunate enough to have to live in a slum area, where it is impossible to keep pace with dirt and decay.

That dear old-fashioned maxim, 'A place for everything and everything in its place', really is a great time-saver, if you can stick to it amidst the distractions of normal family-cum-working life. But I think of another old adage, 'What the eye doesn't see the heart doesn't grieve over', not only when I look round my own home and observe that books and papers have awaited tidying for days while I have been writing or attending committees, but also when I visit the homes of young friends, where the family's anoraks, schoolbags, books, briefcases and wellies litter the hall and the little ones' toys have strayed into the sitting room, bathroom and loo. I know that some young mothers continue to agitate themselves about this, but I assure them that some of the very nicest women I have known have very untidy homes. And remember, the sun doesn't always show up the dust on the mantelshelf or the smears on the window panes. What the eye doesn't see . . . And does it really matter about the house being a bit unkempt if the inhabitants are happy in it?

Homemaking does not equate with housework; cleanliness does not equate with godliness. It is not true that 'where there's dirt there's danger' (as we used to be told in my young married days), unless the dirt is decomposing matter that can breed germs and attract flies, or even mice and rats. Household management is a skill or sometimes an art, but it is not a science. One of the most thought-provoking books I have read in recent years is *For Her Own Good* by Barbara Ehrenreich and Deirdre English. Their chapter 'Microbes and Housework' is positively mind-blowing to any woman reared in the old traditions of unceasing dusting, sweeping and polishing. It tells the story of Ellen Swallow Richards, who wanted a career in chemistry and wished to continue to study at the Massachusetts Institute of Technology. The professors patronisingly permitted her to study separately from the men students, in a segregated laboratory, without the possibility of a degree, no matter how well she did. But they also asked her to sort their papers and mend their braces so that she shouldn't become 'unwomanly'. She, poor misguided creature, kept 'all sorts of things such as needles, thread, pins and scissors around' so that the masculine hierarchy couldn't say 'study spoilt me for anything else'.

So what did she do, this frustrated scientist? In 1873 she founded a new 'science' of her own, which she labelled 'oekology' . . . and as the made up Greek word oekology didn't catch on, she turned it into 'domestic science' and generations of girls studied this pseudo-science whose main purpose was to convince women that household management was a career, in fact *the* worthwhile career for all women. Home Economics, as we more often call it now, is still a subject highly approved in many schools and institutions and by education authorities. In the early 1970s I was asked by a *Guardian* colleague if I would help towards the maintenance of a young cellist who had been refused a grant by her local authority to study at the music school, Chetham's College, in Manchester. I agreed the more readily because at the time I knew a young woman who, after completing three years at a training college *on a grant* studying 'home economics', got a job as *au pair* in the household of a professional woman with one young child!

One influential aspect of Ellen Richards's campaign to establish homemaking as a science was the emphasis on the germ theory of disease which transformed 'dilettantish dusting' into a sanitary crusade against 'dangerous enemies within'. In *Household Economics* published in 1907, an American author, Helen Campbell, asserted that the 'old household crafts have been taken over by men, but cleaning can never pass from women's hands. To keep the world clean – this is one great task for women.'

There is a comical pendant to all this moral fervour about hygiene in the home which was certainly still around when I was a youngish homemaker. In 1976, English and Ehrenreich wrote to six professors of home economics at three American universities, asking several pertinent questions including, 'Is it known today what is the best technique for cleaning surfaces, such as countertops, in order to prevent contagion within the family?' and 'What is actually known about the actual effectiveness of house cleaning in maintaining family health?' It proved a pretty fruitless exercise. One woman professor went so far as to recommend bleach for countertops, another cited two studies which indicated that 'a relationship exists between cleaning methods and the removal of bacteria.' So the authors were left none the wiser, and most sensible women will hold to the view that it is more important to clean the inner bits of the tin opener and the base of the food mixer properly than to poke behind the bookcase for a small accumulation of dust.

It is sad that so many women still have guilt feelings about housework left undone or done by some other woman for payment. Possibly the unacknowledged, scarcely comprehended thinking behind the Wages for Housework campaign is to elevate housework into a proper job, respectworthy because it attracts a proper payment. Only *paid* work rates as part of the GNP (Gross National Product). Is there perhaps an analogy with Ellen Richards's determination to turn housewifery into a science?

I was rebuked myself by the present editor of the *Guardian* when, in reviewing my first book, he suggested that women like me were 'pursuing a quest for self-fulfilment which often seems to hinge on a daily charring treasure scrubbing back home'. All the women like me, I am sure, felt inclined to question him about his progress to the top of the journalistic tree supported by a devoted wife at home and diligent phone-answering, message-taking, letter-answering females in the office. No doubt he and all men like him would protect themselves by the argument that it is their *duty* to work and to do the best they can in their career for the sake of their families. No self-fulfilment in it for them, then, at any other person's expense?

A woman writing to the *Guardian* women's page as late as 1979 described how when she acquired her 'treasure', Edna, a feminist friend was aghast. 'How can you make another woman clean your loos, wash your floors, empty your kitchen bucket?' In vain did the author of the letter, Jennifer C., protest that Edna *liked* housework and sang as she did it. 'It's a cop out,' said the feminist friend. Did such feminists never ask themselves whether they, or their husbands, felt guilt at paying a man to mow the lawn or dig over the vegetable plot or prune the trees? Or clean the windows? And if not, why not? Because the man's contribution to the running of the home and garden is a matter of choice. Traditionally, and still, in many people's opinions, a woman's part in homemaking is not. It is her moral obligation, whatever else she may choose to do in addition.

Perhaps today's newly married couples will see it differently. If the washbowl and the bath are smeary or the paint around the door handles grubby, perhaps the husband will think it as much his job as his wife's to do something about it? Things are changing. Many a husband nowadays takes on the Saturday shopping in our part of the world. Younger men may take one of the children with them. Older men, I observe, are very efficient. It used to be said that butchers did well out of male shoppers because they could always persuade them to buy the most expensive cuts. I doubt if that is true now.

At almost all levels men are much more integrated into the life of the home than they used to be. The steel factory worker may not wash the baby's nappies or wheel her out in her pram, but he is likely to be involved in DIY, decorating, carpentering and servicing mechanical gadgets. All the men I know take a day-to-day interest in the lives of their children. It could be said that almost all the men I know would rate as middle-class – but it is usually in the middle classes that new trends start and gradually percolate through society.

So men reading this book, as well as women, may be feeling some irritation at my apparent assumption in writing this chapter that all that needs to be done in the home is cleaning, washing and cooking. Of course, I have left writing about the major purpose of the home until the last. It is to rear and socialise children. A modern mother is spared much of the toil of her foremothers thanks to disposable nappies (at a price), easily washable little one-piece garments, ready-to-serve foods in tins and packets, baby slings and bags, for those who like them, which allow her to get on with her chores with her baby comfortably on her back – or front. (When Lois Mitchison wrote in the *Guardian* long years ago about a 'baby bag' she had discovered, it produced an unending stream of enquiries.) But in fact babies are not now so much work-makers as time-consumers. They have to be kept under surveillance – mostly entirely by the mother – for twenty-four hours a day, and however dear and precious this tie is, it can be exhausting in a way that domestic labour seldom is.

The men, and some women, who say that women's place is

in the home must be reminded that the section of the population most prone to serious depression is the isolated mother. And instead of working on possible solutions to this sad problem, society has exacerbated it by tolerating the building of high-rise flats. As a delegate to a recent Labour Party conference cried out, 'Who but a man would put a mother in a tower block with nowhere for her children to play, no nursery, no laundry, and far away from the shops?' There *could* be communal nurseries and even nursery schools in flat blocks and housing estates. I have seen such provision in a Danish block of flats, with staff paid by the local authority. Why has there been so little pressure here for this?

I believe that every child is or should be an asset to the community and that therefore the community should be willing to provide some support for his or her parents . . . if only because when today's babies are grown men and women they will have to provide support for over nine million pensioners, of whom it is forecast (for 2001 AD) that more than 900,000 will be over eighty-five (and another estimate is that one in five of the over eighty-fives will need total care). These old people will include many who have not and perhaps never have had a child to care for them. Isn't it time we gave more thought to the home life of the old, as well as of the isolated mother?

Actually, the old and the isolated mothers share many problems. Shopping gets increasingly difficult – for many people a bus ride is needed to get to the nearest chemist, hardware shop, haberdasher's, shoe repairer, dry cleaner's. Homes need these service shops *handy*. Now we are expected to meet all our homemaking requirements in the nearest shopping precinct, which may be a couple of miles away . . . nothing for the family with a car, but an impossible trudge for young mothers with a pushchair and the elderly with a shopping trolley.

'Home' is not a self-sufficient unit as it was once upon a time. It needs a variety of support services, practical and psychological. Nor is it just a structure where people eat, drink, sleep and watch television. Because so many of us do seem glued to the Box, we are perhaps in danger of forgetting how much having a home matters, to people of all ages. It is the place where people feel they *belong*. Home, they say, is where the heart is. I am thankful I have always had a home.

9

A joy for ever?

Every fully adult human being knows that life isn't fair. Some of us are born with a silver spoon in our mouth, some are born with spina bifida. Some stumble in front of a car and are maimed for life, some produce best sellers at the age of sixteen. It's the luck of the genes as well as the luck of the draw. There is nothing so unfair as the way nature hands out brains, but the next most unfair thing is the way she hands out looks. I reckon that since the world began a few humans have arrived destined to be really beautiful — and most have not.

Of course, ideas of what beauty is change from culture to culture, century to century. Rubens loved women fat, El Greco loved them thin. But I am prepared to wager that if you were dropped down in a village in the rain forests of West Africa or amid the Eskimo igloos of Greenland, or in Outer Mongolia or in Tierra del Fuego, you would quite quickly recognise which of the local population, totally unfamiliar though their physiognomy might be, had the quality of beauty. It shines. It gives the person an aura. Look down the row of seated passengers in an underground train and now and again you will see a face that has this magical quality. 'The face that launched a thousand ships' is not just a poetical myth. There are faces that have inspired quite irrational and fanatical devotion. Helen of Troy must have been one such. Perhaps Mary Queen of Scots was another.

In our day, beauty's power has not been over princes and

parliaments but just over people, as individuals, and in the mass. With the coming of the mass-circulation newspaper, the cinema, television, the beauty has become internationally celebrated for nothing much except being a beauty. Before my time, for instance, there was Lily Langtry. Since my early youth there has been Lady Diana Duff Cooper (Lady Diana Manners, daughter of the Duke of Rutland, when I first heard of her). Then most of the world-famous beauties were film or TV stars – like Marilyn Munro or Elizabeth Taylor. I don't see how the rest of us can help wondering sometimes how it must feel to know that when you come into a room heads will turn and conversation halt, or that members of the other sex will yearn to possess or to belong to (men can have this charisma, too) this inimitable human being.

I suppose even the most beautiful women are sometimes disappointed in love, but over and over again they must be aware of young men pining for the glimmer of a smile from them. There are the radiant creatures who have only to *be* to stir the heart. So if beauty is so clearly power, isn't it only natural that women should seek it? After all, for many and many a generation, it was the only power that most women could exert. They had no power of riches, no power over employees, servants or slaves. Their only real power lay in manipulating men, and so, apart from a few heiresses who could buy themselves a desirable husband, the only woman who could command men was the woman who could use the sexual power of her beauty. The preoccupation of women down the ages with 'beauty aids' – kohl, mascara, face powders and creams, hair colourants and pomades – is perfectly understandable. But why have aids to so-called beauty been accepted which by the standards of any other age and culture were not merely disfiguring but *cruel?* How could men impose them on their womenfolk? How could women accept them and even insist on them, as sure-fire beauty enhancers, to their young daughters?

The most horrific example in a civilised society was the Chinese practice of binding the feet of little girls into 'lotus hooks'. No one who has read Emily Prager's story, *A Visit from the Footbinder,* could ever forget the horror of the mutilation of 'Pleasure Mouse', a child of six, snatched from her happy life of running, skipping and cuddling her dolly. This was the technique:

The footbinder took hold of the child's right foot, and leaving the big toe free, bent the toes beneath the foot and bound them down with a long silk cloth. She then took a second cloth and bound it tightly around the bent toes so that the heel and toes were brought together as close as they would go and the arch of the foot was forced upwards in the knowledge that eventually it would break, restructure itself and foreshorten the foot.

'Pleasure Mouse's' mother cried to the child's father, 'You men are so cruel.' To which he replied, '*Men* took from you your ability to walk? Is it the man who pulls the binding cloth to cripple a daughter's feet? No man could do a thing like that. No man could bear it.' But we know that for 1,000 years the 'lotus hook', only about three inches long, had a quite incredible sexual fascination for men and was regarded as a status symbol by women. It was not until the late nineteenth century that 'natural foot' societies began to spring up, and not until the beginning of the twentieth century that the custom rapidly declined.

How could such a highly civilised people as the Chinese, whose arts, learning and inventiveness are the admiration of the world, let this hideous custom persist for so long? And what persuades some tribes to make their womenfolk develop elongated necks like giraffes', and others to fatten up their women like pigs for the slaughter? And what, indeed, animated the young women of prosperous Victorian England to lace up their corsets so tightly that they could hardly breathe? My mother, born around 1875, was five feet seven inches tall and was just like me in build. My waist has never been less than twenty-six inches, and now, alas, is more like thirty-two. My mother's waist when she was a girl, she said, was eighteen inches. Goodness knows what damage this tight lacing did to her lungs. She died of pneumonia at the early age of fifty-seven.

If she had been a public school girl she might have had an even severer regime imposed on her than she imposed on herself. Alison Adburgham, one of the wisest and wittiest fashion writers of our times, related in *Punch* in 1955 that, 'Less than a century ago girls at an English boarding school were sealed into their stays by their mistress, who only released them on Saturday nights for purposes of ablution. It was said they suffered no hardship beyond an occasional fainting fit and it was claimed that a waist of 23 inches at the age of fifteen years could be reduced in two years to 13 inches.' In France a fashion magazine, *Le Follet,* told in 1859 of a young woman whose very tiny waist had been admired at a ball – and of how three days later she died, three of her ribs having pierced her liver.

The worst discomforts I have imposed on myself for the sake of following fashion were forcing tight cloche hats over my 'earphone' hairstyle (plaits coiled over the ears and fastened with large hairpins which the hat pressed into the tender skin), and too-small shoes. We were not as obsessed with small feet as the Chinese, but I think that when I was young shoe manufacturers simply did not recognise that a woman's foot could be bigger than size six (and even size six was thought pretty shameful), and so my size seven foot became misshapen and I not only have to endure bunions but also crossed toes. I could never endure the pain of all my weight being forced on to my big toes by high heels, so more than once in my lifetime I have protested bitterly at the damage stiletto wearers are likely to do to their feet as well as to carpets and lino.

Undoubtedly the fashion that has done the most damage in our times is the cult of slimness. Anorexia nervosa was little more than a name to me until, in 1974, after I had retired from the *Guardian,* I was briefly editing the women's pages of the

Observer while a permanent new editor was being sought. I printed an article I had received from a woman working at the BBC about her anorexic daughter. The response startled and horrified me. Letters poured in from other mothers and from young women themselves describing this deadly condition. There was even, heartbreakingly, a letter from a little girl of eleven. Whatever starts young women – the sufferers are mostly females from comfortable homes and are likely to be intelligent and successful at school – on a course of self-starvation? In a deeply thought-provoking book, *The Art of Starvation,* Sheila MacLeod, a former anorexic, contends that self-starvation is by no means the same thing as overdoing a slimming diet. It is, she thinks, a rebellion against a home situation and a compulsion to establish control over the one thing that really belongs to her, her body. Certainly anorexics prove to themselves the strength of their will. They not only refrain from food, often elaborately deceiving family and schoolmates, but also take strong purgatives and induce vomiting. Some of our *Observer* correspondents confessed to quite frequent gorging followed by drastic measures to throw the whole lot up.

Anorexics look at themselves in the mirror and see the skeleton only just covered with flesh as beautiful, pared of all grossness. A *Guardian* reader in 1983 related how 'being slim was the only way I wanted to be, the only way I saw to be sane and happy. I had purged and destroyed the hateful pudgy thing I used to be and now I was something entirely of my own creation.' Sheila MacLeod comments on the fact that self-starvation almost invariably leads to the cessation of menstruation: 'I had become pure and clean and therefore superior to those around me.' Her analysis of the desire to make oneself in one's own desired image is convincing.

But what starts the belief that losing weight deliberately will achieve an access of power? Only, surely, the current obsession with slenderness. The one sure-fire recipe for success for a women's magazine, I am told, is a series of articles on a new slimming diet. Fortunes are made out of dietary aids and books and classes. Not because fat is unhealthy, though in excess it may be, but because 'slender' is beautiful, and 'chubby' is 'comic' or even 'ugly'. Almost all current fashions are designed for the slim, and the current craze for tight-fitting jeans is particularly hard on growing girls whose thighs are well covered. Useless to tell them that in other societies their comely, well-rounded figures would be much more admired than 'skellingtons covered with skin'. In the swimming baths their schoolmates poke fun at them, and a year or two later they convince themselves that no boy will look twice at a fat girl. They just don't believe you when you say that most men like 'a nice armful'. One can only hope that the current tendency towards 'please yourself' dressing will in time extend to body weight and shape.

Looking back over the years, picturing the clothes I have worn, I feel quite certain that the trend has been towards freedom – both from physical constriction and from iron convention. In my early years, social convention was even more important than the dictates of fashion. The length of your skirt, the fit of your bodice, the shape of your neckline were almost an indication of your moral standards. To show an ankle, when my father was a young man, indicated lack of virtue; so, right up to my middle years, did wearing a top which not only outlined the shape of the breasts but also the nipples. My mother, a great knitter, always produced jumpers which were safely but very unbecomingly baggy. Last summer, on a Mediterranean beach, I was interested, rather than embarrassed, to cast an eye on all the young women who were swimming and sunbathing topless. Does it seem comic to young readers that this was the first time in all my long life that I had contemplated other women's (half) naked bodies? I don't think it would seem comic to my teenage grand-daughters. They are almost as prudish about their bodies as we were. They, I am pretty sure, will grow out of this phase a great deal more quickly than we did.

This 'cover up' custom applied to gloves for a very long time – not, I suppose, for reasons of modesty but of presumed elegance. I remember the *Guardian*'s delightful Paris fashion correspondent, Phyllis Heathcote, commenting in an article in the sixties that on schoolchildren's visits to Paris there was 'never a pair of gloves between them', something which she clearly thought rather ill-bred. And I remember too my friend Nesta Roberts of the *Guardian* saying, when I suggested that the gloves she had mislaid were probably on her desk in the office, 'But I *never* go out without my gloves.' I should be very shaken if I found that that was still true!

In my mother's middle years one also covered one's face, not with a yashmak but with a veil tied over the hat and under the chin. In her snapshot album I have a photograph of her with such a veil, adorned with little black dots. Rather fetching, really, but it must have been a very tiresome fashion for women who like me always have to have glasses on their nose. A photograph of my mother's War Seals Committee, a fund-raising group in Leicester during the First World War, shows not only fine hats with veils, but also large fur muffs. (Before the war, suffragettes found muffs very useful for concealing the little hammers with which they smashed shop windows.) How long is it since muffs went out? Or, come to that, spats for men? I can remember my brothers wearing them in their young manhood, but I doubt if my husband ever did.

It is entertaining to look back over the years and recall all the fashion changes one has lived through. I think what I am most glad about – apart from the general sense of freedom of choice one has now – is the revolution in underwear. I grew up wearing thick woolly bloomers, on top of woolly combinations and a woolly vest. Some of us wore 'liberty bodices' but I doubt if any of us wore a brassière. If one wasn't quite old enough to wear a fiercely boned corset, one wore a suspender belt, and tights didn't come in until the late forties. I still have a few pairs of stockings, dating from the sixties I suppose, but having got rid of the constriction of the suspender belt, I am disinclined to don them, even though some are very jolly – crimson, or cream with a gold pattern! My stomach bulges, and that makes me cross and embarrassed. I know I ought to do muscle-toning exercises, but there are many more interesting things to do, and comfort is precious. I do wonder from time to time whether the scraps of cotton, silk or nylon for which young women pay so much to pull over their breasts and buttocks are adequate to provide a little comforting warmth. But at least they don't cause the awful itches which used to plague me under my layers of wool.

Fashion is, I suppose, very largely dictated by the clothing industry's need to persuade us to discard some of our garments and acquire replacements. How many times in my seven decades have I seen skirts go up and down? I grew up in the age of the tub frock – a most unbecoming, straight-up-and-down frock ending just above the knees. It was so skimpy that when you sat down it tended to rise up and reveal your knickers – acutely embarrassing then, when you were sitting on a tram. Not until the arrival of the mini in the sixties were dresses so short, or so unflattering, except to the few with beautiful long slender legs. The time of the mini was a wretched period for the middle-aged and elderly, who knew they would look figures of fun in dresses which ended well above the knee and dowdy in mid-calf-length clothes. This was when I was driven into trouser suits, which were a very blessed escape. I still wear trousers, of course, but for comfort rather than for elegance, and topped by shirts and sweaters.

The tub frock gradually retreated. My first proper evening dress, around 1926, was of powder-blue silk lace, and though knee-length in front, it dipped to ankle length at the back. The longer skirt was on its way in, but I think it was the mid-thirties before it dropped below mid-calf length.

When I married, in 1937, I wore, for the register office ceremony, an ankle-length dress of slate-blue georgette with little buttons from neck to hem, a little matching hat and a long, slim-line grey and blue check tweed coat. During the preceding years I had been very broke and my only fashion indulgence had been rather saucy hats - you could buy, then, a charming hat for five shillings at C and A's. When K and I went on a delayed honeymoon to Russia, I wore what has always been my favourite hat — a straw boater with a navy ribbon round it. Years later I bought a similar hat, rather larger brimmed, in the market at Faro, Algarve, Portugal. It is still with me, and well known to my friends, having travelled with me to China, Malta, Aegina, Crete, Corfu, Rhodes, Italy and Ibiza. It is looking a bit shabby now, but I should hate to part with it. I think my hats were the nearest I ever got to sexy dressing (men used to comment on them with a twinkle).

Clothes were not a preoccupation during the war (I think with revulsion of the revolting maternity clothes I wore and the appalling maternity corset!) But, with clothing coupons, Utility also came in, and surprisingly some of the Utility clothes were, after strict war-time austerity, quite delightful. I had a charming navy flannel suit with a rather nipped-in waist and a full-flared long skirt. Of course, skirts went up again and down again. I think rather affectionately of the very long topcoats that were worn in the early seventies. Still in a wardrobe I have a very long black coat in which I went on a Women's International Day march and was photographed with Jill Tweedie, looking, I must admit, remarkably dowdy with a big black hat, ungainly boots, overloaded hold-all and, for what reason I do not now remember, a balloon! In some future very cold winter I think I shall probably venture out after dark in this all-enveloping garment.

The problem of clothes is as intriguing as the problem of 'beauty'. I have always been convinced that the naked ape clothed himself as a protection against the weather, though a little later he must have found a need for somewhere to stow his tools or his equivalent of sandwiches. Surely the first 'garment', except in very chilly climes, was some kind of a string around the waist? (Where do today's nudists keep their handkerchiefs?) But in the most primitive cultures men and women wear 'clothes', beads, feathers, shells or whatever, and tattoo or paint their faces and bodies, purely as adornment. Why? It seems to have been one of the earliest impulses of our primitive ancestors. Are we innately programmed to adorn ourselves to attract the opposite sex? Or since we learned that the reflection in the pool was of our very own self, have we grown increasingly narcissistic?

It is hard to refute the charge that today's women are narcissistic. Look along the rows of women's magazines on a station bookstall. Almost every one has a cover picture of a woman's face. When I have asked women magazine editors why, they all say that this is their trademark, that they would not be recognised if their cover showed a flower arrangement, a sailing ship, a litter of spaniel pups, or whatever. But though I can almost always distinguish the *Cosmopolitan* girl from any other, I could certainly not identify *Company, Options* or whatever if it were not for the printed title. The cover girls *must* be projections of our fantasies about ourselves.

The artist John Berger once wrote, 'Men look at women. Women watch themselves being looked at.' Look closely at those cover photographs, and indeed at all photographs of professional models. They are all aware of being looked at, and almost always of being looked at by men . . . the very slightly parted lips, the mock sullen look, the ravishing smile. Aren't they all, in their different ways, somehow saying to men, 'Come on'? And so, one surely has to admit, do a lot of our clothes . . . the deep cleavage, the slit skirt, the clearly defined bosom. Such clothes, surely, are overtly 'sexy'? Not necessarily the worse for that, so long as we don't complain if they produce a sexual response from men. When Anna Ford, television news announcer, complained bitterly at a Women in Media press conference that when anything was written about her it was 'almost always to do with my body, and what I am wearing' (she called this 'body fascism'), it was this complaint that got all the headlines – which we resented, for she is a clever, professional woman who made a very good speech. But at the time she was wearing a deeply slit skirt. Did she expect that to be noticed or not? If not, why did she wear it? And if she did expect her skirt to be noticed, she surely can't have thought it would only be by women who would say how nice and comfortable it looked?

Over the centuries there have been many cultures in which men have imposed sumptuary laws designed to keep women plainly and unprovocatively dressed. The yashmak and the chador persist to the present day in Moslem cultures, along with purdah and that hideous assault on our sex, female circumcision. In our times well-meaning revolutionaries have endeavoured to release women from subservience to fashion by imposing upon them what is virtually a uniform, as in China. The uniform of white shirt, blue trousers and grey jacket is well fixed in all Western minds, but in my travel diary written during my holiday visit to China in 1978 I find this passage: 'The younger women in Pekin are very apt to wear skirts, shortish and usually pleated, often navy but sometimes other colours. Many now wear coloured, patterned shirts. White is still "uniform", with navy trousers, but some of the men wear coloured shirts, including our guide.' One significant fact we noted was that all the children we saw in Pekin were gaily dressed in very colourful clothes. Could they bear to go into the navy and white uniform when they grew up?

As long ago as 1958 Lena Jeger (now Baroness Jeger) was asking why the Chinese 'who glory in colour and form . . . and whose traditional clothes have rich, strong colours and are far from practical in style' could limit themselves to the universal jacket and trousers, 'making it almost impossible to differentiate men from women from behind'. Lena talked to both men and women, and one Party official told her, 'It is time that our girls looked like girls again. It is time they dressed with beauty and variety.' Things had changed so very little twenty years later, and an anecdote Lena related probably explains why: 'At a conference on how to get people out of uniform, a painter, Chang-Ting, related how his wife made their sixteen-year-old daughter a flowered frock to wear on a public holiday. She put it on, but when we went out she insisted on wearing her grey uniform jacket. There's public opinion for you!'

Obviously public opinion has an immense influence on what it is 'right' to wear. In western civilisation today the chief moulders of public opinion are commercial interests, through advertising in the media. A report by Jill Tweedie in the *New Statesman* in 1973 about the women of Moscow, where she lived for some months, asserted that the most remarkable factor about the way Soviet women look was the *absence* of advertising: 'Without a single Twiggy, a sole beauty queen, a tiny piece of cheesecake on that whole sixth of the earth's surface, no profit-motivated standard of female beauty exists . . . which gives your actual woman-in-Red-Square an almost unnatural ability to be herself, free from inferiority feelings.' The result, she observed, was the Soviet woman's total unself-consciousness about her shape and weight. 'In the Moscow swimming baths changing rooms,' she wrote, 'the decadent porn-soaked Westerner shrinks in blushing alarm from the tons of nude flesh that perambulates itself without the faintest attempt at concealment. Stomachs so pendulous as totally to conceal genitals spread themselves happily on benches, consorting contentedly with breasts that cover navels.'

Feminists have two problems to resolve about their clothes and self-adornment. One is the belief that it is wrong to lavish on one's personal appearance money which might be directed towards feeding some hungry Third World child. There is a

simple answer to that one, for those who choose to accept it –
buy your clothes at an Oxfam shop. (As indeed I very often do,
finding great pleasure in mixing and matching the shirts,
pullovers and skirts I pick up there and at 'good' jumble sales!)
The other problem is almost insoluble. How do you achieve a
measure of self-adornment and elegance that will please your
own image of yourself without appearing to be setting your
stall out to attract the eye of every passing man? Perhaps the
only answer to that one is to grow old! Jill Tweedie, ten years
after her Moscow sojourn, was writing:

You don't have to signal a social conscience by looking like a
frump. Lace knickers won't hasten the holocaust. You can ban the
bomb in a feather boa just as well as without, and a mild interest
in the length of hemlines doesn't necessarily disqualify you from
reading *Das Kapital* and agreeing with every word. Stick up two
fingers at the Puritans, kick up two silver heels, come up with all
frills flying and remember – the art of exterior decoration is light
years older than Paris. It is an ancient human right and
delight . . .

A right and delight explored by the Punks who astound their
elders by, as it seems to us, deliberately 'uglifying' themselves
with their half-shaven heads, glued-up vividly dyed hair and
mask-like make-up. That, I suppose, is their rebellion against
the conventional adult world. It is perhaps not more odd and
unpleasant to adult eyes than the remarkably foul language of a
teenager scrupulously careful and elegant in every detail of her
dress is to adult ears!

Perhaps we should laugh at ourselves more about our
attitudes to dress, be more confident of our own personal
integrity? A *Guardian* feature by the fashion editor Brenda
Polan and the artist Shari Peacock contained some entertaining
and memorable insights. As, for instance, the 'cliché feminist'
in sweater, huge boots and boiler suit who says, 'I know some
so-called feminists are now claiming that fashion is not a tool of
male oppression. They claim they are enjoying it as an

expression of their own sensuousness. They are lying to themselves.'

Probably we all lie to ourselves to some extent about our interest in our appearance and are reluctant to admit how much compliments from the other sex enhance our ego. But my best compliment for years was from a granddaughter who watched me on a small TV programme and said, 'Granny, you *did* look pretty.'

10

Interlude

Increasingly, as I have been writing this book, I have wanted to make plain the non-sexist attitudes to me and to my mother of my father, my husband and one or two other members of my family. The best way, I thought, would be to let them speak for themselves through extracts from the many letters I have saved.

R.G. Waddington (my father), a teacher who became a full-time journalist by way of founding and editing a weekly newspaper, *The Wyvern*, in Leicester:

August 31, 1923 (on my success – 1st class 1st division – in the Oxford School Certificate examination, equivalent of today's 'O' Levels): We are all very proud of you. Mamma pretends to be very alarmed but she is just as proud as the rest of us that her daughter has done so well. Johnnie says you *will* have to take his exams for him now . . . and don't go reading a lot of books while you are at Auntie Frieda's. Give your eyes and your brain a good rest, as I have no doubt that Miss Heron (headmistress of the Wyggeston Grammar School for Girls) will want to work you hard when you get back to school.

W.C. Bates (the eldest of my mother's brothers), who emigrated to the United States, and became a very successful consultant in the motor trade in Boston, Massachusetts. I visited him there in 1929. This letter was written on the death of my mother:

March 8, 1931: In all my life there was never anyone quite like
my sister; in all my life I never had so real a pal. Time, distances,
long lapses between letters seemed to make no difference. Always
there was a strong bond between us that never faltered or dimmed,
and still find it difficult to believe that so great a scout has passed
on.

In 1931 I joined the *Bolton Evening News*, and for a year,
until he died on Good Friday 1932, my father wrote to me a
chronicle of his doings each Friday afternoon and I put a letter
in the post to him on Sunday afternoon. The first of these
extracts indicates that it was not from my mother alone that I
acquired an example of 'public service'. The second shows that
his ambition for me was great, and in this instance was fulfilled
after twenty-five years!:

1932: Every night between office and bed I have had 2 or 3
engagements. I think I have done four Leicester Pageant meetings,
a British Association guide book meeting, a technical college
meeting and a Rotary Club Rag Book meeting. Besides that I have
attended the Lit and Phil, a chamber music concert, an LSO
concert and tonight I am going to the Little Theatre for "And So
To Bed". Added to those few things I have had to look after an
Associated Board of Music exam and have had a lot of work to do
for next Tuesday's "Dream of Gerontius" (by the Leicester
Philharmonic Society, of which R.G.W. was honorary secretary).

I should like to see you settled in a bigger place than Bolton. If
you could manage the *Guardian* I should be very proud of you.
Not that I am destitute of pride already.

K Stott, journalist, northern editor of the *News Chronicle* at
the time of its demise in 1960, and an assistant editor of the
Daily Mail, Manchester, until he died in November 1967. He
was called up into the Royal Navy in 1941, and after training
served for a year in the North Atlantic on convoy duty. After
commission training, he joined a mine-sweeper corvette as a
second lieutenant and sailed for the Mediterranean in April
1943, a fortnight after our daughter was born. She was more

than two years old when he returned. We wrote to one another several times a week during the war years, numbering the letters. Not one was lost, and the collection has now been handed over to the Imperial War Museum:

Oct 25, 1941: One thing gives me vast pleasure – W.R.R.'s obvious fear of losing you. . . . He has an obvious instinct to lean on you for ideas, for articles and for that balance that is needed to keep things going. . . . I certainly think that the work you are doing in getting into the minds of working class women and ultimately putting Women's Outlook on to the public bookstalls is far more important than going round police courts and inquests for the *Leicester Mail*.

Nov 8, 1941: People just don't seem to think of women for jobs like editing the Co-operative News but when it is brought to their notice say 'Good Lord, why didn't I think of that. So away with modesty and on with your battle dress.

Nov.24: I always feel a second-hand glow at compliments to my Talented Totty . . . . the Board must be brought to think that they would not be doing anything in appointing a woman as editor but that you are asking a favour of you in offering you the job.

The job of editing the *Co-operative News* and its allied publications was *not* offered to me, for the specific reason, I was told by the editor I should have been succeeding, that it would not do to have a woman. K was ashore at this time, and I have no record of his feelings except this one splendidly angry comment:

Why on earth men like Alf Barnes [chairman of the Co-operative Press Board and of the Co-operative Party and Member of Parliament] and Woods [The Rev. George Woods, also an MP and member of the Co-operative Press Board] pose as intelligent democrats beats me – they see every woman in a good job as a menace and yet are completely satisfied to be put into Parliament by women's votes. I think if I held these views I'd just pack up politics and start earning an honest living again.

When in April 1945 I was offered a job as 'parliamentary sub-editor' on the *Manchester Evening News*, K said he was as excited as I was:

I have no doubt you can eat the job, and it certainly seems to be right up your street. I know you will never be really satisfied until you get back into daily journalism . . . and so good luck to you and heaven preserve you from police court pars.

Two months later, in the Royal Naval Hospital, Bristol, K dreamed of the days when the war would be over again:

When I am a civilian again we will sit down and assess our prospects for the future – whether we are going to London. *Your* job now is quite as big a factor as mine.

As a pendant to the *Manchester Evening News* episode, I must quote with excusable glee from a letter from the editor, T.E. Henry, who brought my stay there to a close by telling me, plainly and honestly, that I could not expect promotion because 'the succession had to be safeguarded and the successor must be a man'. The letter was written to the *Guardian*'s managing director, Peter Gibbings:

Mary wanted to sub hard news in a tough man's world. I threw the stool, the bucket and the lot at her, made her a splash sub and she loved it. Just to show no weakness was permitted I made her sub also the live Parliamentary copy, for the Late Night Final, which was exacting, deadline, high-speed work for sure. She thrived on it all! She wasn't going to permit any frail womanly foibles on any account, so it is appropriate that when today she receives the Granada TV award for Women's Guardian she should start a series on women's liberation. She is well qualified. I reckon she started it – in the *Manchester Evening News* subs room.

So Tom Henry, whom I shall always remember with con-sid-erable affection, was not as chauvinist as he appeared in 1950. No one knew better than my brother, R.W. Waddington, why I wanted to be a sub. My brother, whom we called Johnnie, was a sub-editor in Leicester until he developed tuberculosis. The letter from which I quote, written in an affectionate teasing vein which my brothers always adopted towards me, was the last he wrote to me. He died in the autumn of 1950:

Why is it so desperately important to you that you can do subbing? (Damn it, any reasonably intelligent and liberally-minded journalist can do that.) Why is it now so important that you should find out whether you can make 'any kind of success in the writing kind of journalism'? Good Lord, don't you know that after 25 years in the racket? What do you want? Fame, pots of money, individuality, what? I don't understand this unsettled fluttering around. All this, of course, doesn't prevent me from wishing you all the luck and happiness in the world in your new job. [This was a rather short-lived term as local government correspondent of the now defunct *Daily Dispatch*.] I hope you'll get an awful lot of satisfaction out of it, because, to my way of thinking that's the only real standard of measurement of what a job's worth.

This little interlude cannot be ended without a paragraph from one of K's letters from the Mediterranean that I regard as the happiest summing-up of the felicity of a true partnership marriage:

June 21, 1943: Did you notice that by some odd error I sent the cable to Miss Waddington? One would imagine that after all these years I should have sent it to Mrs Stott at her home address! Still, I value the independence of Miss Waddington just as much as I prize the thought that she is Mrs Stott, so things couldn't be better. I am in love both with Miss Waddington and with Mrs Stott, and wouldn't part with either of them for the whole world.

11

Growing old

Somewhere along the line I stopped using all those self-defensive phrases and words for my age . . . 'I'm getting on, you know!'; 'Not so young as I was'; 'Quite elderly'. Now I say – perhaps a little too firmly, to assert that I am not afraid of the truth – 'I'm seventy-six.' This usually brings the polite reaction, 'Good Lord, you don't look it,' but I honestly prefer the statement to be received without comment, for it is better just to be a person, of any age whatsoever.

It is a release to shed embarrassment about your years; not to feel that you may be pitied, patronised or just written off as 'past it'. If it weren't for a few obvious disadvantages it would really be very nice to be old and somewhat remote from the battle. So many things that mattered terribly when we were young matter hardly at all when we are old. A dozen times a day we who are old forget a name, a word, an incident, why we came out of the sitting room into the kitchen. It stops bothering you overmuch after a while, for though it really is maddening when you have a blank spot about the name of the person to whom you are talking, someone you know perfectly well, you learn not to panic and to ignore the blank. The name, the word, will quite suddenly be in front of your mind again.

I know nothing about the physical nature of the brain, but I find myself picturing all those whorls and coils imprinted with everything that has happened to us, all that we have consciously learned and read, as if on electronic tapes. When I look at my book cases and see the hundreds of books I have accumulated, and think that in my head there are hundreds of times as many 'records' of things past, I think it is no wonder that those mental 'electronic tapes' get a bit blurred or a bit tangled up from over-use. So I stop fussing and sometimes even feel exhilarated at all that history, all that past experience, that I have got stocked up there. The zoologist, Desmond Morris, asserts that people who live to ninety or even 100 and enjoy it are 'almost to a person anti-nostalgic', and I think this may well be true. But I find I increasingly like being a sort of living history book.

People seem to think of us as being *diminished* by being old. But I think there is now a lot *more* of me than when I was young. I go back as far, in memory, as a coronation procession for King George V; I remember making ugly drawings of suffragettes; I remember the outbreak of the First World War, the recruiting posters stuck all over our bedroom, including Kitchener with his staring eyes following you around the room: 'Your King and Country Need You'; the awful wartime food, especially my mother's horrible oatcakes, which I secreted in my pocket and then flushed down the lavatory; the soldiers' and sailors' club where we helped to serve mugs of cocoa sweetened with condensed milk; being brought down to the dining room one night when there was an air-raid warning so that we could, if the worst came to the worst, thought my mother, all die together.

I remember an eclipse of the sun in 1927, when I was twenty. My father took us to watch it on the Yorkshire Moors near Giggleswick — the clouds raced with the sun but receded just in time so that we saw the moon's shadow cover the sun, surrounded by the dazzling, leaping flames of the corona. The world turned bleak and grey and the birds all fell silent and fear stalked the earth. I remember the coming of radio in my teens. My Uncle Frank made us a battery radio set, and when we had collected it from his sister's house in Cheshire where he was staying, my brother stopped the car in the middle of the Derbyshire Moors and switched on. Just at that moment the chimes of Big Ben peeled out through the darkness. No one who remembers the way Big Ben came into our lives could cease to regret that now on radio he is cut down to a single strike.

In my teens I heard Fritz Kreisler play and saw him march on to the platform at the De Montfort Hall, Leicester, trailing his violin behind as if he were a cavalry officer leading his horse. I heard Pachmann talking amiably to himself and the audience as he played Chopin. I heard Tetrazzini and Dame Nellie Melba, and saw Sir Thomas Beecham stop in his tracks, turn round and glare at a latecomer creeping to her seat. In choirs I have sung under the legendary Henry Wood, as well as Beecham, Malcolm Sargent and, at the Dartington Summer School of Music, Benjamin Britten conducting his cantata, 'A Boy was Born'. I heard W.B. Yeats and Sean O'Casey lecture. And I got Winston Churchill's autograph when he was Liberal candidate for West Leicester. And so much more . . . like a living picture gallery all around me.

In the years before writing, the old must have been the repositories of all known human experience, treasured in a way we need not treasure the old today. The BBC must have fabulous archives of the history of our times, and now Help the Aged is developing slide tape sequences about the Great War, 'Living Through the Thirties' and 'World War II'. Help the Aged field workers have told me that for some old people these sequences revive distressing memories, but I should have thought that most would be more inclined to preen themselves on remembering that they were there, and that they know something which younger people do not and cannot. Harold Nicolson wrote that one of the great joys was the joy of 'recognition' . . . probably because it usually means knowing something other people don't know! And if these old memories do sometimes bring tears to the eyes and a pain in the breast, is that such a very bad thing? Grief welling up out of the past can be a sort of release, as I found once when walking along a sunny promenade in the beautiful Greek resort of Nauplion. Suddenly I was drowned in tears — I had last walked there a dozen years or more earlier, with my husband. My Greek friend took my arm without comment and let me weep on, understanding that the tears filled some need, and that when that passed I was probably calmer and more serene for letting the grief, which during the everyday business of living has to be so rigidly hidden, rise to the surface.

On the bad days when we are exasperated at forgetting something as simple as our own telephone number, let us remind ourselves of how much more we remember than we forget! Social workers are apt to point out to me that I have had a good deal more interesting life than most of their clients. I don't deny my luck, but surely everyone's life is interesting to himself or herself? Remembering about those awful oatcakes is, in its way, as interesting to me as remembering about the Sunday morning when the R101 airship crashed in flames in France with the Air Minister among the dead.

Let me not deny the disagreeable things about being old but now list them firmly, and put them in their place. Not being able to run more than a very few yards. But then, if I had been to keep-fit classes or gone in for jogging, I should probably still be able to take part in one of those marathons which bring thousands on to the streets . . . people older than me complete the course.

Being afraid of falling over — this is a nasty one. Twice I have stumbled, fallen sideways and broken my upper arm by banging it against a wall. The first time it was my right arm when I went with my daughter on a 'restorative holiday' after pneumonia, in Lanzerote, in the Canary Islands; the other was broken only yards from my home, when I tripped over an uneven paving stone. (This second fall led to a memorable exchange with a hospital doctor when I presented myself to have my fracture checked. 'Right arm?' he said. 'No, left arm,' said I. He looked at the X-ray again. 'Right arm?' 'No, left arm.' At last the penny dropped. The X-ray department had sent up the X-ray of the previous fracture, so I had to be X-rayed again, and very displeased I was.) So now if I stumble my heart races, I feel hot and cold by turns and I shiver as I go on my way. No answer to this, is there, except to be careful how I go? A friendly doctor told me I could probably strengthen my bones by taking plenty of milk and cheese. Milk I do not much like, but I try to remember to have plenty of cheese — though I learned long ago that the views of nutritionists and doctors on diet differ noticeably.

Seeing less well, hearing less well, even chewing less well because of false teeth, are all a nuisance. There must still be a lot to be discovered and transmitted to opticians about aids to vision. Though my glasses enable me to read without strain, provided the light is pretty good, I find great difficulty in seeing across the road, so that I fail to recognise acquaintances or bus numbers, let alone read street names, until I am within a yard or two of them; I also have a special pair of glasses which enable me to play the piano. Yet my friend Gertrude, 100 years old in May 1984, had an operation when she was ninety-nine for a cataract, with only a local anaesthetic, and can read as well as anyone. She has even started painting greetings cards again. Surely more might be done to help people like me with difficulties in distance vision?

The hearing problem is more of an embarrassment for me than a serious problem. If one is in a meeting and the speaker has not learnt to project her or his voice, one just goes off into one's private thoughts, which may be just as useful, perhaps, as the thoughts of the speaker! There are spectacles with hearing aids fitted in. Could those not be made readily available for people with only a moderate hearing loss?

The stiffening of the joints is another problem. You learn

certain tricks, like pressing your hands on the thighs when about to get up from an armchair, but getting out of the bath is apt to remain a problem. People in later middle age would certainly be well advised to have handles installed on either side of the bath so that when they are beginning to become old and stiff they have something to grab hold of and to lug themselves up with. No one wants to think of himself or herself as aged and 'decrepit', but I thank my lucky stars daily that in my sixties I moved into a flat which had had many conveniences of this kind installed during the occupancy of my predecessor, also a rather old lady.

Then there is the experience most of us have, of tiring more quickly, of falling asleep after meals, of *wasting* precious time. I don't know what is to be done about that, except organising the day so that you make full use of the mornings, the afternoons *or* the evenings, whenever your own energy is at its peak. My best bit of the day is after I have breakfasted; my worst after I have lunched. People differ; they have to work out their own programme.

Most old people mind *looking* old, in more or less degree . . . having lank grey hair, sparse white hair or no hair at all; having a wrinkled skin with tell-tale brown 'freckles'; having a paunch, a pot belly, or pendulous bosom, a sagging jawline or a double chin. To see yourself unexpectedly in a full-length mirror — that old man's stoop, or dowager's hump; or to catch a view of yourself in profile — that beaky nose and scraggy throat — can be a nasty jolt. I think it is worse for women than for men because we are apt to mind more the loss of physical attractiveness. The power to charm depends initially on looks for very many women, and losing that charm must be hard to accept. Men's power to charm, depending so much more on personality and lifestyle, can actually increase as a man gains wealth, prestige and 'experience'. Assets like these seldom, alas, win a successful woman a string of younger admirers.

It is not surprising that so many older women spend a good deal of time and money on their faces, hair and figures. Those petal-like complexions that in age are crosshatched with wrinkles must have helped to make cosmetic manufacturers' fortunes. Hair colourants are acceptable now at any age, and fill shelf upon shelf at the chemist's. One has, I suppose, to make up one's mind – is the end result worth all this time, trouble and expense? Does one really want to emulate Barbara Cartland's pink, fur and pearls image? Would one's life be happier or more interesting? Not for me, it wouldn't, but people have to decide for themselves. If the reason for 'beauty cure', admitted or unadmitted, is to establish a physical relationship with a man (or men), the odds are very strongly against success for women in their sixties, let alone their seventies. Every widow and unattached elderly woman should bear in mind the stark statistic that there are three million widows and 800,000 widowers in Britain. Not enough chaps to go round . . . and those who are free, and interested, have plenty of choice among young women and assume that it is some law of nature that a man can and should find a mate younger than himself. I think this situation is changing and will change still more as time goes on: there are more men than women in younger age groups, and as women are tending to lead more stressful lives and to smoke more and drink more, they may be running more risk, I fear, of early death from heart disease, lung cancer and such diseases currently more prevalent among men. The balance of the sexes in the population is changing and is likely to change further. Men are likely to have less choice, women more.

One more disagreeable aspect of growing old is that ageism is probably more prevalent than either sexism or racism. People from ethnic minorities I meet at little seminars on ageing, even a taxi driver who drove me home from a London Broadcasting Company phone-in, insist that in their cultures – Chinese, Hindu, Pakistani, Caribbean – the old, and especially old women, are valued for their wisdom and knowledge. It is certainly not so here. In politics you occasionally find male leaders of seventy or more – Ronald Reagan, notably, though Michael Foot's failure to retain the leadership of the Labour Party was probably due mainly to the fact of his age. But the departments of state, I discover, have a tacit rule that women over sixty will not be recruited to quangos (quasi non-governmental organisations), royal commissions and the like. One of the reasons I hope that the House of Lords will survive is that it is the one place in which the elderly – even the very old like my Lords Shinwell, Soper, Fenner Brockway and my Lady Wootton (the only woman who has ever sat in for the Lord Chancellor, on his woolsack) – are listened to with respect, even reverence.

Social workers always insist that the worst problem of old age is loneliness, so it must be very widespread and often very, very sad. People who have lost a lifetime partner always have an inner loneliness, unless they have the exceptional good fortune to find another dear and loving friend with whom to share the rest of their life. I don't believe there is any substitute for the pair bond, and when death severs it the survivor, even if like me he or she is fortunate enough to find friends, interests and reasons of all kinds to go on living, must always be aware of being 'alone' in a way those who have remained partnerless are not.

But all that said, why do I claim that being old is in most ways acceptable, and in some ways very enjoyable? Many of the things you have always enjoyed are still there to enjoy. The coming of spring still lifts your heart – the daffodils under the cedar tree, the grass becoming quintessentially green, the forsythia outside your bedroom window turning to a blaze of gold, the magnolia blooms opening as if they were living mother-of-pearl. If you have no garden, there are other people's trees and flowers. I remember walking down our road a few years ago and finding an old man with a dog standing in a sort of stunned rapture at the beauty of an ornamental pink-blossomed cherry tree.

If music has been your special thing, age is no barrier to continued enjoyment – indeed, so far as *listening* is concerned, we have riches unknown to our forebears in radio, TV, gramophone records and cassettes. I have been discovering with delight, this last year or two, that I can record from my 'music centre' onto tapes, even old tapes, music that particularly pleases me, and then play it back whenever I choose. The newer machines, like mine, do not accommodate the old seventy-eight records. Perhaps some enterprising Age Concern or Pensioners' Link or Help the Aged groups might install an older model at one of their centres so that old people could bring their treasured seventy-eight Clara Butt, or Paul Whiteman or Maurice Chevalier, record it on tape, and sit happily of an evening listening to the music of their youth. To think that I still have records of Elizabeth Schumann, Fritz Kreisler, Alfred Cortot and so forth never heard any more – to say nothing of a record I myself made of a song my very remarkable Uncle Harry wrote when he was well into his sixties, a setting of Shakespeare's 'Fear no more the heat of the sun'.

Singing and playing an orchestral instrument are wonderfully companionable pursuits; so is hobby painting. Almost all my happiest holidays since my husband died have been with painting groups. And, of course, the greatest value of hobbies like this – or it might be pigeon racing, old-fashioned dancing, bowls, fishing or flower arranging – is that they make us friends. I know I am very lucky indeed to be able still to sing in a small choir. The unreliability of my voice now sometimes drives me to distraction, but the fact that after something like sixty years of singing in various choral groups I am pretty sure to come in on the right note at the right time tends still to make my dear fellow altos grab my arm and hiss 'Please sit by *me*.' Skill in any hobby is a bond with our fellows, even in great old age.

Confidence in being your own woman, your own man, is one of the pleasant aspects of being old. This may, of course, not be quite so deep-rooted as we like to think – human beings seldom slough off all self-doubt or sensitivity, and we may come upon intolerance and ageism even in sons and daughters who find a parent's reminiscences boring or who habitually exclude them from conversation round the dining table. But we don't, surely, have to be slaves of fashion ever again, either in dress or possessions. Very few of my elderly acquaintances, whether male or female, are inhibited about going to Oxfam shops or even to jumble sales to pick up coats, shirts or jackets. I should never now, I think, be embarrassed by arriving at a function in a hat when everyone else is hatless, or by wearing a mid-calf skirt when everyone else is wearing floor-length creations. Gloves now are for comfort, not for elegance. I see no reason at all to follow fashion in buying new domestic equipment unless it has been clearly shown to me in the kitchen of a friend or relation that it would suit my lifestyle. I see no reason to repine because I can't afford 'up-to-date' furniture or furnishings. What I have will see me out very comfortably, and so should all of us say who are growing old.

Best of all the good things that have happened in my old age is the readiness of young women friends to give and to *show* me affection. (I wonder if young men are so generous in their comradeliness to men old enough to be their fathers and grandfathers? I hope they make them feel as welcome as my young female friends make me, giving me a little kiss and hug on meeting and parting.) Customs have changed in recent years, and I am very thankful for it. I know that it is not because I am nicer that I receive more evidence of liking and affection in my seventies than I did in my fifties, it is just that there has been a change in social mores, owing partly to the fact that the women's movement has given young women

greater feelings of fellowship, sisterhood, comradeliness, call it
what you will. (If anyone gets up to give me a seat on the bus
or tube it is almost always a young woman nowadays.) And
partly because the cult of youth has its pleasant as well as its
unpleasant side, the young do not feel so in awe of us as we
were of our grandparents. And if you are in a strong position,
as the young are in many ways, you can afford to be chivalrous
to the less advantaged, can't you? I also find that old people are
rather nice to one another too – meeting in the post office
drawing their pension, in the butcher's buying their half-pound
of mince or single chop, even passing in the street, they are apt
to greet one another in a friendly kind of way, as if to say, 'We
old 'uns must stick together.' I like it. I find the world a much
friendlier place than it is reported to be by a good many social
workers.

And so I have to admit that part of my enjoyment of my
autumnal years is a product of my lifestyle since my retirement.
Many of my young friends are deeply involved in the same
causes as I am involved in, as well as in the same leisure
pursuits. I think it heartens them to know that a woman in her
seventies still cares about what they care about. Walking to the
tube station from a small committee meeting recently with a
colleague of eighty-three and a woman of barely fifty, I was
delighted to hear the younger woman burst out, 'I think it is
wonderfully inspiring to find so many of our members (in the
Fawcett Society) still so active and energetic as you two.' And
we, of course, feel heartened and even exhilarated by their
enthusiasm for the causes we have worked for for so long.

Sometimes I find myself saying something like, 'If you're
lonely, it's your own fault', which must, especially to kind and
concerned social workers, make me sound rather like the sort of
middle-class suburban Tory living in the prosperous south-east
who asks the unemployed why they don't get on their bikes
and go and look for a job. I *do* count my blessings, of which far
the most important is good health. I have had too many friends

whose old age has been ruined by arthritis, Parkinson's disease, some degree of paralysis after a stroke, even total incapacity, and one very dear friend whose mind has completely gone — the most awful affliction that can befall any of us, or our families. The gerontologist, Dr Alex Comfort, has pointed out that though medical science has made immense progress in conquering and controlling the infectious diseases (like tuberculosis, which killed my brother and hundreds of thousands of other quite young people in the first half of this century), it has scarcely made any impact on the degenerative diseases. Even cancer, it seems to me, is not so much to be dreaded as the mysterious virus, or whatever it is, that causes the onset of senile dementia.

But there are, thank heaven, a great many more old people in tolerably good health, able to get about, look after themselves and *do something for someone else* than there are old people who are dependent on others for their survival. I know it is a bee in my bonnet, I know I am in danger of being a bore about it, but I do fervently believe that the 'young old' should be a resource for society in helping to look after the 'old old'. Pensioners are apt to get angry with me when I write, or say at seminars, that we owe some duty to the community for the right to a pension which, if not exactly generous, keeps us from having to be dependent on our children, or go into a workhouse. 'I've worked all my life,' they say, 'and I've paid all my insurance contributions and never asked for help from anyone. I'm *entitled* to retire now in comfort.' I suspect that actuarially we do get more in pension and benefits than we have in fact paid for, but that isn't really the point. The point is that we are all members of a community. The community owes all its members support, and each member of the community likewise owes all the others some degree of concern. 'Each for all and all for each,' as the old socialists used to put it. This concern for one's fellows seems to me the essence of morality. At the very least, shouldn't we be prepared to give as good as we get? There is in fact a very dismaying fact about this final quarter of the twentieth century – the proportion of *very* old people in our community will go on increasing until at least the year 2001 AD. So if we say, 'I've done my bit; it's up to the state to look after me now,' what we are really saying is that the shrinking population of taxpayers, who usually have children to educate and mortgages to pay off, must pay in rates and taxes for seeing that we get an inflation-proof pension, transport concessions, rate and rent rebates and reduced fees for every activity we undertake, from hairdressing on Mondays, to LEA classes and courses.

No one is saying, least of all me, that the newly retired ought to be 'conscripted' into service for their older brothers and sisters. It is just that many older people, who have never enjoyed exactly luxurious lives and are glad to be finished with dreary and not very well-paid jobs, have not yet learned how very much we are still needed by society, and how good it is to feel needed. Once when I was taking part in a study day on ageing, a fellow lecturer said that he did not think it right that old people should undertake services for the community without pay. I spoke up rather tartly: 'There are other ways of being paid than in money.' One is paid in affection, gratitude, esteem and, very importantly, in *self*-esteem.

I would have thought it was far more fun to take part in *serving* at an Age Concern 'pop-in parlour', or a pensioners' luncheon club in the church hall, than to just turn up every week to be waited on. One of the most enterprising and enjoyable local ventures I have heard of is TAP – Tooting Action for Pensioners – run by a small group of local people whose outstanding spokeswoman is the vivacious, energetic Olly Hollingsworth. TAP sends representatives to Greater London campaigns for improved pensions and benefits, and also tackles basic local problems like the hazard of broken paving stones by surveying, photographing and reporting on them to the local council. In Wandsworth there is a 'Dial-a-ride' service for pensioners, and not only for necessary visits to the doctor, the clinic or the shopping centre. Says their leaflet: 'Dial-a-ride is not just for necessary trips; use it for fun. Go to the park or the pubs, the shops or the zoo; visit a relative or get involved in local community affairs.'

Isn't this sort of participation better than having things done *for* you? Sometimes I have a flicker of irritation over the unconsciously patronising attitudes shown towards us by some well-meaning educationalists. I am sure I am not the only stroppy septuagenarian who is tempted to say, 'I could probably tell *you* a thing or two, my lass.' I may claim to know a bit about writing and talking and editing; similarly, many a retired man knows an immense amount about various crafts and DIY skills, and many an elderly woman could instruct her juniors on, say, the women novelists of the twenties, as well as various domestic arts. Is it very mean of me to feel, sometimes, that educating the elderly, and educating social workers to care for the elderly, sometimes looks as if it is one of the few growth industries in the UK? Information keeps coming my way about projects for the benefit of 'the elderly'. Most of the ideas are truly worthy, but most of them are by Them for Us. FREE (Forum on the Rights of Elderly People to Education) sets out to be a clearing house of information on all aspects of education in the later years; to bring together the people concerned in our educational opportunities, and 'to promote continuous assessment' (oh dear, jobs for the boys); to advocate 'a greater share of resources' for older people, and to evaluate work in progress, identify and promote good practice, etc. . . . (more jobs for more boys? – and the girls?) So many of these projects, it seems to me, are concerned with discussing and evaluating services for the elderly rather than with helping the elderly to help themselves.

I always rejoice when I hear of a contemporary, male or female, enrolling for an Open University course or, indeed, any local education authority class. If I hadn't so very many other more pressing things to do, I should dearly like to take a course in Chinese . . . not that I could ever, I think, learn to speak it, but that I might be able to learn to write those beautiful, flowing characters and learn to understand how in one culture, like ours, writing is built on symbols for individual sounds, and in another on symbols for things, ideas or people. But it seems pretty silly to me that so many authorities have an age limit for their tutors. Who better to instruct the elderly than the elderly themselves?

Sociologists and social workers are also apt to think that they know better than we do what we really want. 'Old people want *choice*,' they proclaim with generous sympathy and total conviction. 'Choice gives you dignity, and to provide free choice, cash in the pocket is always preferable to hand outs and "benefits" however generously administered. The only guarantee of independence, dignity and freedom from patronage or charity is a secure income.' I agree that these sentiments sound admirable (and I have used this line of reasoning myself when arguing that what women need for a happy and successful marriage is economic independence.)

But in the case of pensions and benefits for pensioners, the argument has a flaw. The retirement pension may be meant to be a secure income; it could even be so if politicians insisted that it should really keep up with prices. But to people who grew up in a time when inflation was only a word that had something to do with blowing up balloons, *it does not feel secure*. Inflation presses upon the old not only financially but psychologically, and I am inclined to think that the psychological impact may be the worse of two evils. If you grew up before the war, were actually married and running a household before the war, you remember that a bag of coal cost two shillings (10p) and that you knew how many bags you needed per week. Eggs were a shilling (5p) a dozen. Half-a-crown (12½p) was a good substantial sum. You could get a very good lunch for that in the brasserie of the Midland Hotel,

Manchester.

Yes, I know that in those days the retirement pension was still ten shillings (50p) a week. A very good salary was £400 a year – less than a quarter of my current state pension. But what the post-war people do not seem able to comprehend is that our *thinking* about the cost of goods induces a kind of panic non-buying. We can't believe that we are the sort of people who can pay £100 or more for an overcoat (though in my younger days my winter coats always cost £20 or more, on a smaller income than I now operate on). Some elderly people now give up buying a daily newspaper, not because they really can't afford it – a TV licence costs almost as much – but because it seems monstrous to pay 23p for what used to cost 2d. We can remember the days of the penny stamp, and now sadly prune the Christmas card list – a treasured way of keeping in touch with friends all round the country – because the government's £10 bonus is hardly enough to cover the cost of postage, let alone the cost of the greetings cards.

Yes, our thinking is not exactly rational; in fact it does sometimes feel as if our mental processes, in relation to the cost of living, have gone on the blink. But there it is. If organisations concerned with the welfare of the aged convince the government, any government, that £2 on the pension is better than subsidised bus passes, I don't believe they will be doing us a service. We don't like subsidised bus passes because they are 'charity'? Nonsense. You should see the jolly ladies queueing up at those booths on stations or in the big stores where you can photograph yourself when the time comes round for the renewal of the Greater London free bus and underground travel pass. They are as merry as grigs, and they will go and visit their friends and relations right on the other side of London, or make a daily jaunt to the nearest big shopping centre, just for the fun of it and because it's free. I knew a distinguished critic who was so delighted with his free bus pass that he used it to explore all the areas of the city he

had never known before. 'If you had something like a bus pass
for free, or a half-fare pass on British Rail,' I want to ask
people who lead the 'old age' organisations, 'wouldn't *you* use
it? Would *you* swap it for a pound or two in the pocket?' I
certainly would not. I value this benefit so much that I think
that all the concerned organisations ought to be campaigning
for equality of treatment right throughout the country. There
are a number of local authorities which do not provide a penny
towards the cost of pensioners' travel even to the doctor, the
clinic or the hospital, and others who hand out only a small
number of travel tokens.

Everyone knows that one of the worst threats to the health
of the aged is inertia. It is when you feel that you can't be
bothered to go out that trouble sets in. Too much trouble to
go shopping, so you stock up on cheese and tinned corned beef
and never cook a decent meal for yourself (let alone a
nutritionally well-balanced meal). You can't be bothered to go
out, so you never make contact with new friends, or even keep
regular contact with old ones. But if you have that lovely free
bus pass – isn't it a shame not to use it? How many of us
really care to look a gift horse in the mouth?

So if subsidised travel is a good idea for keeping people lively,
interested and active, isn't subsidised *heating* a good idea, to
keep our very aged friends and relations safely warm and snug
during the wintry weather? I seriously believe that inclusion in
the pension book of a clutch of coupons with which any fuel
bill could be paid, in part or in whole, might save many deaths
from hypothermia every winter. Gas and electricity bills creep
up and up in the offices of British Gas and the electricity
boards. Not many elderly persons, like me, have the will or the
ability to keep track week by week of how many therms or
electricity units we are using. Many old people must dread the
quarterly bills and therefore switch off the heat and retire to
bed to keep themselves warm. I myself on cold winter days
often wrap myself in a floor-length quilted polyester coat rather

than switch on the central heating before evening. I know it is possible to get a heating allowance, but few of us like doing this, and applications of this kind are not easy – as my experience with my local rating authority suggests.

Being a single householder on a not very large income, I decided to enquire whether I might be entitled to a rate rebate. My enquiry was made just after I had paid my spring instalment. Months went by and the autumn demand arrived. After I had written to enquire plaintively, 'Do I have to pay or do I not?', a kind and courteous employee of the rating office called, checked over my income and outgoings and took away certain documents which he returned quite promptly. But still no news from the borough treasurer's office until the next spring rate demand fell due. I then was told that on a rate demand of £426.60 my rebate was £4.29.

Hilariously amused, and resolving never to put myself, or the borough treasurer's department, to the trouble of making or assessing any further application, I wrote to the borough treasurer:

I think perhaps your staff should be congratulated on taking only ten months from the date when I first raised the question of my eligibility for a rate rebate, and thanked for enabling me to settle my account before the next rate demand arrives shortly. I also think the rating authority's generosity should be acknowledged. £4.29 is probably enough to buy a new hot water bottle and a pair of leg-warmers, to help to ward off hypothermia.

Needless to say, I had no reply. When, two or three months later, I heard a former chairman of the National Association of Widows tell *her* story of a rate rebate to the association's annual conference, I wondered if I had not been a trifle too sarcastic. Her munificent rating authority had awarded her a rebate of *48p per half year*.

Is it any wonder that some of us feel that free or subsidised transport passes have immediate, positive value whereas rebates on this and that are hardly worth the worry and the difficulty of applying? Or that we would like to see heating coupons? And free telephones for the very old? (In the 'select' area where I live, I came home from the National Association of Widows conference to our local British Rail station to find that all four telephone kiosks in the vicinity had been vandalised. My daughter or any of my local friends would willingly have given me a lift home but I could communicate neither with any of them nor with a taxi rank. So, at the end of a tiring day, I had to lug a heavy case three-quarters of a mile to my home. Extra cash *isn't* everything a pensioner needs!)

Oh well . . . I am truly thankful to be old in the eighth decade of the twentieth century and not in the first or second centuries AD. I also believe that we who are old now are better off than those who will be old in the year 2001. The Office of Population Censuses and Surveys estimates that in that year there will be more than two million people between the ages of seventy-five and eighty-four, and 845,000 aged over eighty-five. These figures are expected to increase until at least 2011 AD . . . because our mothers and fathers, in the first decade of this century, were tending to produce large families (as Mary Goldring most entertainingly pointed out in a Radio 4 'Analysis'). But at the time of writing, the size of the average family has shrunk to 1.8 children – not enough to replace the existing population, and certainly not enough working citizens to support comfortably, either in taxes or in personal services, the vast population of pensioners there will be.

So let those of us who are already elderly and old be thankful if we have good health and are able to keep on our feet; let us remain involved in the community and keep a strong sense of our identity. I am *ME* as much as I was at twenty or thirty. More 'me', in fact, because of all that experience stored up in my brain.

My mother lived only to see one granddaughter. She never heard a grandchild say, 'I love you Granny; take care.' She missed the very interesting and rewarding years a woman can have in her sixties and seventies. I am sure young women would have shown her as much affection as they have shown me. I wish she'd had what I have. I wish *all* men and women of my age had as good health and as many friends as I have. Though you have to work for friends, luck also plays a big part in the possibility of keeping them.

The other day I saw a poster in a women's centre in London, showing a very old woman and her thoughts. 'Old age isn't calm,' she was thinking.

Fires burn in the bodies of old women
Flutes sing in their ears and
they fall in love now and then.

That's right.

12

Going places

Thank goodness I grew up in a family always willing to go places. What a poor, impoverished old age it would be if I hadn't got this crock of gold to dip into, this memory bank of seventy years of holidays. Our family never went to the same place twice. 'Abroad' wasn't for us, probably because of shortage of money, but in my childhood travel was by rail and sea and there were no package holidays to alluring places in other lands. But Mother did her best. We rented cottages in various places she thought sounded interesting – preferably by the sea, with a nearby promontory – but inland during the First World War when the coast was thought unsafe. I can remember very clearly a holiday in 1916 near Ross-on-Wye, where we paddled in a stream opposite the house and I stuffed my school bloomers full of hazelnuts from a tree on the opposite bank; and a later one at Clynog, North Wales, where I made myself very sick by eating too many winkles gathered from the rocks on the shore.

The best of these early holidays was during the summer after the end of the 1914-18 war. We took a farmhouse a few hundred yards from the fine, five-mile-wide bay of Hell's Mouth, near the end of the Lleyn Peninsula, not far from Pwllheli, North Wales. Day after day the sun shone. We went down to the beach and paddled, and I learned to swim, and Johnny dug pools in the sand and filled them with large jellyfish he scooped up with his spade. Mother was furious if she spied any other human beings along the shore — except on the day when the mackerel came in following a shoal of minnows and the people from the isolated farms round about were alerted and joined us in slapping out the fish with any implement that came to hand. Imagine *any* sandy beach deserted for long sunny hours round our coasts today! It is a sad thought that as more of us enjoy holidays in lovely places, the more we are likely to spoil them for one another.

Mostly we spent our childhood holidays in Wales; once, almost disastrously, we went to Dunoon on the Firth of Clyde — the weather was wet and bitterly cold, but there was a piano in the house and Mother and I spent a lot of time playing Brahms' Hungarian Dances together. Apart from this, the first time I set foot out of England was when, in 1929, aged twenty-one, I sailed across the Atlantic to Boston, Massachusetts. This happened because my mother's mother had died, leaving her a small legacy which she divided among her three children, arranging that my little portion should be spent on going to visit her favourite brother, Charlie, who had emigrated when not much more than a lad.

Charlie's eldest son, Carlton, had come to England to visit us all, and I was to travel back with him in the S.S. *Laconia*, an eight-day boat from Liverpool to Boston. Of course, it was the only way of crossing the Atlantic then, and now that we can fly within a few hours distances that took as many days then, I would not go by boat any further than across the Channel, or possibly the North Sea. Much as I love the sea, I am too impatient to savour 'foreign' sights. Besides, life aboard ship is like living permanently in a posh hotel or a residential club. It has nothing to do with my normal lifestyle. On board the *Laconia* we spent most of our time eating, as I remember it. Huge breakfast, elevenses, lunch, afternoon tea, dinner. No doubt a healthy twenty-one-year-old enjoyed every mouthful, but the mere thought now makes me feel slightly sick.

We were not so weight conscious in the 1920s as we are

now, and having gorged myself on board ship, I gorged with even more enthusiasm when I reached the United States. Uncle Charlie's wife was a very good cook, and the cafés and drugstores served meals and snacks which I could not resist. I learned about clams, baked swordfish, corn on the cob and gorgeous salads such as those of ham, cream cheese, pineapples and lettuce, which would be quite commonplace at a party today but was a gastronomic revelation then. And sundaes. On my way from Uncle Charlie's home at Cambridge to his office in downtown Boston I would almost invariably stop off for a banana split or similar. I can't imagine what I must have weighed when I got back home.

Uncle Charlie was an assessor for a car insurance firm and part of his job was to examine the damage to wrecked cars all over New England. So he took me with him to Concord, to Lexington, to Louisa May Alcott's home and through many of the little towns and villages of Massachusetts with their elegant white churches, their white clapboard houses and their front lawns sloping to the road with never a hedge in front of or between them . . . so unlike the little boxed-in front gardens of the sort of terraced house I was used to.

This was a 'sociable' visit, of course, and I met many of my uncle's friends. It was during that strange Prohibition era, and I was staggered at the frequency with which they offered me alcoholic liquor. We were almost a teetotal family; apart from the occasional bottle of cider, wine and spirits were never seen in our house. (I imagine that when the uncles visited, either at our home or at our grandparents', they had to nip out to the pub if they wanted a drink.) No one ever talks now of the Prohibition years – even of the awful results of trying to impose total abstinence on a whole nation, especially one so culturally diverse as the USA. But I remember very vividly my visit, one sunny day, with Uncle Charlie to his bootlegger, who hung out in the woods somewhere in the countryside outside Boston. No doubt he thought it unseemly that his young niece should be involved in this expedition, so I sat in the car until he returned, but I have often wished that I had seen that secret still. (I don't even know if it distilled gin or whisky, for at that time I drank neither.)

I had my twenty-second birthday while I was in the US, and Uncle Charlie gave me a stupendous birthday treat – a trip by boat down to New York, chiefly, I think, so that I should be able to stow away the unforgettable picture of New York Harbour, sailing past the Statue of Liberty. Flying into JFK airport is a very trite and inferior experience. We were very happy trippers – for Uncle Charlie's sake, mostly, we went up the Woolworth Building, then, I think, the tallest building in the world. For my sake we went to one of the avant-garde theatres, which he, the American, had never heard of and I, the English provincial, had. We went over to Statten Island, one of the most exciting ferry trips anywhere, for the view it provides of the New York skyline. We walked down Wall Street, then a fearfully gloomy canyon, for the skyscrapers of the period were not stepped back to give a little light and grace but shot straight up to the sky. Nothing, I think, will ever make me *like* New York. Even during the week or so I spent there with K in 1963 I hated the noise and the dirt and the lack of architectural grace, but I have to admit that at night, with all the windows of the high apartment blocks lighted up in a fantastic mosaic, it is one of the architectural wonders of the modern world.

The American holiday K and I had together in 1963 took us from New York to Washington, Boston, Atlanta, New Orleans, right across to Albuquerque, New Mexico and Santa Fe, and on to Los Angeles and San Francisco. K then had to return home, but I, having an extra 'sabbatical' month's leave from the *Guardian*, went on, mostly by Greyhound bus, to Fresno in California, Reno, Salt Lake City, Sioux Falls, South Dakota, Buffalo to see the Niagara Falls, and back to Washington, Boston and New York. How absurd it is of us to jeer at Americans who 'do' Europe in two or three weeks' vacation, when in similar time we cover far greater expanses of the earth in America – and almost as great a variety of cultures.

What stays in my mind most vividly of this eight-week 1963 trip? First, two culture shocks: one in New Orleans, so beautiful with its white-pillared residences and its wrought-iron balconies, so charming and so friendly – but it was the first time I had seen overt racial discrimination; the first time I had seen the sign on a public lavatory, 'Whites Only'. The other shock was in Los Angeles which was, to me, a complete non-place, a vast area of houses and apartment blocks divided by motor roads. No centre. No history. This impression was not dispersed, despite visiting the attractive University of South California and the famously beautiful Beverley Hills suburbs, when I returned in 1969, for when I stayed with a hospitable friend on Wiltshire Boulevard there was, so far as I ever discovered, no way I could get to a post office, a drugstore or any useful little shop, unless she took me by car.

On this second visit I did at least escape the horror of a Los Angeles smog, all the more scary for being faintly yellow and not thick black like our Manchester fogs but so acrid as to bring stinging tears to the eyes and a choking sensation in the chest. I have never experienced anything like it elsewhere (though the atmosphere in Pekin is pretty nasty and is apt to inflict on tourists a particularly unpleasant sort of cold, with temporary loss of voice). But then, so much of the United States is stunningly beautiful: the red rocks rising up from the New Mexico desert like ancient, crumbling castles; the thin, clear air of Santa Fe and its strange adobe houses, and Los Alamos with its memory of nuclear fission looming frighteningly in the distance; San Francisco, its pastel-painted houses like some charming old English seaside town – Southwold, perhaps, or Lyme Regis – climbing up from the harbour; a bungalow in Albuquerque, home of a friend's brother, festooned in the magical blue of morning glory, which

I had never seen before. (In the little Greek Island of Simi I saw morning glory covering the cone-shaped roof of a public shelter. I suppose a visitor from warmer climes might think the way our pure white convolvulus runs riot over waste ground and hedges just as miraculous.)

Though my visual memory is so poor, I always remember flowers – hedges of pink roses in Stresa, by Lake Maggiore; many-coloured mesembryanthemum in the Scilly Islands (our last holiday before K was called up into the Navy); mimosa in Nauplion in the Peloponnese; hibiscus in Rhodes; autumn crocuses in Corfu; acres of dazzling golden gorse in Sutherland; blue squills on the cliffs near Saint David's, Wales; daffodils in Gloucestershire; primroses in Cornwall. Of course we used to go on bluebell walks and even cowslip walks in May in the fields and woods of Leicestershire when I was a child.

I don't think I envy anyone their holidays – though there are still a few places I long to see before I die, like Troy and Bali and Peru. Almost all mine have been so special, like my second trip abroad. This was a singing party to Yugoslavia in 1930, organised by a leading London baritone, Frederick Woodhouse, who had served in Serbia during the First World War. He recruited singers from choirs all over Great Britain, including my father and me. I was then twenty-two and fancied a Mediterranean cruise, but Mother was very uneasy about what I might get up to and welcomed the idea of the singing holiday with Father as chaperone. So, actually, did I, for singing was then, as it still is, my greatest pleasure. After travelling across Europe we started rehearsing in Venice, then continued sailing down the Adriatic to Dubrovnik and were welcomed at sunset in the harbour with flowers and a brass band. Sir Arthur Fagge was our conductor, Reginald Paul our accompanist, and Ida Cooper our soprano. We sang, naturally, a programme of English songs, from 'The Agincourt Song' and 'Summer is icumen in' to Elgar's 'As Torrents in Summer'. The Yugoslav choirs sang their songs to us. It was all marvellous — the floodlit castle floating, it seemed, in the sky above Ljubljana: the 'rout' in a baronial hall at Zagreb (nearest thing to a 'groaning board' that I am ever likely to see); the integration of Diocletian's Palace into the front at the seaside town of Split. But what I recall as one of the most sheerly beautiful moments of my life was Frederick Woodhouse and the soprano Ida Cooper, singing, in the cathedral square at Dubrovnik under a starlit sky, to a vast, hushed audience, Purcell's exquisite duet, 'My dearest, my fairest'.

It was a long time before I had another singing holiday — apart from those eager-beaver weeks at the Dartington Summer School of Music, rehearsing choral works in the morning, listening in at master classes in the afternoon and attending concerts in the great hall in the evening. But in 1980 Calliope Bourdara, then President of the Women's Union of Greece, whose summer tour for feminists from all over the English-speaking world I had enjoyed the year before, sent me a brochure about letting her large villa on the island of Aegina. It enumerated the attractions of the villa and its studio chalets, and added, as a sort of afterthought, 'There is a piano for practice.' 'Wouldn't it be wonderful,' I said dreamily that evening to the friend who gave me a lift to our choir practice, 'to get up a singing party to Aegina?' And that is what we did — eight of us in the villa, two in one of the chalets. The singing was not very serious, mostly part-songs and Negro spirituals (though we didn't do too badly with the Fauré Requiem), but the like-mindedness of the company was enchanting. One day we asked Calliope what was the correct way to address our friend the wine merchant. 'Kyrie,' she said. Immediately six lusty voices sang out: 'Kyrie eleison, eleison . . .'

One of Calliope's chalets was occupied by a wealthy Greek refrigerator manufacturer and his wife. They struck up a friendship with members of our party and invited us, *all ten of us*, to pay an overnight visit to their home on the island of Hydra. And we did. Two couples had bedrooms, the rest of us slept on banquettes or the floor and were wakened at dawn by the donkeys, the cocks, the hens and the church bells. It was wonderful; and I think that this small group of people who didn't really know one another very well when we came together, but who sang and swam (sometimes naked at midnight!) and walked and talked together, will remain friends for life.

For me Greece, its historically superb mainland and its countless islands, is the nearest to an ideal holiday country. I have a strong sense of history and am profoundly moved by classical remains, in Athens, in Delphi, in Corinth, Epidauros, Mycenae, Delos, Lindos or wherever. How can one not have a sense of the past, walking where Socrates and Plato and Sophocles and Aristotle and Demosthenes and Phidias and Euripides – and perhaps even Homer – walked and talked and orated and prayed? I suppose if you never did Greek at school; never read Greek myths or history, never came upon J.C. Stobart's book *The Glory That was Greece*, so influential in my young days; never even read Leonard Cottrell or Mary Renault's marvellously evocative novels, you could go to Poros or Skiathos or Spetses without a thought beyond sunlit seas and warm sands, fetta, black olives, ouzo and retsina. You might not bother to take a caique from Mykonos to contemplate those stone lions, like sentinels guarding the one-time busy port of Delos. You might regard Knossos as just a little break from sunbathing at one of the Crete resorts, and perhaps never even notice the ancient stone throne of King Minos, 3,000 years old if it's a day.

And how many happy holidaymakers at Nauplion, a charming resort in the Peloponnese, come upon the fusty little museum which houses a real, original Linear B tablet, of the kind that baffled antiquarians and linguists for years (What was the language? What did the scratchings mean?) until a young Cambridge researcher proved that 'Linear B' was not a different language from Greek, but an early ancestor.

So my mind jumps across the world to ancient China where I saw another extraordinary treasure in the history of written language in a small archaeological museum at An-Yang. This was a collection of the oracle bones on which the scribes of the Shang dynasty (1600 to 1100 BC) used to carve inscriptions. For many years peasants in the area north of the Yellow River, turning up pieces of bone while they were ploughing, had assumed them to be dragons' bones (probably ox bones) which had various notches cut into them. Dragon bones were thought to be very efficacious medicine, especially for nervous diseases. And so it came about, we were told at the An-Yang museum, that in the late nineteenth century a Chinese professor who took great care of his health noted that some of the 'dragon bones' in his medicine chest were not just casually notched but carefully inscribed. The bones were used for divining by being split by a red-hot bronze point. The way the bone parted gave a rough and ready 'yes/no/perhaps' answer to the question. But those small, neat scratchings were found to be the questions the diviners had asked, and they provided for later historians and etymologists a 'dictionary' of 2,000 characters and clues to the history of this whole dynasty. In this little An-Yang museum I feasted my eye on these very bones, some large shoulder blades, some quite tiny fragments, but all having rows of characters perfectly legible to any person who understands the Chinese pictograph form of written language, though at least 3,000 years old.

Perhaps people not quite so fascinated by the history of language as a journalist and writer is likely to be may identify more closely with my awe at the observatory at Deng-feng. In this beautiful quiet place, the founder Guan-Xing discovered that the earth goes round the sun. That was in 1279, three centuries before Copernicus, and then Galileo, tried to convince the European 'establishment' of the same truth. What an incredible people the Chinese are – they first used gunpowder in 1000 AD and predated Gutenberg's use of movable type by nearly four centuries. Their paintings, sculptures, pottery are beyond compare: can anyone who has ever seen them forget the great stone beasts — lions, elephants and camels — which line the 'spirit way' to the famous Ming tombs? Television has brought us wonderful pictures, in recent years, of hundreds of pottery warriors recently excavated. But at the head of the Huan River, the bones of 2,000 slaves immolated alive were found. How many people died, one wonders, in erecting the Great Wall, 3,000 miles long and the only human artefact identifiable by the astronauts who landed on the moon? Probably it is because the tourist is so overwhelmed by the marvels of this unknown land — China has only in the last few years begun to welcome visitors from the West and to become a 'tourist attraction' — that one feels so keenly there the cruelty of man to man. (Egyptians and Greeks have also been cruel to slaves and others, and the cruelty of the race which has produced such a vast amount of the world's great music was, in the slaughter of the Jews in the gas chambers of Auschwitz, surely at least as horrible as that which practised the immolation of Chinese slaves. And this happened in an era we had thought of as 'civilised'.)

You can't travel far without being aware of the hideous side of human nature. In 1972 I went with a party from the Press Club of London to 'the Holy Land', a small strip of land at the eastern end of the Mediterranean which has perhaps been more fought over, more desecrated by bloodshed, than any area in the world. Battles have been fought here in the name of religion for at least 3,000 years. It takes an imagination, or a faith, much stronger than mine to visualise Jesus of Nazareth stumbling up the Via Dolorosa with his cross, for now it is jam-packed with little shops draped with kaftans and necklaces of carved woods and the Stations of the Cross are squashed between a butcher's and a greengrocer's. It is hard, too, to believe in 'Christ's' tomb in the Church of the Holy Sepulchre, so often built over, so over-adorned, so often wrangled over by

Catholics, Greek Orthodox, Armenians, Syrians, Copts and Abyssinians. We were told that because of the wrangling of different religious denominations over the rights to 'possession' of a wall or a ceiling or a pillar in this most holy place it was in danger of disintegration.

When I was there, Jerusalem had for some time been administered by the Israelis. Most of our party came filled with compassion for the sufferings of the Jews and a burden of guilt for Dachau and Auschwitz, but we were shocked by the numbers of Arab beggars we saw – blind old men and beautiful children, stretching out hands for alms. We could not relax totally in this unhappy land, and I doubt if any of us returned home either a convinced pro-Israeli or a pro-Arab. Since then the Middle East has continued to be torn apart by Christian/Jewish/Moslem conflicts. Is this what religion is all about?

Human violence does not compare with nature's violence – yet. Since Hiroshima there has always been the possibility that one day it will, but so far we have not perpetrated anything to equal the boiling over of Mother Earth's seething interior, or the uncontrollable juddering we call earthquakes. So I am glad I have seen, at a safe distance, a volcano in action, for it seemed to put the human race in its puny place in the universe. This was Hekla, Iceland's volcanic mountain, which was in eruption when I went in June 1969 to attend the first music festival organised by the pianist Ashkenazy and his Icelandic wife. The music was splendid – the Ashkenazys had recruited Daniel Barenboim, Jacqueline du Pré, Victoria de los Angeles and other world-famous musicians. But living in a land where the sun does not set was also exhilarating. When you came home from a concert at almost midnight and saw the children still playing out and a householder mowing his lawn there seemed little point in going to bed and strangely little need for sleep. Once I sat on the rocks on the seashore and painted the sky as the sun went down, and rose again.

It was fascinating to learn about this strange island's history from an old friend of my Co-operative days, Audur Jonasdottir, whom I had met at an international conference in London in our youth. She took me about, showed me the tiny parliament house, the vast plain where the Thingvettlir, the oldest parliament in Europe, had met, and the lava fields where we picnicked with her family amongst the scrubby vegetation. I wandered off and was scaringly lost for half an hour or so. We saw the geysers showering boiling water around, but the most terrifying sight was the little mud pools in the grass where the water was boiling and bubbling like soup in a pan, so close to the surface is earth's inner cauldron here. All Reykjavik's homes have piped hot water from the hot springs – you soon get used to its sulphurous smell, like bad eggs!

Of course, all the tourists went to see Hekla in eruption – not Audur, though, because her husband, a geologist, had been killed in its previous eruption. It was dead of night when we got there, which of course meant an eerie half light. There in the distance were the flames, spurting up and up, dotted with chunks of rock being hurled high into the sky. The whole earth as far as one could see was covered in thick black powdered ash, and moving along slowly was a snake of 'coke', the lava trail, ten feet or more high and wide, and within like the furnace of some monster central-heating boiler. We stood almost within touching distance of this terrifying snake of fire remorselessly shoved along by the invisible power of the volcano.

Though Iceland is a gay and spirited place in summer with its green and scarlet corrugated-iron roofs and the houses' green-grass thatches, it is basically strange and bleak, with no real trees, no mineral deposits at all, and nothing one could call 'architecture'. So it seems a more bearable scene for the devastation of an erupting volcano than sunny, fertile Italy, populated by one of Europe's most influential peoples, both culturally and politically. Twice I have been to Pompeii: once with K in 1938, the year after our marriage, in the course of a £30-a-head 'train cruise' which took us to Stresa, Milan, Venice, Florence, Naples and Rome, and once with a happy party of painters staying at Massa Lubrense on the Bay of Naples. My romantic approach to history made it inevitable that I should people those gracious villas and the rutted stones of the long streets where the chariots raced up and down with handsome men and women walking and talking and sitting at ease in the frescoed dining rooms. In 1938 some of the more lewd friezes were shut off from the eyes of lady tourists; in 1982 all was visible, but nothing shocked even my old-fashioned sensibilities. It is the things like the bakers' ovens, the *cave canem* paving stone, the acanthus and the herbs still growing in the carefully laid-out gardens that are apt to touch a raw nerve . . . for here people, mothers and fathers and babies and pet dogs and cats, were immolated or burnt to death under the deadly bombardment from Vesuvius and the inexorable crawl of the lava.

Pompeii was only one day out in an exceptionally happy painting holiday during which a small group of us painted all morning, ate sandwiches and snacks on the hotel's flat roof at lunchtime, painted a little more, and then met on the jetty for a blissful swim in the harbour each day at four o'clock. One of the most fortunate chances of my later years was discovering an enjoyment of painting – actually through K, who was advised by a friend to take it up as a hobby. I took my paint box on several holidays with K – to Aldeburgh, where we went almost every year to the Festival; to Dolgelly at Christmas, where I painted with gloves on, to the great amusement of K and my brother, and to a holiday cottage in Seine-et-Marne lent to us by the distinguished war correspondent, Clare Hollingworth. So when K died and I was faced with the bleak prospect of holidaymaking by myself, it seemed a possible answer to go on an organised painting holiday. From 1969, when I went with a Galleon party to Bandol on the Côte d'Azure, I have been on a painting holiday almost every year, or at least have taken paints with me to break off for a day or half a day in order to bring home a souvenir more precious than even the most professional photograph.

'What do you do with them all?' people ask me. I used to ask the same question before I became addicted, pointing out that if your hobby is *singing* you are no trouble to anyone – you have no fruits of your labours to dispose of, no souvenirs beyond a few scores and a few programmes. But as I type I can see on the facing wall two paintings of Lindos, Rhodes and one of Rhodes itself (done in blissful shade in a near gale at the foot of one of the columns that mark the entrance to the harbour, which legend said was bestrode by the Colossus); one of the Great Wall of China, where the mist was so heavy, after days of blinding sun, that the distant watch tower came and went as the mist thickened and dispersed, and a view of the snow-capped Pyrenees, seen with astonished delight from a farm gate in the northern Spanish village of Berdun. I really went overboard painting those louring mountains, that purple cloud, those orange fields. So next day, imaginatively drained, I said to the tutor, 'What shall I paint?' 'Paint me a door,' he said, and I did, a fine handsome door in Berdun's little main street. And now I have six pictures of doors and gateways over Piano No. 1 in the spare room – Berdun, Mdina (Malta), Massa Lubrense (Italy), Brixlegg (near Rattenberg, Tirol), Rhodes and, probably my favourite, a carved doorway to a crypt behind the little lake at Agios Nilolaus, Crete, adorned with the winged lions of Venice with their delightful pussy-cat faces.

I always have six little paintings on the wall facing my bed on which I can rest my fond gaze when I wake. They are quite often changed. One painting tutor asked me why I used only half the sheet in my very large book. 'Because that is the size of my frames,' I said firmly. It must have seemed a daft answer to him, but if you have, as I have, a couple of dozen frames measuring ten by seven and a half inches, that is the size you paint, isn't it? All these little frames have detachable backs, so my picture gallery is not static – no one looks at pictures which stay on the wall too long. Now if I choose I can have pictures from Lake Maggiore, Majorca, Ibiza, Corfu, Rhodes, Crete, Mykonos, Aegina, Palamos (Spain), the Algarve, Rumania, Hungary, northern California, the Vienna Woods, Lanzerote (Canary Islands), the Dordogne, Normandy, Yugoslavia, the Tyrol, Delos, Aegina, Iceland, Israel – and, of course, the British Isles, from the Channel at West Wittering, to Ben Loyal, Sutherland. I am quite surprised by the number of churches I have painted, from Orford in Suffolk, to Castle Cary in Somerset; from Budva in Yugoslavia to Ratfeld in the Tyrol; from Eloundi (Crete) to Paleokastritsa (Corfu); from St Paul's (Malta) to Lindos (Rhodes). I like domes, and better still I like towers and steeples which have a bell-filled arch with blue sky behind. Oh well, I know traveller's tales pall, but I am very glad that my amateurish watercolours are on my walls and in my desk drawers to compensate for my inadequate visual memory.

'Going places' does not mean painting, or even photographing, for everyone. For many it means lying on some Mediterranean beach and acquiring a gorgeous tan – which to me, at my age, seems a ridiculous waste of time. For others it means gastronomic exploration. (That can be interesting in France, as I found on a very happy holiday by car with friends to the Dordogne.) Though I would always choose holidays in Greece rather than in France, I have to admit that apart from fetta, black olives and some kinds of fish (not, oh not octopus!), Greek food is not to be compared with French. (Nor, in all honesty, have many Greek villages the charm of the villages and little towns of the Dordogne, which are comparable in our own country only with the lovely mellow limestone villages of the Cotswolds.)

'Going places' may mean anywhere from San Francisco to Pekin, Reykjavik to Heraklion. But it may also mean going just outside your own front door, if you live in surroundings comparable with mine. Just down the road from me, in the south-east London suburb of Blackheath, is Morden College, a 'collegium' for 'forty needy merchants' designed by Sir Christopher Wren for a city merchant trader, Sir John Morden, in 1695. Wren, surely the greatest of English architects, also designed the Ranger's House on the other side of the Heath and the Astronomer Royal's house in Greenwich Park. So our architectural tradition is exceptionally distinguished. The domestic architecture of the Cator Estate, on which I now live, we largely owe to Sir John Cator, who commissioned the Paragon, a handsome crescent with large four- or five-storey houses joined by colonnades. From across the Heath, these houses look like stately pepperpots, but the curve of the crescent is pure Georgian elegance.

Many of our roads are tree-lined, notably Blackheath Park, along which John Stuart Mill used to walk home from the station between spreading chestnut trees – even vaster now, of course, than in his day – and up-thrusting limes. We have splendid acacias, even in the middle of a handsome council estate. We have noble copper beeches and cedar trees (one in front of and one behind our own house), but what is so remarkable about our gardens is that beautiful, remarkable plants 'happen' without human intervention. Some aeons ago, I imagine, Blackheath must have been under water, for our soil is spangled with little pebbles of all colours. It is not exactly fertile, and yet astonishing things happen here. In a crack between the flags and the little wall outside my front door, a beautiful bush, nearly two feet high, has appeared – some kind of a broom, with little glossy leaves and yellow flowers. We have squirrels, dear silly creatures, who drop acorns and forget where they have put them, so that little oak trees shoot up in the borders. Holly saplings and cotoneaster and berberis are like weeds, and so are bluebells, foxgloves, a charming blue creeping bellflower, wallflowers, violets and pansies. Even our worst enemy, alkanet, which has a root as strong and as long as a parsnip, has blue flowers as bright as borage, and it is only after the flowers have faded that one can bear to dig it out.

My home is truly called a garden flat, so that when I look out of my bedroom window, or into the mirror in the hall, I can see grass, trees, forsythia, fuchsia and the great cedar trees where rooks perch and squirrels race up and down. One day in the hot summer of 1983 I saw just one little bright blue butterfly flitting above the French beans. My mind raced back at least twenty-five years to a similarly hot summer and a field by the river Barle in Somerset, where I was walking with our dear black mongrel dog, Snuff. The whole of that field was covered with similar little bright blue butterflies, as on a fluttering, gauzy bedcover. I don't think I ever saw one, between then and now. Where, oh where have the blue butterflies gone?

Going places has been one of the greatest joys of my life. I hope I shall go to many more far-distant places. But if I become too frail to travel very far, may I still find some new thing, a strange lily, a seedling silver birch, or, as my neighbour found this summer in her rose bed, a trio of healthy tomato plants sown by our friends the birds!

13

Going where?

At sixty you are elderly. At seventy-five you are indubitably
old, even if kind friends endorse your own feeling that you are
not any age, but simply 'you'. 'Old' means not only that you
are conscious of a sort of fading but that you also begin to
grasp the obvious fact that as each birthday arrives the odds on
its being your last increase. Your grandchildren are appalled if
you speak of death. 'Don't be morbid,' they beg. But it is not
morbid. To come to terms with a disagreeable fact is the
reverse of morbid.

But is it so disagreeable? We are all going to die. I am old so
it is almost certain that I shall die sooner than you. Is that such
a very terrible thought? What can be frightening is that there
is no way of knowing how or when we shall die, or what
death means. We picture it hopefully as a gentle drifting away,
preferably during sleep. Will there, even then, be a moment of
recognition: 'This is it'? Or will all those years of joy and woe,
achievement and failure, love and the rejection of love, be
obliterated in an instant with no chance to glance back any
more than to look forward?

It is not morbid, I think, but salutary to recall how family
and friends have died . . . of heart attacks, predictable or totally
unexpected; tuberculosis, pneumonia (neither a killer now);
various forms of cancer; Parkinson's disease; massive strokes,
mercifully fatal, or lesser strokes, perhaps even scarcely
observed, gradually reducing a human being to a barely

functioning carcass; arthritis, causing ever more and more excruciating and incapacitating pain, often controlled, like cancers, to the point of hastening as well as easing the end by merciful doctors. When you read over this long list, can you help asking yourself whether we should not be allowed the right to choose when and how we go? Should we not be able to decide when the spirit and bodily strength are both flagging, when our mission here seems accomplished, when we are ready to hand over, when we can believe that children, grandchildren and beloved friends can learn to manage without us?

Dear sons and daughters, do you really want to condemn us to a long-drawn-out death, to years of perpetual pain, or even to years of senile dementia? Do you think we would really prefer to have to depend on you to feed us, bath us and clean us up when we are doubly incontinent to being allowed, or even legally helped, to spare you this burden and us this shame, and decide when to make an end?

But is it an end? When we are old, should we not let the imagination wander? If death is the cessation of life, what is life? The lungs inflating, the heart beating, the brain instructing the nervous system? My little *Concise Oxford Dictionary* defines life as a 'State of ceaseless change and functional activity peculiar to organised matter and especially to the portion of it constituting an animal or plant before death'. The concept of life must include the mosquito that drives you frantic on holiday in the sunny south, the earwig that comes in from the garden on a dahlia, the daddy-long-legs that scuttles around the bath, the moth fluttering round your bedside lamp, and the maddeningly buzzing bluebottle. If you swat or spray these small creatures you are extinguishing life. Does it matter to you? Do you, as I do, tend to carry out the creatures you cannot frighten off, on a piece of paper or rag, and release them in the garden?

If you feed the blackbirds, as I do, do you reflect that apart from gorging a remarkable amount of bread and biscuit, they also swallow worms? Nature is essentially 'cruel' in that one creature battens on another creature and kills it for food. Most human beings eat meat, fish and poultry. I am horrified at the idea of eating blackbirds, but though greedy pigeons also eat up my breadcrumbs and biscuit, I should not be shocked at eating pigeon pie. Even the most ardent conservationists would not hesitate to destroy a poisonous snake or tarantula. Is there anything qualitatively different about the 'life' that animates the ant, the antelope, the weevil, the whale, the cobra, the cormorant, the mouse and the man? There seems to be no overriding, reasonable view of the sanctity of life in Mother Nature's scheme.

My own rather childish view of 'life' is that as it is what animates us, so it is something like an electric current. What switches it on, then, and what switches it off? Does this current persist somewhere in the atmosphere after it has ceased to animate some particular body, or does it simply 'run down' like an overworked battery? The oddities of 'static' fascinate me. You can get a tiny 'shock' from kissing your granddaughter's cheek. When you pull off your tights and pants at bedtime, they may cling, and sparks will fly when you pull them apart. What's more, the static in the tights will make them cling to the wall for minutes, not seconds. Has the static then exhausted itself, or has it been absorbed into a persisting current somewhere?

There are more dramatic examples of this mysterious 'electrical' current — for that is what I choose to call it. After reading about Yuri Geller's spoon-bending feats I lay in bed one Sunday morning gently stroking an old silver-plated pair of sugar tongs. My hands are not at all strong. I have to take nutcrackers to untwist screw-top bottles. But after ten minutes or so the metal of the tongs was warm and soft, and I bent it right back. How? The journalist Ann Shearer described very engagingly in an article headed 'The Psi Adventure' how at the Psychical Research Society's centenary conference at

Cambridge, she took part in two metal-bending parties: 'My fork and my spoon became very hot and a rush of energy through me to them softened them so that I could bend them in a way I certainly couldn't normally and never had done before . . . What's more,' she added, 'at one of these parties over half the seventy or so people in the room did the same or more.'

In my childhood we often had table-rapping sessions led by my mother, and I know, without any doubt whatsoever, that the mind can transmit something to the fingertips which can transmit something to the 'inanimate' wood of the table. Not very long ago I sat down at a small table in the dark with a friend. I knew perfectly well when he was 'helping' the table to move, and when it was moving because of some current that was transmitted from our fingers to the wood. To deny the reality of such phenomena is as obscurantist as it was to deny that the earth could be moving around the sun.

What I wonder about is whether there is, in fact, a life force, whether it absorbs the tiny trickles of 'life' that cease to animate matter on this earth, whether they retain their small identity within the whole, and whether, in fact, there is anything we could visualise as personal survival. How one wishes, as one grows older, that one could think this is possible, so that the dialogue cut off so long ago with husbands, wives, brothers and even parents could be resumed. Nonsensical though it must sound, I often 'talk' to my mother, who died at the age of fifty-seven in 1931, so that I am now quite old enough to be her 'mother'. If only I could tell her what has been going on in the half century since she died, and she could tell me what is going on where she is – if she is – and assure me that there is still something there for me to *do* so that I could travel hopefully.

Looking for another Tennyson quotation, I found this:

Ah Christ that it were possible
For one short hour to see
The souls we loved, that they might tell us
What and where they be.

Tennyson called death 'crossing the bar' — putting out to sea from the familiar harbour of our life on earth to the great unknown, uncharted ocean . . . to me a much more helpful image than any of a Christian hereafter, let alone 'heaven'. The Christian Church today has not succeeded in finding any image to replace the old concept of heaven as a place inhabited by angels and guarded at the gate by Saint Peter. Even the thoughtful and imaginative clergy I have met refuse to construct an image of the hereafter for us. They say it is as impossible as for the butterfly to picture life as a chrysalis. But could they at least not remind us that life has meaning because of death, just as light has meaning because of shade, and happiness because of pain? Long years ago I was walking along the seashore at Barry, during an interval in some trade union conference, with Ian Mackay, one of the most admired and loved newspaper journalists of his time, known as 'The Great Bohunkus'. The sun shone, I was just a little in love, and I said in glad surprise, 'Oh I *am* happy.' Ian looked at me shrewdly and said, 'If you know you are happy, you must have been very *un*happy.' And so I had. The shadow not only frames but validates the sunlight. Death gives meaning to life.

Does anyone now believe that death is a sort of doorway through which we pass from one known place — our home or hospital bed — to another place, not heaven or hell, not known, but somehow definable? And if we can't define what that 'place' may be, isn't it likely that most of us will come to feel, whether or not we can put the feeling into words, that there *isn't* really any 'place' at all — in fact not any kind of continuing life at all? Most Christian clergy, I believe, encourage their flock to believe that a loving Father will take them into his care now, at death, and hereafter. But I fear that doesn't really mean very much to me.

I look up at the night sky and see hundreds of stars, a few of which are planets in our own galaxy, but many more of which are millions of light years away. Then I ask myself how I can relate Jesus of Nazareth, called the Son of God, and his life, his miracles, his crucifixion and his resurrection to those incomprehensible immensities. This is not to deny the 'divinity' of Jesus Christ, or any other being in human form who may have communication directly with the creator. If a creative force or principle does animate the cosmos, why should it not communicate more closely and purposefully with some animate beings than with others?

It is difficult to look even at the planet we know, let alone the universes we see at night with the naked eye, and not be aware of the marvels of creation, from the tiniest scarlet pimpernel or speedwell, perfect in colour and form though apparently quite useless in nature's scheme of things, to the mighty spreading oak which grew, centuries ago, from an acorn hidden by an absent-minded squirrel. Can such marvels have happened purely by chance? Where the squirrel dropped the acorn may have been chance, but can the power of the acorn to produce the oak tree, or even the squirrel's part in the distribution of the acorns, be just an accident of evolution? There seems so much evidence of *design* in the cosmos, which the observations of scientists seem more and more positively to confirm, suggesting the evidence of logic and purpose. And if there is logic and purpose, surely there must be *mind*? And if there is mind, mind of a power beyond the power of human minds to comprehend, must there not be what millions of human beings throughout the centuries have called 'God' and to whom they have humbly worshipped and sacrificed?

Arthur Koestler wrote in his last letter, before taking his fatal overdose: 'I wish my friends to know that I am leaving their company in a peaceful frame of mind, with some timid hopes for a depersonalized afterlife beyond the due confines of space, time and matter and beyond the limits of our comprehension. This "oceanic feeling" has often sustained me at difficult moments and does so now, while I am writing this.' The eminent scientist, Sir Fred Hoyle, made it plain in his book

The Intelligent Universe that he believes in a creator and thinks this the most rational explanation of the universe. He thinks the idea that life evolved from a 'primordial soup' is about as likely as the idea that the scattered debris of a Boeing 747 could be reassembled by a whirlwind. He admits that he doesn't insist on the idea of a mighty creator, but he does insist that there is life outside the earth.

This is the sort of certainty I wish could be communicated by other scientists, by philosophers and by ministers of every religion, as well as by psychical researchers whose experiences and findings are so often pooh-poohed by ordinary men and women as well as by scientists with minds as closed as those of Galileo's contemporaries. Listening to a radio discussion of Sir Fred's ideas, I heard this sentence: 'Composers are reaching out for the universal intelligence.' And for me that is the strongest assurance that there *is* a universal intelligence; that there is mind and purpose, and that the tiny spark that animates the human mind is *not* doomed to extinction at the moment of death.

My passport to the life hereafter, if such there be, will not be baptism, confirmation, confession, absolution, the last rites. It will be the great glory of music, the knowledge that it exists all round us and in us, even when we cannot hear it, and will always exist. Even 100 years ago no one knew or believed that the sound waves, which carry speech as well as music, could be picked up and carried thousands of miles through the atmosphere. More than sixty years ago, when radio broadcasting was very young, I heard on a crystal set, through headphones, in a boarding house where I was staying near Victoria, a live performance of Bach's St John's Passion. The 'miracle' of the glorious sound was not greater than the miracle of the power of the human mind to imagine and set down such a complex pattern of sounds, so profoundly moving, so profoundly logical, so profoundly of both mind and spirit.

So there is my faith, that because there is Mind, there is

Purpose; that when the spark of life that animates me flickers out, it may not mean that it is 'dead'. It may be animating some new manifestation of what on earth was Me.

Sometimes I have thought of famous last words, and what I would like to be my own last utterance. Quite simply, I think:

THANK YOU